Understanding AI, IoT, 6G, and the Infrastructure Revolution

Understanding AI, IoT, 6G, and the Infrastructure Revolution

Walter Goralski

MERCURY LEARNING AND INFORMATION
Boston, Massachusetts

Publisher: David Pallai
MERCURY LEARNING AND INFORMATION
121 High Street, 3rd Floor
Boston, MA 02110
info@merclearning.com
www.merclearning.com
800-232-0223

W. Goralski. *Understanding AI, IoT, 6G, and the Infrastructure Revolution.*
ISBN: 978-1-50152-292-5

The publisher recognizes and respects all marks used by companies, manufacturers, and developers as a means to distinguish their products. All brand names and product names mentioned in this book are trademarks or service marks of their respective companies. Any omission or misuse (of any kind) of service marks or trademarks, etc. is not an attempt to infringe on the property of others.

Library of Congress Control Number: 2024946870

242526321   This book is printed on acid-free paper in the United States of America.

Our titles are available for adoption, license, or bulk purchase by institutions, corporations, etc. For additional information, please contact the Customer Service Dept. at 800-232-0223(toll free).

All of our titles are available in digital format at *academiccourseware.com* and other digital vendors. The sole obligation of MERCURY LEARNING AND INFORMATION to the purchaser is to replace the files, based on defective materials or faulty workmanship, but not based on the operation or functionality of the product.

This one, most of all is, for Camille. I searched for her a long time, but she was worth it.

CONTENTS

FOREWORD

In an era where the digital infrastructure evolves at an unprecedented pace, understanding the intricacies of networking technology has never been more crucial. It is with great enthusiasm that I introduce Walter's seminal work on this subject—a comprehensive guide that embodies both the depth and breadth of expertise needed to navigate all the layers and deployment models of modern networks.

Walter's profound knowledge in networking technology, whether it is IP, Ethernet, Optical Networks and even AI is not merely academic; it is the result of years spent on the front lines of the field, engaging with the challenges and breakthroughs that shape our digital world. His journey through the labyrinth of network protocols, infrastructures, and innovations has equipped him with a unique perspective that is as insightful as it is practical.

While working together with Walter on *The Complete IS-IS Routing Protocol* I used to refer to him as "Professor." As you delve into these pages, you will realize why. Walter's ability to demystify complex concepts and present them with clarity and precision makes this book an essential resource for anyone interested in the future of networking technology. His contributions to the field are not just academic but also practical, offering readers the tools and perspectives needed to excel in an ever-evolving technological landscape.

Walter has done it again and put together a comprehensive book that is easy to read at all proficiency levels. It is a reflection of his exceptional expertise and a beacon for all who aspire to stay ahead in an ever-connected digital world.

Have fun reading it, I certainly did.

Hannes Gredler
CTO, RtBrick Inc.

PREFACE

This book was written for the same reason I have written all my other books: There was no book available that fully satisfied my curiosity about the field . In some cases, this was no surprise because my interests were always on the cutting edge of what was possible to implement. It seemed clear that there should be books about configuring routers that included both Cisco and Juniper Networks devices, or residential DSL. Therefore, I wrote those books. By the early 2020s, a comprehensive book that surveyed the latest and greatest breakthroughs and developments and explained how they all fit together to create the modern networking infrastructure that is used every day was needed. Existing books were either too narrowly focused or did not explore the topics in appropriate depth .

This book required drawing on every bit of experience gained over the years in areas ranging from mobile networks to security and privacy. Unlike the "deep dive" books I've previously written on SONET/SDH or the TCP/IP family of protocols, this book had to be broad rather than deep. Delving too far into any single technology would result in a a 500-page volume.

Each chapter is as much a history lesson as it is an exploration of the latest developments in the field, from photonics to cloud data centers to cryptography. After all, that is typically how we learn. We do not learn about modern conics without discussing Apollonius of Perga, who died around 190 BCE. There is no number theory as the foundation of modern cryptography without Pythagoras. We learn where things have come from so that we can understand why they are the way they are today.

Ethernet is a good example. It is everywhere, even after fifty years, mainly because of the foresight of a group of engineers who created the IEEE 802 . They made "Ethernet" (actually, IEEE 802.3 with pieces of the original Ethernet) easy to add features to as times changed. A good rule of thumb formulated over the years is that only simple technologies succeed; complicated methods almost always fail.

The career behind this book has included many years working for Silicon Valley companies, as a contractor for IBM, as a professor at a major U.S. university, as a doctoral candidate in the early days of AI, and as a course developer and technical trainer .

Hopefully, this unique background has resulted in a book readers will find equally unique and enjoyable.

This book is an educated person's guide to how modern technology fits together and enables the modern world to function. The book does not claim to be comprehensive in any of the areas covered, but it is intended to introduce the basic concepts that all these technologies are built on.

The audience for this book includes, but is not limited to, anyone who is knowledgeable about one of the key areas of technology covered and wants to learn more about others, as well as gain insight into how all these various technologies came together to create the network infrastructure that none of us could live or work without.

Every chapter in this book is covered in much greater depth by books that are 500 pages or even 1,000 pages long. However, this book focuses on how these technologies came to exist in their present form and how they function together as a (mostly) seamless whole.

There are no complex equations in this book, only a few simple ones. Familiarity with terms like mega- or giga- is required, but the key points are supplied by tables in an appendix.

This book is a good fit for students, especially those in engineering or technical fields; interested managers responsible for acquiring, implementing, and using these technologies; and general readers who just want to understand how the global public Internet came to function as it does.

CHAPTER OVERVIEW

This book explores seven key technological areas that form the foundation of the global public Internet today. It not only describes technology at a high level but also shows how each technology evolved into its modern form and contributes to the overall network infrastructure we all benefit from.

Each chapter begins with a strong historical introduction to technology. There are two reasons for this emphasis. First, this practice gives newcomers a glimpse into what people who have been working in the field for a long time already know, so that those less familiar with the history have some context in the area. Second, it is always a good idea to understand how things have come to be in order to understand how they might change—or not—in the future.

For instance, the Ethernet LAN technology recently marked its 50th anniversary. Despite its age, Ethernet-based technology is entrenched in almost every network product made today. Not only is this a testimony to the foresight of the IEEE 802 LAN committee, founded in February of 1980 (802), but it shows how flexible standards can be. This is not true of all commonly used networking practices, as this book points out.

The chapters in this book can be read in any order by readers with a minimal technical background. However, this book has a logical flow to the chapters, with the major points of each suggesting issues that are brought up and explored in the next. As a whole, the book forms a journey from a vehicle on a highway to deep into the Internet and then back again.

CHAPTER 1: MOBILE NETWORKS

The first chapter in this book explores mobile networks and smartphones—really a form of pocket computer—that are the common mobile platforms used today. There is some history of the cell phone, but only so the progression through cellular network generations becomes vivid and understandable. This includes a first look at layering for network protocols. The basics of layered networks are covered here, so that those who studied them years ago have a kind of refresher and those who never learned them at all can have a complete grasp of why network layers exist. Details of the development of some of the key aspects of 5G and 6G networks are explored.

CHAPTER 2: IPV6

The second chapter focuses on the essential features of IPv6. Oddly, IPv6 has been around since 1995 or so, but the lifetime of IPv4 has been extended by a series of tricks and workarounds. User equipment manufacturers and customers might not use or care much about IPv6 yet, but service providers certainly have to pay attention to IPv6 now.

CHAPTER 3: PACKET OPTICAL FIBER LINKS

The third chapter examines the characteristics of packet optical networks, particularly backhauling.

Backhauling is the term used to describe how data to and from a mobile platform finds its way to the streaming servers, clouds, and other types of data centers and back. This backhauling work is done by high-capacity fiber optic links, often called IP-over-DWDM (Dense Wavelength Division Multiplexing). Today, a common term is *packet optical* because routers and switches no longer must convert light to electricity to access the packets. Packet optical links pass traffic from continent to continent without the long propagation delays of satellites and without the risks of the outages that satellites must deal with.

CHAPTER 4: CLOUD DATA CENTERS

The fourth chapter of this book explores virtualized clouds and "big data" data centers.

Fiber optical cables get digital information from the cell tower to the cloud data center. "The cloud" is the place where most of an organization's data is stored on servers and manipulated by apps (applications). These apps are written in a high-level language, many times in graphical drag-and-drop environments, and not by highly trained programmers typing away in front of multiple monitors. The apps usually also reside in the cloud. The cloud is often run by a separate organization than the owner of the data, but not always.

CHAPTER 5: IOT AND M2M

The fifth chapter investigates the impact of IoT and M2M on the modern network.

More and more of the bits flying back and forth over these mobile and other wireless networks come from and go to not people, but *things*. So much so that the terms Internet of Things (IoT) and Machine to Machine (M2M) were invented to cover these circumstances. Many people have automated their homes to a greater or lesser extent. Video doorbells display who is at the door, and thermostats adjust themselves through remote cell phone control. M2M applications are similar but generally involve much more than just sensors. Factory floors are run by M2M applications, as are the networks that gather automotive statistics from cars and trucks on the highway.

This chapter also investigates passive optical networks (PONs) as a popular foundation for an architecture called *Industry 4.0.*

CHAPTER 6: AI AND ROBOTS

The sixth chapter addresses AI and robots. This chapter attempts to separate the current AI hype from reality, but there are more questions here than answers. The chapter examines some of the claims for modern robots and the role that AI plays in this field and on its own. How independent should these creations be? Should they always have a human "in the loop" or at least "on the loop" to override decisions, especially in military applications?

This chapter includes the basics of large language models (LLMs). LLMs form the basis of all popular implementations of natural language processing (NLP) and all the generative AI (GenAI) chat apps.

CHAPTER 7: SECURITY AND PRIVACY

The seventh and final chapter focuses on security and privacy, both for individuals and the infrastructure itself. No matter the reason why a mobile user reaches out, something comes back to the user. The information flow must be secure so that users can be confident that the result of their transaction with the network is valid. Privacy must make sure that information is kept under the control of the originator, not necessarily the organization that gathers it. This had widespread implications for finance, health care, and other fields.

The chapter covers the basics of public key infrastructure (PKI) and introduces elliptic curve cryptography (ECC) without delving into complex mathematics.

END MATTER

The book concludes with an appendix detailing the important powers of 10 that appear repeatedly in the text.

It also has an acronym list of all but the most acronyms in the fields covered. For example, ROADM is listed, but not AI or PC.

W. Goralski
November 2024

ACKNOWLEDGMENTS

Every creative person knows that they are not the sole creator of a work. There may be one person's name on the painting or one person's name on the book, but they know that there was more than one person involved in the journey to the finished product.

First and foremost, thirty years ago, Jay Ranade of McGraw-Hill and an editor named Steve Elliot asked me to write a book based on what was then a promising new technology called asynchronous transfer mode (ATM). He had seen an article I had written about its overhead for TCP/IP in *Network World*.

Steve guided me through a series of books, and Steve was the person who conjured up this book. He and his colleague Jennifer Blaney gently weaned me from the bad habits I had picked up between books and led me back to solid ground.

May there be more books and experiences like this!

Chapter 1

MOBILE NETWORKS

OVERVIEW

In today's world, almost everyone requires multiple Internet connections at home, in the office, in the car, and at work to function, plan their lives, and entertain themselves. Wired connections have been replaced by wireless solutions, especially for mobile platforms such as cell phones and automobiles.

WHAT YOU WILL LEARN

This chapter delves into the generations of mobile networks. It often seems like the next generation of mobile devices and networks is being developed and perfected even before the current generation is widely available. While there is some truth to that, all networks that impact nearly everyone in the world to some extent require careful planning and consideration before trials are attempted.

The topics covered include:

- The impact of mobility
- The role of WiFi
- From car phones to cell phones
- Mobile network generations
- Mobile network architecture

- Protocol stacks and their functions
- The modern world of mobile networking

THE IMPACT OF MOBILITY

Cell phones have been in existence since the 1970s, but they looked very different from the pocket-sized smartphones we are familiar with today. Early cell phones required a backpack for batteries, which only lasted a few hours and included a full-sized landline telephone handset with a three-foot-long whip antenna. The evolution of smartphones is a prime example of one of the themes of this book: the cell phone could not have become a pocket-sized device without advances in battery technology, smaller speaker and microphone design, and an improved fractal-like antenna that folded in on themselves in a compact fashion. A breakthrough in one area could only go so far until other areas caught up. There were always counter arguments to deal with as well: one point made about smaller cell phones was that people would lose them more often.

Early cell phones made life much easier. The key people with the bulky backpacks were usually members of critical customer support teams or other employees who needed to be reached wherever they were at any time of day or night. Without the mobility and convenience offered by cell phones, contacting a support specialist could go like this:

1. A customer calls the vendor to report an issue with new hardware or software.
2. The customer is told that the specialist needed is off-site at a meeting.
3. The customer calls or is transferred to the place where the specialist is.
4. The receptionist there tries to locate the specialist, either using an intercom page or knowing the conference room where the meeting is being held.
5. The customer rings the phone closest to the specialist, who presumably answers.

These five steps become one with cell phones: dial the number and the specialist's phone rings.

Cell phones also improved safety once they became small enough in the early 1990s to be taken everywhere. Not only could those in distress call for assistance wherever they were in a service area, but they simply made life much easier. Before cell phones, a sales representative might fly into a strange city late on a Sunday night. At the rental car counter, they often had only a one-sheet area map to guide them to the hotel and company location for Monday morning. If they got lost in an industrial park, they had to try and find a pay phone to call the hotel for directions while alone, in a dark area, late at night, outside their car.

Before there were portable smartphones, there were car phones. Car phones became popular in the 1970s, but they were simply big "walkie-talkies" that only operated in the range of a central radio tower, usually in a metropolitan area like Manhattan. There were only a few frequencies that could be used, so capacity was an issue. There was a push-to-talk button, so you did not have to say something like "over" when you were through speaking. All in all, car phones were not really telephones but were built to look like telephones because that is what people expected and were used to.

The equipment consisted of a couple of big metal cabinets in the trunk of the car (which filled most of it up). Cables connected to the telephone handset under the dashboard, and there was a 15-inch antenna mounted on the roof of the car.

Users had to call the mobile operator and request to place a call: "Give me corporate headquarters, please." These early mobile phones cost ten times what a regular "land line" cost to have and use. If someone wanted to call the car, that required reaching a regular operator and then the mobile operator, who asked for the number of the car (car phones did not use regular phone numbers at first). Later services let you dial the number directly.

The point is that all the technologies in this book changed social norms and altered people's behaviors, often in ways that were unforeseen and might be harmful to children or other groups.

A NOTE ABOUT WiFi

Wireless communications, specifically the wireless local area network (WLAN) technology known as WiFi, was once seen as the primary competitor to cellular networks. However, most modern smartphones now come equipped with both mobile cellular link capability and WiFi.

Many users often keep both WiFi and their cellular phones enabled simultaneously, along with Bluetooth for keyboards and earbuds. This quickly drains the battery, and there are times when it is much less expensive to use the free public WiFi than to use up a limited monthly data allotment on a smartphone.

WiFi will not be discussed in depth here, except to mention that it has evolved as much as mobile cellular services. In the early days of wireless LANs, the equipment shared the same public frequencies—no license required—much like those generated by microwave ovens.

Since 1995, mobile network speeds have significantly improved, with experts predicting that by 2035, mobile networks and WiFi systems will merge to achieve speeds of up to 1 Tbps. In simpler terms, a user could download in a single day all the data that users downloaded at 1 Gbps over the past three years (or 3,000 years at 1 Mbps).

FROM CAR PHONE TO CELL PHONE

All generations of cellular mobile telephony services originated from central radio tower systems. The breakthrough occurred when technology advanced enough to allow users to move between cellular towers without dropping calls. For engineering purposes, cell towers were strategically placed to cover over the area of a six-sided polygon (a hexagon, like wargamers sometimes use). These hexagons were packed side-by-side across a service area.

Cell tower coverage is more of an amorphous blob with edges that ebb and expand due to weather, temperature, sunspots, and a variety of other factors. Cell phones usually had to pick the "best" (strongest) signal between two towers, or occasionally three. In a jet aircraft, above terrestrial obstacles, a dozen or more cell towers could compete for the ability to carry a call, and roaming at jet speeds stressed the handoff system. In the early days of cellular communication in commercial aviation, there were concerns about whether cell phone use could interfere with the plane's electronic systems. As a result, airlines simply banned cell phone use during flights. Although most interference issues have been resolved, airlines are still hesitant to allow passengers. to use their phones without activating "airplane mode," due to the potential for tension and arguments among in the cabin, much as on commuter trains. Trains often have "cell phone-free" cars for those who wish for some quiet.

The frequency spectrum used for calls was spread out among several cells to minimize interference between calling channels with the same frequencies. A common practice in early mobile phone systems was to use a seven-cell pattern, in which a central cell was surrounded by six other cells. Another used a series of twelve cells to accomplish the same thing. This "footprint" was then replicated throughout the service area. However, this reuse pattern had its limitations, as many early systems had to limit the number of simultaneous phone calls in a cell to about fifty. For instance, during a sports event that ran late and saw 20,000 or more people leaving the venue, only the first fifty or so people were able to call home and say they were on their way.

Delivery services appreciated the convenience of having voice communication in their vans but found calls often dropped, even when they were completely at a stop. This occurred because cell towers would hand calls off for reasons other than roaming. A call could shift due to atmospheric conditions as signals faded or strengthened, or as a cell with many calls in progress sought to shift some to towers not as near to maximum capacity.

Voice quality was also an issue. The Bell System prides itself on the clarity of its voice services. However, when analog mobile phones were introduced, voice quality was not up to par. During conversations, there was a lot of chaotic interference and hissing, making it seem worse. It was more like intercom chatter rather than conventional speech communication.

In 1980, an AT&T® study made a prediction that cell phones would be a niche market in comparison to the established landlines that were ubiquitous in households and businesses. An executive announced that there could be as many as 900,000 subscribers by the year 2000. He was only 99% off; the actual number was 109 *million*. It is important to note that what the executive was really saying was: "I cannot believe that many people will pay a premium for the worst voice service they could ever have."

Of course, the problem with the prediction being so far off was that people were not buying voice service. They were buying the *convenience* that mobility in communications provided. Once marketers realized this and recognized that consumers were willing to pay a premium for even the smallest upgrades every few years, the popularity of cell phones took off.

There is a valuable lesson hidden in this simple example: the success of any new technology is not only based on saving money for service providers or customers (or both), or on doing things more efficiently. Much depends on the cultural value of the new technology.

Early mobile networks in the late 1970s were proof-of-concept services. They worked but did not become commercially viable until the billing software caught up with the technical hardware in the early 1980s. Flat-rate services were always popular with customers, but the carriers always favored per-use plans that often resulted in *sticker shock* at the end of the month.

There were other reasons for the giant AT&T Bell System to aggressively market cellular service. Regulatory rules had mandated that the expensive long-distance revenue be shared with the local phone company because no local phone calls could be made during a long-distance call. However, with an AT&T mobile phone used to connect long-distance calls to users, the new rules allowed AT&T to keep every penny.

MOBILE NETWORK GENERATIONS

It is common to refer to the evolution of mobile networks and cellular telephony in terms of "generations" using terms such as 4G, 5G, and 6G. Today, these are mostly marketing terms. However, the standards describe the features of each generation vary comprehensively. Therefore, they are worth reviewing.

Each generation of mobile networks poses a special challenge to those wanting to learn more about them. First, the names for basic network components all change, although the functions are similar. Therefore, the cell tower itself, initially called the base transceiver station (BTS) in 2G, became Node B (NodeB) in 3G, then the evolved Node B (eNodeB) in 4G, and now the gNodeB (gNB) in 5G.

Second, these differences are important because, generally, each new generation is backward compatible with the older ones. In other words, a 3G phone should still work on the 5G network. Finally, there are as many specialized implementations of mobile architecture in each generation as there are confusing diagrams to try and explain it to perplexed newcomers.

Mobile networks have three main pieces: the radio network situated in the field, the servers and support equipment at the service provider's premises (with links to the Internet), and the intermediate infrastructure that links these two components. Advanced features like network slicing, virtual cell towers, and other items are additions—sometimes crucial additions—to the basic function of the network, which remains connecting users to servers and to each other.

Mobile network generations have followed a general pattern. First, they allow a user of a cellular smartphone to reach out and access features of the global public Internet. Then they allow users on the global public Internet to reach out and access features of the user of a cellular smartphone. This evolution might sound trivial, but it is really fundamental.

The generations of mobile network service can be loosely described as follows:

"1G"—the first generation of cellular mobile networks—was introduced in 1983. No one called this type of mobile network "1G" because no one knew there would be subsequent generations. It supported analog voice bandwidth and did not support any type of data. The phones were bulky, like the famous Motorola® "brick," which weighed about three pounds (mainly the battery). You could drive while on a call with them, but it was hard to make turns, and service was often cut out under bridges or when a handoff to another cell tower failed (which was often).

The important things to know about 1G networks are:

- It was an analog system, similar to the public switched telephone network (PSTN) it was based on.
- Like the PSTN voice network, you could use modems to push digital data over the voice lines, but only at speeds up to 2.4 kbps. If you could somehow find a server that stored movies in HD back then, it would take about *one month* to download a single movie.
- There was no international calling.
- It was not called 1G, but the Advanced Mobile Phone System (AMPS) in the United States.

2G—after mobile networks gained popularity, the radio signal was digitalized in 1991. This digitization increased capacity and made more efficient use of the radio spectrum. The Global System for Mobile Communications (GSM) standard was introduced. Phone conversations became digital, and text messaging (short message service, or SMS) was initiated, although not all low-end devices supported such messages. This was the start of various *enhanced* services so that one carrier could say, "My service is better...." Sometimes, these were called 2.5G services.

The important things to know about 2G networks are:

- The network was now digital, not analog. Voice was carried as a stream of digits.
- Data speeds could go up to 64 kbps. That HD movie could now be downloaded in about 17 hours.
- Voice quality improved due to digital service, and this generation supported the SMS text service, which used control messages to carry short user text messages.
- International service became possible in certain countries.

3G—the many flavors of 2G networks led to the formation of the 3G Partnership Project (3GPP) in 2001 to standardize the generations of mobile networks. The universal mobile telecommunications system (UMTS) was standardized by the 3GPP and was widely used around the world. For the first time, mobile users came online and browsed the Internet.

The important things to know about 3G networks are:

- Handsets supported other network features like GPS, WiFi, and Bluetooth.

- MIMO (multiple input, multiple output) is used as an antenna technology: multiple antennas are used at both the source (transmitter) and the destination (receiver) to reduce errors and improve throughput.
- Data speeds range from 125 kbps to 2 Mbps, depending on distance to the cell tower and interference. That HD movie could now be downloaded in about an hour.
- Voice quality became close to landline quality but still used PSTN circuit-switching connections, even though the voice was digitized.
- Video conferencing and 3D gaming became possible using packet-switching data.
- Global roaming became feasible.

4G—in 2010, the fourth generation of mobile networks was defined by the International Telecommunication Union (ITU) as 4G. Now mobile users could stream movies as easily as to a laptop or tablet. The 3GPP, which blithely moves from generation to generation without a name change, also created a standard to provide a context for the "long-term evolution" of mobile networks (LTE).

The important things to know about 4G networks are:

- Mobile TV channels could be streamed directly to cell phones.
- Data packet speeds reached up to 200 Mbps, but more often about 100 Mbps.
- The HD movie could download in about 2 minutes or use live streaming.
- Global roaming is easy.

5G—standardized in 2019, 5G offered lightning-fast downloads and a new radio spectrum to increase bandwidth. However, 5G also came with limitations in terms of distances that early users found vexing, to say the least.

The important things to know about 5G networks are:

- That HD movie could now be downloaded in 4 seconds.
- There is more bandwidth available due to the new radio spectrum. However, these frequencies do not travel far or penetrate buildings very well.
- The system often requires *fronthauling*, the process of adding smaller radio relay stations where needed to get the signal to the central cell tower site.
- Cell towers now boast over 100 antenna ports to boost tower capacity.

- Innovative techniques like bouncing signals off buildings to reach *shadowed* areas help service access from even the lowest powered and smallest devices.

6G—the upcoming mobile network standard. It is tempting, and not totally wrong, to describe the 6G mobile network as "5G plus AI." But 6G is far more than just applying AI to an existing 5G network.

It would require many pages to detail all the services and features that 6G mobile networks support. Here are some highlights according to the Institute of Electrical and Electronic Engineers (IEEE) and other standards groups:

- **New Service Offerings**: 3D hyper-accurate positioning, localization, and tracking (think of finding and rescuing stranded motorists or hikers in bad weather); interactive mapping, digital twins or replicas, digital healthcare and enhanced body networks, and automatic detection, protection, inspection, and industrial control (things like shoplifting prevention).
- **Enhanced Network Features**: Trusted AI as a Service (AIaaS), seamless coverage, satellite integration, support for high altitude platform stations (HAPS balloons or drones), service continuity, environmental sustainability and energy efficiency, and efficient service coverage.
- **Enhanced Human Communications**: Services include extended reality, immersive media, telepresence, teleoperation (which will require better sensory communication), and intelligent interaction and sharing (for things like chip and circuit design).
- **Enhanced Machine Interactions:** These services include support for a network of factory robots and their control, autonomous machines, uncrewed aerial vehicles (still controversial), and massive, low-energy hyper-connectivity (think of all these drones that light up and make figures in the sky).

To bring all these things to reality quickly, research is progressing in:

- AI for mobile networks
- Cloud communications applied to the mobile network
- Low-power devices and green technologies
- Advanced MIMO and beam forming (giving active areas more bandwidth)
- THz communication (a previously impossible bandwidth range)
- Visible light communications (*free-space optical* without fiber cable)

There are other areas, of course.

MOBILE NETWORK ARCHITECTURE

What do 5G and soon 6G networks look like in terms of architecture and components?

6G networks look much like 5G networks in that regard. According to the 3GPP standards, the architecture of a 5G mobile network is remarkably simple. Figure 1.1 shows that there are only three main pieces. The figure adds details to the architecture established by the 3GPP and is available at *https://www.3gpp. org/technologies/5g-system-overview* (from 2022).

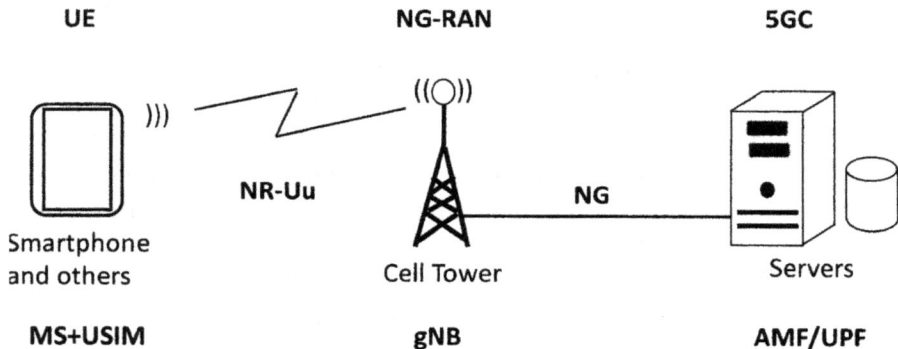

| UE | NG-RAN | 5GC |

NR-Uu   **NG**

Smartphone and others   Cell Tower   Servers

MS+USIM   **gNB**   **AMF/UPF**

FIGURE 1.1. Overview of 5G architecture.

Now, those who have searched for information when trying to learn more about mobile networks will find it hard to believe that this is the official network architecture. Yet it is.

The whole thing seems much too simple. This is another lesson to learn about networking: the simpler it is, the better. Only the simple stuff has a good chance of working well; the more complicated it is, the more things can go wrong, and at the worst possible time.

This chapter has already pointed out that there are only three big pieces to a mobile network. These are the radio network in the field, the servers and support equipment at the service provider's premises (with links to the Internet), and everything in between. This is exactly what the figure shows: the user equipment (UE) accessing the network, the servers and support equipment (the 5G Core: 5GC), and everything in between the next generation radio access network (NG-RAN).

Here is what all the other acronyms mean:

The UE consists of the mobile station (MS) and the universal subscriber identity module (the USIM card) that holds all the information needed to identify (and bill) an individual user. The USIM also implements the security, authentication, and ciphering functions on the user end of the network.

The central feature of the NG-RAN is the gNB, where "g" stands for "5G" and "NB" for "Node B," which is the name (from 3G) used to refer to the radio transmitter. The radio interface to the UE is called New Radio Uu (NR-Uu). The "Uu" is merely an interface designation and not an acronym. For some services, where fronthaul is needed to reach the UE (inside a steel building, for example), the gNB splits into a gNB-Central Unit (gNB-CU) and one or more gNB Distributed Unit(s) (gNB-DUs), linked by what is called the F1 interface.

In practice, there are lots of RAN variations. The IEEE distinguishes centralized cloud RANs (C-RAN), heterogeneous cloud RANs (H-CRAN or just H-RAN) for load balancing traffic, fog RANs (F-RAN; more on fog networks after we talk about network layers), distributed RANs (D-RAN), and more. Most have a line here or a box there a bit different than the others. If you isolated these different RAN variations onto flashcards, shuffled them, and handed them out, most people would have a hard time matching the diagram to the acronym, even those who were supposed to know without looking them up.

The 5GC has a lot more than what is represented here by the AMF and UPF entities, but these are the vital ones. The user plane function (UPF) handles the user data and makes sure it gets to and from the right source and destination. The access and mobility management function (AMF) is for signaling and accessing the UE and the NG-RAN. The reference point between the access and the core network is called "NG" (architectural reference interfaces are not really acronyms, but most think of it as "Next Generation").

Although not shown in the figure, the 5GC architecture relies on a service-based architecture (SBA). The architecture elements are defined in terms of network functions (NFs) rather than by "traditional" network entities. Any given NF offers its services to all the other authorized NFs or to any "consumers" that are permitted to make use of these services.

If the network architecture is so simple at heart, why do some mobile network diagrams look so complex? One reason is that each vendor will emphasize a different part of the architecture depending on what software or hardware they are selling. If the vendors sell anything that has to do with cell towers, then expect a lot of detail in the gNB portion of their figures, and the other pieces shrink toward the margins.

There is a disconcerting tendency among some vendors to make their mobile architecture diagrams as complex as possible. They try to include as many acronyms, boxes, and interface lines as they can. Some do not even bother to explain the acronyms they use. It is all a way of saying, "See, we thought of everything."

The Mobile Network in Action

What kinds of features are supported by modern mobile networks like 5G and 6G? Here are some of the things that mobile networks are used for today.

Smart Systems: Smart systems are devices that contain processors capable of many advanced features that add some degree of "intelligence" to the basic functions of the device. Examples include:

- Smart Wearables
- Smart Mobility
- Smart Parking

Water Quality: Water quality monitoring is the ability of mobile sensors to relay information about the quality of a body of water to some central location.

Utility Management: Utility management is the sensing of problems or conditions of underground utilities such as electricity, natural gas, water, and anything else that can flow into a building.

Automotive Systems: Automotive systems are a key part of modern mobile networks. Communications capable take on various forms, such as:

- Car to car (collision prevention)
- Car to other services (such as a towing service)
- Traffic control (longer green lights in congested directions, rush hour modifications, and so on)

eHealth Services: Health-related network features provide for such features as:

- Traffic priorities for ambulances and paramedics
- Health condition monitoring (insulin levels, oxygen content, pulse, and so on)

Domotics: Domotics is defined as monitoring or controlling home (domicile) features such as lighting, climate, entertainment systems, and appliances.

Home security (visual doorbells) and access control locking and alarm systems are also part of domotics. Devices include:

- Smart refrigerator and freezer
- Connected house

Entertainment Systems: Entertainment systems are not the same as large-screen televisions. These are:

- Virtual reality (VR) gaming
- Fine-tuned gambling (betting during a game as scores and conditions evolve)

Smart Grid: The smart grid means monitoring and control or major utility distributed, for example, of:

- Electricity
- Natural gas

Security and surveillance: General security and surveillance are also included in a modern mobile network. Cameras are often installed on traffic signals or even on the sides of buildings.

SUMMARY OF MOBILE NETWORK FEATURES AND CAPABILITIES

Each generation of mobile networks has seen bandwidth increase and latency (a form of network delay) decrease. These tendencies are illustrated in Figure 1.2.

How does a 5G mobile network deliver the features it supports? There has been tremendous progress in several areas when it comes to the specific technologies that form the foundation of these networks. Here are a few:

- Flexible radio access technology (RAT) and waveforms include more types of physical layers to support older and newer radio technologies. All these combine to support "ultra-low" latencies never seen before.
- New spectrum has opened up millimeter wave (mmWave) ranges, from 6 GHz to 100 GHz. Microwave small cells can complement sub-6 GHz macrocells.
- MIMO (multiple input-multiple output) cell towers support "massive MIMO" with 100 or more antenna elements on the base station. (MIMO already supports 64 full duplex send-receive channels.)

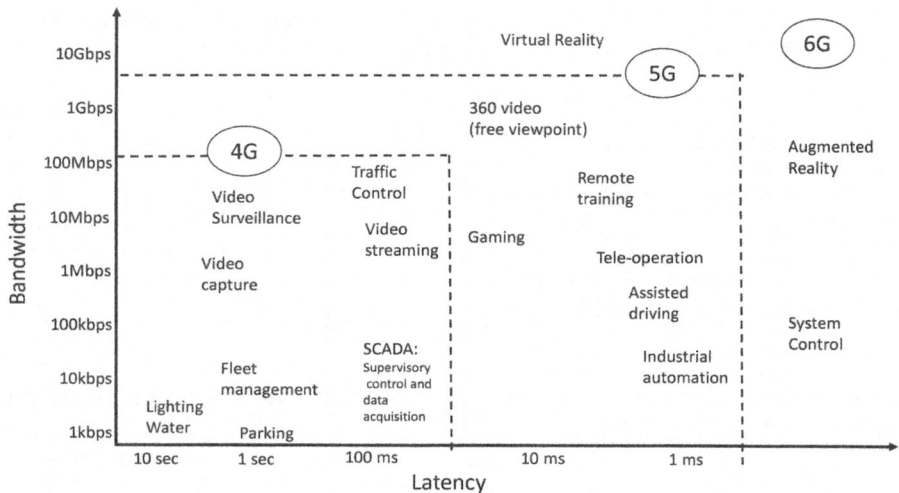

FIGURE 1.2. Key features of 5G and 6G networks.

- New advances promote alternate architectures for backhaul networks (wireless) and access integration.
- Virtualization concepts such as software-defined networking (SDN) and network function virtualization (NFV) have applied cloud and fog features to mobile networks. Edge computing brings data storage and computes tasks closer to where the data is created and used.
- Network slicing allows multiple networks, both virtualized and independent of each other, to share a common physical infrastructure. Each slice (portion) of the network can be allocated based on the needs of the application or customer. For example, cars can use one slice for engine telemetry and another slice for streaming entertainment for the passengers. Newer mobile networks do not limit these different quality of service (QoS) needs only in the backhaul and core potions of the network but also onto the radio portion of the mobile network, right to the end users.

HOW MOBILE NETWORKS FUNCTION

It is time to look at how mobile networks work in 5G and beyond. The TCP/IP packets that run over the global public Internet and the radio signals that span the air between your cell phone and cell tower at first seem so different that connecting them seamlessly—and quickly—appears impossible.

But before we can look at the path of information between a cellular device and a Web site, there is more to know about networks, protocols, and layers.

NETWORK LAYERS

All network protocols are structured in layers. It was not always that way. Early programming languages like COBOL included statements that let programmers send bits out of a physical port on the computer. The syntax was normally something like `write(port 2$, "testing 123")`. When this program was run, the external port 2$ (whatever that was) would spit out the bits representing the string testing 123 from an output *buffer*, which is a portion of memory devoted to telecommunications. As for the receiver at the other end of the link, a program run there would wait until some bits of interest showed up at an external port there. A statement such as `read(port 3$, BITSTRING)` transferred the bits from an input buffer to a variable named `BITSTRING`.

However, this simple sender-receiver network is more complicated than it might seem. Is there a wire attached to the sending and receiving port? Are the bits disappearing into a *bit bucket*? Even if there was a wire connecting sender and receiver, what if it broke while the bits were in their way? And what about other types of errors, such as bit errors? How can the receiver alert the sender that the bits have arrived safely? And so on.

Even if the listening process received the bits, does the content make sense? Some chips store bits in a different order, and whose responsibility is it to re-order the bits? Is "123" a string for printing or a numerical representation to be used for mathematical manipulations? What if there is no direct connection between sender and receiver? What if, in addition to the "end systems," there is one or more "intermediate systems" that have to know somehow to pass the bits along to the ultimate destination?

All of these issues could be solved by many lines of code in every program that sent and received bits. Usually, there is only one communication port on the end system, the network interface. If a single "all done in this program" is actively using the port to stream a movie, for example, how can another program use the same port to send email? It is not possible. There is no multiplexing in this simple network case.

In any case, modern operating systems do not allow user programs to directly access hardware. Applications must go through the operating system. This makes the centralization of networking tasks as a series of layers in the end and intermediate systems the only way to make a network function.

Another benefit is that layers isolate the software to some extent, preventing problems at one layer from causing side effects elsewhere. Layers are also, at least in theory, interchangeable, as long as they comply with all relevant standards. This should allow customers to use a layer from one vendor and another layer from a different layer, but in practice, this is rarely done.

The problem is seldom one as clear cut as the car not starting. Older networks, from the 1960s and 1970s, failed all the time, but the causes were usually clear and the remedy easy to implement. Modern networks do not fail as much as they seem slow down but continue to deliver packets and messages. Yet, the data might go to the wrong destination or be corrupt once it gets there. Therefore, the networks do not often fail, but the issues are often hard to diagnose, and the fix is not always clear (or even known with certainty).

Once the issue of layered protocols has been resolved, the question remains as to how many layers there should be and what exactly they should do. Various network protocol *models* developed to answer these questions. In the mid-twentieth century, every computer vendor had their own proprietary layered models for computer communications. They were proprietary because you could only buy them from the vendor, and in many cases, there was little documentation as to how they worked internally. As a result, for a long time, only IBM computers could talk to other IBM computers, and the same was true of computers from Digital Equipment Corporation (DEC), Wang, and so on.

As networking became more common, pressure began to mount to allow computers from different vendors to interoperate. One international organization, with the input of all major computer companies throughout the world, developed the Open Standard Interconnection (OSI) reference model (OSI-RM). It was "open" in the sense that all specifications were published for anyone to implement and no one got to say, "Mine is better than yours." There are people today who are convinced that "open" means there are no patents or intellectual property considerations for components to worry about, or that it is free, but none of those things are true.

Networks have come a long way. Networks have undergone significant changes over the years; when they were first introduced, it was common for them to only operate during typical working hours.

THREE PROTOCOL STACKS

Any deeper investigation into mobile networks must begin with the concept of *protocol stacks*, the collection of network layers that work together as a *protocol suite* to deliver data from one end of the network to the other.

This section will compare the layers of three protocol stacks: the OSI-RM, the mobile network, and TCP/IP. Understanding how these work will help readers figure out how networks as different as radio-linked cellular networks with quickly-moving devices can attach to older networks like the global public Internet, where network addresses are intimately connected to a device's fixed location. The three protocol stacks are shown in Figure 1.3.

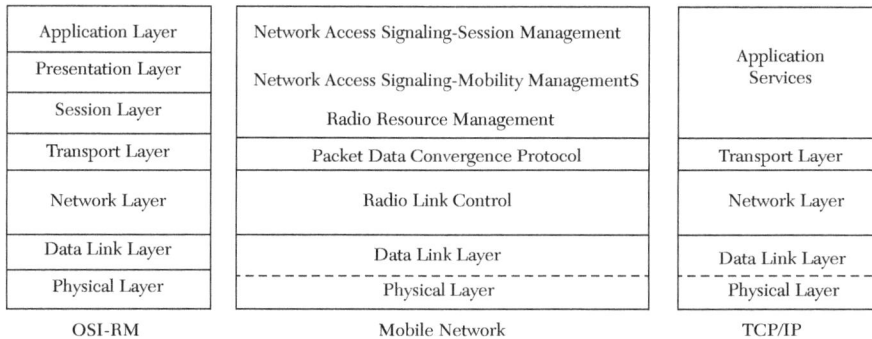

Application Layer	Network Access Signaling-Session Management	Application Services
Presentation Layer	Network Access Signaling-Mobility ManagementS	
Session Layer	Radio Resource Management	
Transport Layer	Packet Data Convergence Protocol	Transport Layer
Network Layer	Radio Link Control	Network Layer
Data Link Layer	Data Link Layer	Data Link Layer
Physical Layer	Physical Layer	Physical Layer
OSI-RM	Mobile Network	TCP/IP

FIGURE 1.3. Three protocol stacks.

THE OSI-RM

The OSI-RM is a seven-layer model that assigns distinctive names and numbers to its layers (the reason for both names and numbers is unclear). Today, models are often used as a learning tool to introduce the layers and functions of TCP/IP. This section also includes the layers of mobile networks. The OSI-RM is shown in Figure 1.4.

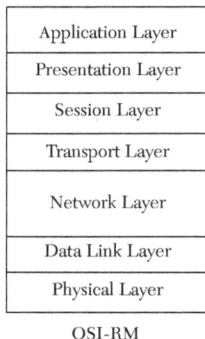

| Application Layer |
| Presentation Layer |
| Session Layer |
| Transport Layer |
| Network Layer |
| Data Link Layer |
| Physical Layer |

OSI-RM

FIGURE 1.4. The OSI-RM Layers.

The OSI-RM was developed by the International Organization for Standardization. Their standards are abbreviated as ISO (meaning "equal" in Greek) to emphasize the equality of implementations based on the standards. The model was developed in the late 1970s and first published in 1984 as ISO 7498. The current version, jointly published with the International Electrotechnical Commission (IEC), is ISO/IEC 7498-1:1994.

Layer 1: The Physical Layer

The physical layer involves the physical communication medium and the related technologies necessary to transmit data across that medium. Data communication is essentially the transfer of digital and electronic signals through various physical channels like fiber-optic cables, copper cabling, and air. The physical layer includes standards for technologies and metrics closely related to the channels, such as defining what a 0 and 1 bit are "on the wire," any additional bits for error detection or correction, data transmission speeds, connector type, and so on.

In simple terms, the physical layer "spits out bits."

Layer 2: The Data Link Layer

The data link layer focuses on the structure of the *frame*, which is a first-order bit structure. A frame is the final form of bits before they are sent and the initial form when they are received. It is important to note that frames do not contain bits that instruct a receiver, "This is the first frame of a series. Wait to process it." All frames are processed as they arrive.

Because of flow control (the sender needs to slow down or speed up) and error control (this frame makes no sense; I need to have it resent), these were key focuses of the data link layer. Ethernet is a common standard at this layer. For local area networks (LANs), the data link layer is divided into two sub-layers: the lower media access control (MAC) layer and the upper logical link control (LLC) layer (for all the flow and error control). Nowadays, LLC is often overlooked as flow and error control are handled at higher layers.

Flow control is a local issue for a network: no senders should be able to send faster than a receiver can accept new traffic. Flow control should not be confused with congestion control, which is a global property of the network: no sender is overwhelming any receiver, but there is simply too much traffic in the network. In cases of congestion, it is the *network* as a receiver that tells the senders to slow down. This can be done with the same mechanisms as used for flow control but generated inside the network instead of at a receiving endpoint.

However, the MAC address, often called the device hardware or physical address, is the key part of Layer 2. The MAC frame contains 48-bit source and destination addresses administered by the IEEE and written as a 12-digit hexadecimal number. An example is 00-B0-D0-63-C2-26. The first 24 bits (00-B0-D0) are assigned to manufacturers by the IEEE and form a vendor identifier. The last 24 bits (63-C2-26) are assigned by the vendor and form a kind of serial number for the network hardware.

It is important to note that MAC addresses say nothing about where in the world a particular system is located. To do that, another layer on top of the data link layer is needed.

Layer 3: The Network Layer

Not every system is directly connected to every possible destination except LANs and a few small point-to-point network backbones. Most of the time, a frame has to be relayed through one or more intermediate systems (ISs) to the correct end system (ES). This process requires a global (good all over the world) public (known to all potential senders) addressing mechanism for the global public Internet.

The network layer is where this global and publicly addressed scheme resides. The layer is concerned with concepts such as routing, forwarding, and addressing across multiple connected networks. The network layer address tells every system in the world where the source and destination are located and, even more importantly, what the "next hop" is to move the information closer to its destination.

The data unit of the network layer is called the *packet*. On the Internet, systems put messages inside packets and put the packets inside frames. It is just as accurate to say that "Layer 3 protocol data units (PDUs) are placed inside Layer 2 PDUs," but the common phrase is that packets are inside frames that are sent as bits.

It is important to note that frames only flow between directly connected and linked systems, as on a LAN. At every hop, the frame is processed as soon as it is received. If the information is to be relayed to another system, another frame with different source and destination MAC addresses is constructed to hold the packet inside. In other words, frames travel hop-by-hop while the packet inside flows from source to destination across the network.

The OSI-RM has its own global public addressing scheme, which is used in the IS-IS routing protocol. For most of the Internet, the Internet protocol v4 (IPv4) and now IPv6 are used as the main network layer addressing systems. IP is known as a *best-effort* data delivery system. All of the systems try their best to deliver the packet content, but if things go wrong, it is not the responsibility of the network layer to figure out what went wrong and what to do about it. (Can you see another layer coming to solve this issue?)

The structure of IPv4 and especially IPv6 addresses is quite complex. They deserve a chapter on their own.

The network layer used to be called the *routing layer,* but they changed it to something harder to understand.

Layer 4: The Transport Layer

The responsibility of the transport layer is to ensure that data packets arrive at the ultimate destination without errors or missing packets and in the right order. If any of these error conditions are detected, the transport layer decides what to do to fix it. In the case of streaming data, like a video, the answer might be "do nothing" because if the error is small enough, it will not be very disruptive.

However, if the data is a database record about how many hours you should be paid for—well, it is best to get that right. This way the receiver can ask the sender for a resend of packets until the message is received correctly.

The transport layer can work in a connection-oriented or connectionless manner. In connection-oriented networks, the sender must contact the receiver and receive permission to send data. The sender, through special messages, can even "wake up" a receiver that is not ready to accept data. When data has been exchanged, the connection is closed, like making a telephone call. The nice thing about connection-oriented transport layer services is that they provide an easy way to detect missing or mis-sequenced packets quickly. Connections also provide a convenient place to hang quality of service (QoS) promises from. In fact, standards provide for different service-level guarantees when connections are in use.

A connectionless transport layer is much simpler to implement but can make for a lot of work the layers above it and the applications that rely on the integrity of data they send and receive. One trend today is to make a lot of communications that used to be connection-oriented connectionless because errors are a small fraction of what they once were and end systems have enough horsepower to do whatever they have to do to function properly.

The way you say this is that, not too long ago, the network was smart and the end systems were kind of simple, but now the end systems are so smart that the network can be simple.

The transport layer used to be called the *end-to-end layer*, but, as with the routing layer, people could figure out what it did much too easily.

Layer 5: The Session Layer

Definitions of the session layer tend to be circular: something like "The session layer is responsible for network coordination between two separate applications in a session." Many, like this one, say everything correctly but add nothing useful.

The session layer is in charge of keeping the history of the activity between the two end-system applications that are communicating. It is not continuous: the sender creates a session, uses it, and then drops it when done. During the session, if things go wrong, you can pick up where you left off because both ends of the interaction have all the information they need to determine what needs to be done ("I sent all of this so far…what are you missing?"). Without a decent session layer, every one of those 2 GB movies you download would have to start all over again if a link dropped, even for a second, and even if there was only a megabyte or so left to go (this used to happen all the time in the old days).

In a client-server model network, such as the cell phone system with the end equipment as the client and the other system as the server, it is not unusual for a very busy server to push session information back at the client. This information is often stored as *cookies* from various Web sites, along with any other information the server wants to know when you return. In the past, only the server possessed sufficient power to retain all necessary session information.

Not everything requires a session, of course. Yet, it is there if you need it.

Layer 6: The Presentation Layer

Data comes in all different forms. Computer chips store the data bits in an 8-bit byte in different ways. Some processors used to be called *big-endian* and *little-endian* in a nod to writer Jonathan Swift, and the terms still apply. Before storing data from a file transfer, for example, the presentation layer had to turn those bits around if they arrived in a different order than expected.

NOTE	*They were called big-endian and little-endian from a book by Jonathan Swift. Two nations in Swift's book go to war because they are different as to which end of an egg is correct to crack first. The importance is that early computer scientists were widely read and often had a playful sense about what they were doing.*

Today, content can arrive in a JavaScript Object Notation (JSON), as HTML, or something else. It is the responsibility of the presentation layer to ensure that the receiver application is given arriving data in a form it can use.

Layer 7: The Application Layer

The name of the application layer is a good one, except that there are not really any applications at the application layer. The applications are really *above* all seven layers, and an application like a text processing program runs fine on a stand-alone computer.

But when run over a network, the application layer provides the text applications with all the application program interfaces (APIs) and other tools it needs to run over a network. The application layer supports standard communication *methods*. Therefore, for example, Web browsers communicate using hypertext transfer protocol secure (HTTPS), and HTTP and email clients communicate using post office protocol version 3 (POP3) and simple mail transfer protocol (SMTP).

The Upper Layers

That was a brief tour of the OSI-RM. There is much more to learn, but this is a start.

It is important to note that the top three layers of the OSI-RM, namely the session, presentation, and application layers, were designed to be completely independent and interoperable regardless of their source. However, it is almost universal that all three of these layers are implemented in one comprehensive package.

One way to remember the order and names of the OSI-RM layers is to use a mnemonic, which starts at the top and works its way down:

All People Seem to Need Data Processing.
There is also one for going from bottom to top:

Polly Doesn't Need to Save Puppies Anymore
(There were many variations: several of the activities that poor Polly could now refrain from are no longer considered polite.)

THE TCP/IP MODEL

It is incorrect to think of the TCP/IP protocol stack as different from the OSI-RM protocol stack. It is more accurate to think of TCP/IP as a very successful implementation of the layers of the OSI-RM. The TCP/IP Layers are organized differently and differ in some respects, but TCP/IP was up and running before the OSI-RM was completely defined.

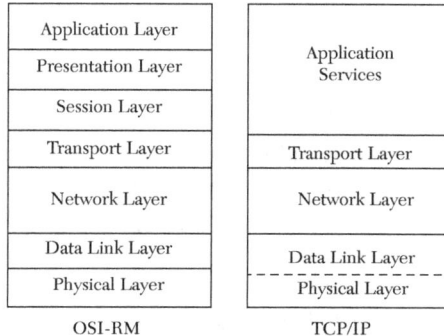

OSI-RM	TCP/IP
Application Layer	Application Services
Presentation Layer	
Session Layer	
Transport Layer	Transport Layer
Network Layer	Network Layer
Data Link Layer	Data Link Layer
Physical Layer	Physical Layer

FIGURE 1.5. The TCP/IP Protocol Layers compared to the OSI-RM Layers.

The Layers of TCP/IP

One significant difference between the OSI-RM and TCP/IP is that TCP/IP does not define anything below the IP Layer, which corresponds to the network layer (or Layer 3) of the OSI-RM. What the TCP/IP standards do is define how to put Layer 3 IP packets into different kinds of Layer 2 frames and how to extract them. This allows IP packets to run over almost any kind of network, as long as there is an RFC (the Internet standards are called, for historical reasons, requests for comments) that covers it.

Even if a new type of network link is invented, such as packet optical, and has a way to send some kind of framed data bits over it, it can still someday be part of the Internet. All that has to happen is convince the Internet gurus to create an RFC for mapping IP packets to packet optical frames.

This may seem like a trivial point, but it is not. The layers below the IP Layer are not as important as the overall flow of packets from one host (end system) to another across the network.

And this layering means that once the packet has been "framed," all the other layers above the IP Layer are along for the ride. Only the IP Layer has to deal with the underlying network link hardware.

It is also important to note that TCP/IP is considered a *peer protocol* stack, meaning every implementation of TCP/IP is considered to have the same capabilities as every other. There are no "restricted" or "master" versions of TCP/IP to be concerned about. Therefore, for example, there is no special server software needed.

However, this does not mean that all TCP/IP applications are "peers." TCP/IP, like many other protocol stacks, is implemented according to a model known as the *client-server model*.

The Client-Server Model

The host systems that run TCP/IP generally fall into one of two categories: one host is the *client* and the other host is the *server*. This is mostly an application issue because most computers today are fully capable of running the client version of a program for one application (for example, the Web browser) and the server version of another program (for example, a file transfer server) at the same time. Dedicated servers are most common on the Internet, but almost all client computers can act as servers for many applications.

A server process usually just sits and waits for the client to "talk" to it. Normally, this client request could be to stream a movie, or to get a page for a client Web browser, and so on. Clients usually have people sitting in front of them to initiate an action, and servers generally wait for some client to request something. The way you say it is "clients talk and servers listen."

The client-server model is not the only way to implement a protocol stack. Lots of applications today implement a peer-to-peer model. Peer applications have the same capabilities, whether used as a client or as a server. Distributed file-sharing systems on the Internet typically function as both clients (fetching files for the user) and servers (allowing user files to be shared by others).

The differences between client-server and peer-peer models are mainly application differences. A desktop computer that runs a Web browser and has file sharing turned on is both client and server but is still not peer-to-peer.

Sockets

Another concept that is essential to understand when it comes to protocol stacks is the *socket*. Sockets are the way a programmer usually implements applications that run over a network. Sockets came about when client-server networking applications first became popular in the 1980s. Early application programmers had never faced this situation before and had no guidelines on how to proceed.

However, all programmers learned how to manipulate files. They knew how to create a file, open it, read from it, write to it, close it, and even delete it. Therefore, the socket interface was invented to allow programmers to treat the network just like a file.

A programmer using sockets could easily create a socket, open a socket, read from a socket (on the server side), write to a socket (on the client side), close a socket, and even delete a socket that was no longer needed.

In TCP/IP, the socket is a combination of the IP address and the TCP port number. Servers use sockets running on well-known ports (Web sites use port 80) so that clients know where to send. Clients are forbidden from using well-known ports in their sockets and are typically numbers with five digits.

TCP/IP LAYERS

The TCP/IP protocol stack is usually presented as a five-layer model. Unlike the OSI-RM, the layers only have names and not numbers. They do not even have to be capitalized.

The bottom two TCP/IP protocol stack layers, sometimes seen as one, are the physical layer and network data link layer. Above the data link and physical layers is the IP Layer itself. The IP Layer creates and routes the IP packet to the destination IP Layer. IP packets are called datagrams in much of the documentation, especially older documentation. IP is the major protocol at the TCP/IP Network Layer (the routing layer).

The Transport Layer of TCP/IP consists of two major protocols: the transmission control protocol (TCP) and the user datagram protocol (UDP). TCP is a *reliable* transport layer added on top of the *best-effort* IP Layer to ensure that even if data is lost in transit, the hosts will be able to detect this and resend the missing information. TCP is connection-oriented (connect, interact, and disconnect), and the data units are called *segments*. UDP is connectionless (just send) and is as best-effort as IP itself. UDP data units are called *datagrams*.

The messages that applications using TCP/IP exchange are made up of strings of segments or datagrams. Segments and datagrams are used to chop up the application content, such as large, multi-megabyte files, into more easily handled chunks.

TCP is reliable because it always resends corrupt or lost segments. When hits happens, TCP stops and waits for a sender to resend the missing information before it can receive anything new again. This is suitable for bulk data transfer but creates many issues for delay-sensitive and streaming applications such as voice or video.

UDP, on the other hand, is a connectionless transport layer on top of connectionless IP. UDP segments are simply forwarded to a destination under the assumption that sooner or later a response will come back from the remote host. The response forms an implied or formal acknowledgment that the UDP segment arrived.

The top layer of the TCP/IP stack is the application (sometimes application services) layer. In contrast to the OSI-RM top three layers, this TCP/IP Layer combines the history of a session, differences in data types, and other application features all together. This is where the client-server concept is important. Applications for networks typically come in client or server versions. While a host computer might be able to run client processes and server processes at the same time, in the simplest case, these processes are two different applications.

For example, a Web server runs on a host whether there is a browser client pointed at it or not. The Web server process issues a *passive open* to TCP/IP and essentially remains idle on the network until some client requests content. When the Web browser (client) process issues an *active open* to TCP/IP, it sends packets to a Web site immediately. The Web site can be the default site for the browser, but if the Web site is not reachable or not running, that causes an error condition.

This is a good place to look at some of the operational aspects of the TCP/IP protocol stack at the TCP and IP Layers.

THE IP LAYER (NETWORK LAYER)

The connectionless IP Layer routes IP packets independently through the collection of network nodes such as routers that make up the "Internetwork" connecting LANs. Packets at the IP Layer do not follow "paths" or "virtual circuits" or anything else set up by signaled or manually defined connections for packet flow in other types of network layers. However, this also means that the packets' content might arrive out of sequence, or even with gaps in the sequence due to lost packets, at the destination.

IP does not care which application a packet belongs to. IP delivers all packets without a sense of priority or sensitivity to loss. The whole point of IP is to get packets from one network interface to another. IP itself is not concerned with the lack of guaranteed *quality of service* (QOS) parameters such as bandwidth or minimal delay, and this is characteristic of all connectionless, best-effort networks. Even the basics, such as sequenced delivery of packet content, priorities, and guaranteed delivery in the form of acknowledgments (if these are needed by the application), must be provided by the higher layers of the TCP/IP protocol stack. These reliable transport functions are not functions of the IP Layer, and some are not even functions of TCP.

Two other major protocols run at the IP Layer besides IPv4 or IPv6 (or both). The routers that form the network nodes in a TCP/IP network must be able to send error messages to the hosts if a router must discard a packet (for example, due to a lack of buffer space because of congestion). This protocol is known as the Internet control message protocol (ICMP). ICMP messages are sent inside IP packets, but ICMP is still considered a different protocol and not a separate layer.

The other protocol at the IP Layer has many functions depending on the type of network that IP is running on. This is the address resolution protocol (ARP). The function of ARP is to provide a method for the IP Layer, which technically knows only about packets, to find out the proper data link layer address to place in the frame header destination field. On LANs, this is the MAC address. Without this address, the network of links beneath the IP Layer could not deliver the frame containing the IP packet to the proper destination.

On a LAN, ARP is a way for the IP Layer to send a broadcast message onto the LAN asking, in effect, "Who has IP address 192.168.13.84?" Each system, host, or router on the LAN will examine the ARP message (all systems must pay attention to a broadcast), and the system having the IP address in question will reply to the sender's MAC address found in the source field of the frame. This target system will also cache the IP address information so that it knows the MAC address of the sender (this cuts down on ARP traffic on the network). The MAC layer address needed by the sending system is found in the source address field of the frame carrying the ARP reply packet.

ARP messages are broadcast to every host in what is called the network layer *broadcast domain*. The broadcast domain can be a single physical group (all hosts attached to a single group of hubs, for example) or a logical grouping of hosts forming a *virtual LAN* (VLAN).

The most important task of the IP Layer is to take care of the global public addressing scheme. This global scheme allows all attached systems to communicate (if permitted) and prevents obvious errors like two devices having the same address.

THE TRANSPORT LAYER

The two main protocols that run above the IP Layer at the transport layer are TCP and UDP. Recently, UDP has been gaining more prominence on the

Internet, especially with applications such as voice and multicast traffic like video. One reason is that TCP, with its reliable resending, is not particularly well suited for *real-time* applications (real-time just means that the network delays must be low and stable or else the application will not function properly). For these applications, data that arrives late is worse than data that does not arrive at all, especially if the late data causes all the data *after* it to also arrive late.

TCP

TCP's built-in reliability features include sequence numbering with resending, which is used to detect and resend missing or out-of-sequence segments. TCP also includes a complete flow control mechanism (called *windowing*) to prevent any sender from overwhelming a receiver. Neither of these built-in TCP features is good for real-time audio and video on the Internet. These applications cannot "pause" and wait for missing segments, nor should they slow down or speed up as traffic loads vary on the Internet (the fact that they do just points out the incomplete nature of TCP/IP when it comes to quality of service for these applications and services).

TCP contains all the functions and mechanisms needed to make up for the best-effort, connectionless delivery provided by the IP Layer. Packets could arrive at a host with errors, out of their correct sequence, duplicated, or with gaps in sequence due to lost (or discarded) packets. TCP must guarantee that the data stream is delivered to the destination application error-free, with all data in sequence and complete. Following the practice used in connection-oriented networks, TCP uses acknowledgments (ACKs) that periodically flow from the destination to the source to assure the sender that all is well with the data received to that point in time.

On the sending side, TCP passes segments to the IP Layer for encapsulation in packets, which the IP Layer in hosts and routers forwards without a connection to the destination host. On the receiving side, TCP accepts the incoming segments from the IP Layer and delivers the data they represent to the proper application running above TCP in the exact order in which the data was sent.

UDP

The TCP/IP Transport Layer has another protocol running at the TCP Layer. UDP is as connectionless as IP. When applications use UDP instead of TCP, there is no need to establish, maintain, or tear down a connection between a source and a destination before sending data. Connection management adds overhead and some initial delay to the network. UDP is a way to send data quickly and simply.

However, UDP offers none of the reliability services that TCP does. UDP applications cannot rely on TCP to ensure error-free, guaranteed (via acknowledgments), in-sequence delivery of data to the destination.

For some simple applications, purely connectionless data delivery is good enough. Single request-response message pairs between applications are sent more efficiently with UDP because there is no need to exchange a flurry of initial TCP segments to establish a connection. Many applications will not be satisfied with this mode of operation, however, because it puts the burden of reliability on the application itself.

UDP is often used for short transactions that fit into one datagram. Real-time applications often use UDP with another header inside called the real-time transport protocol (RTP). RTP borrows what it needs from the TCP header, such as a sequence number to detect (but not to resend) missing packets of audio and video, and uses these desirable features in UDP.

THE APPLICATION SERVICES LAYER

The top of the TCP/IP protocol stack, at the application layer, are the basic applications and services of the TCP/IP architecture. Several basic applications are typically bundled with the TCP/IP software distributed from various sources and are interoperable.

The standard application services suite usually includes a file transfer method (file transfer protocol: FTP), a remote terminal access method (Telnet, which is not commonly used today, and others, which are), an electronic mail system (simple mail transfer protocol: SMTP), and a domain name system (DNS) directory service for domain name to IP address translation (and vice versa), and more. Many TCP/IP implementations also include a way of accessing files remotely (rather than transferring the whole file to the other host) known as network file system (NFS). There is also the simple network management protocol (SNMP) for network operations. For the Web, the server and browser applications are based on the hypertext transfer protocol (HTTP). Some of these applications are defined to run on TCP, and others are defined to run on UDP, and in many cases, they can run on either.

TCP and Mobile Networks

The Internet's transport layer, TCP, was standardized in the 1980s. It offered reliable packet delivery over the best-effort IP protocol at the network layer, plus a mechanism for flow control so that no sender can overwhelm a receiver, as well as congestion control to prevent the network from trying to carry too much traffic.

However, the new 5G and 6G networks, which employ millimeter wave (mmWave) links, pose problems for the way TCP operates. These radio links exhibit "erratic propagation behavior," which can cause problems for TCP's reliability and flow control features.

Various modifications have been proposed to TCP to allow for reliability for applications that require low delays (latency) and large bandwidths. One issue is that TCP is technically an end-to-end protocol (recall the transport layer as the "end-to-end layer") that should run from a host system source to a host system destination. Several modifications to TCP seek to "short circuit" this behavior and run TCP between local servers in the mobile network instead of the source server endpoint, an idea called a "shorter control loop."

In fairness, many of the limitations of TCP were already apparent before newer mobile networks made such shortcomings obvious. For this reason, many applications that would ordinarily use TCP to deliver message segments now use connectionless UDP to deliver datagrams instead. The role of TCP is played by the real-time transport protocol (RTP), which slides in above UDP and below the application services of TCP/IP to deliver audio and video.

THE MOBILE NETWORK PROTOCOL STACK

Here is another look at how layers in a mobile network match up to the OSI-RM and TCP/IP. Figure 1.6 shows the layers of a modern mobile network in between the layers of the OSI-RM and TCP-IP.

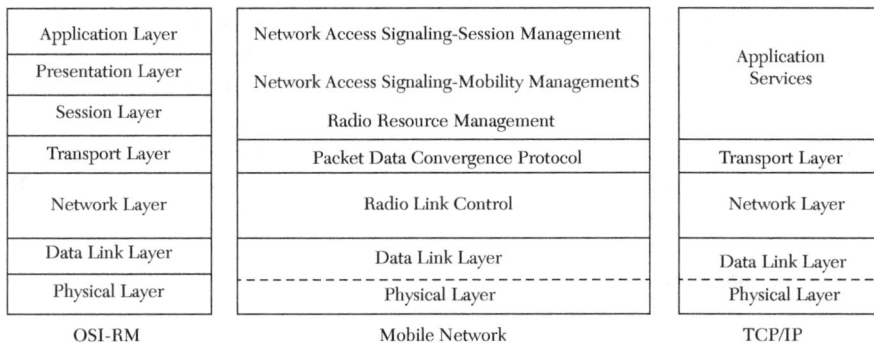

OSI-RM	Mobile Network	TCP/IP
Application Layer	Network Access Signaling-Session Management	Application Services
Presentation Layer	Network Access Signaling-Mobility ManagementS	
Session Layer	Radio Resource Management	
Transport Layer	Packet Data Convergence Protocol	Transport Layer
Network Layer	Radio Link Control	Network Layer
Data Link Layer	Data Link Layer	Data Link Layer
Physical Layer	Physical Layer	Physical Layer

FIGURE 1.6. The three protocol stacks compared.

We are now ready to discuss how a user equipment (UE) client device such as a smartphone can connect to an Internet-based Web server running TCP/IP. This end-to-end connectivity is shown in Figure 1.7.

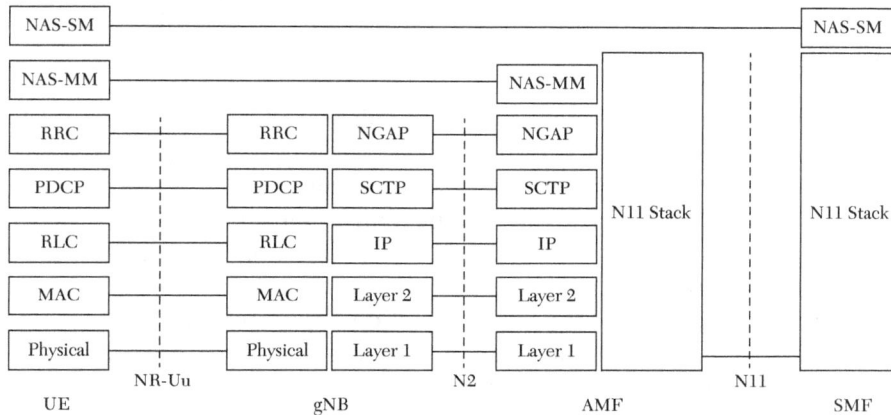

FIGURE 1.7. Mobile networks and the Internet.

There are three main components shown in the figure, although four items are displayed. Compared to the middle portion of Figure 1.6, the two internal pieces of the 5G core have been separated as the access and mobility management function (AMF; note that it is not AMMF) and the session management function (SMF). Technically, these are not nodes on the Internet itself, but servers in the mobile network service provider's network that handle the session with the network and mobility issues as the UE moves around. However, the traffic flow remains the same.

Once the UE attaches to the network and establishes a connection using the network access signaling-mobility management (NAS-MM) signaling protocol, a session is established using the network access signaling-session management (NAS-SM) protocol.

It is the responsibility of the radio resource control (RRC) layer to manage all communications with the cell tower, the gNB device. To accomplish this, it packages up messages in the packet data convergence protocol (PDCP) layer format. A convergence protocol's task is to make everything above it appear the same while allowing differences in the layers below the convergence layer. It is a way of saying, "Things can look different below this layer, but here and above, everything has to look the same: same fields, same parameters, same structure to the data unit."

There can be different types of radio link control (RLC) depending on the type of cell tower it connects to. As in many other stacks, the messages end up organized as frames at the media access control (MAC) layer and sent as a series of bits across the physical link.

These lower layers are matched at the cell tower gNB across the new radio Uu interface (NR-Uu), although technically the interfaces in mobile networks are not acronyms, just designations.

Note that from the cell tower to the mobile provider service point, the backhaul portion of the network, the lower layers are IP (although labeled with OSI-RM numbers, it is likely TCP/IP protocols running here).

The two higher layers are the stream control transmission protocol (SCTP), which provides reliable and in-sequence transmission services for data units sent over the mobile network.

The last piece here is the next generation application protocol (NGAP), a layer that basically takes the place of TCP and transports both signaling and data messages over the backhaul network.

These layers run over the N2 interface.

Now an odd thing occurs: the AMF and SMF connect over the N11 interface using the N11 protocol stack. N11 is special. N11 is a dedicated interface that connects the 5G core (5GC) network to external systems, specifically for interworking between 5G and non-cellular networks, such as the global public Internet.

Therefore, in most cases, the N11 protocol stack is old reliable TCP/IP.

CLOUD NETWORKS AND FOG NETWORKS

Much has been written about cloud networks and fog networks. Both are characterized by virtualization of functions (software-defined instead of hardware-determined) and flexibility in the resources assigned to an entity running that protocol.

Simply put, if these characteristics apply to a centralized group of systems, this is cloud computing or cloud networking. If these characteristics apply to a decentralized (to the edge) or distributed group of systems, this is fog computing or fog networking (or just "fogging"). Fog networks always aim to process data closest to where it is generated or consumed.

THE MODERN WORLD

The next time you're in an automobile, imagine that you are the driver of the four-person carpool on your way to work. Everyone has a cell phone or tablet. The cell phones are on, and some are using their tablets or laptops. Someone is in the passenger seat on her cell phone with her husband to remind him that he has to take their daughter to soccer practice after school. He does not pick up, so she leaves a voicemail and texts him a reminder. In the back are two other coworkers. One is using her tablet to catch up on the latest episodes of a new thriller series she has been watching. Someone comes to the door of her house, and the doorbell signals her laptop. She sees it is a delivery of the gift for her son's birthday and speaks to the person as if she were upstairs. She has them place the package at the door. She goes back to her show, and the rush hour traffic up ahead suggests that she will have plenty of time to finish before they arrive at the office. The last passenger is uploading and distributing his final changes to a presentation that he is giving to his team later that morning on adding more robots to his factory floor.

Each of them sometimes works at home, but they often have to make the trip to the office, if for no other reason than workers and managers with a personal, face-to-face relationship get more work done more efficiently than groups who have never had close contact. Therefore, the networking needs of all four of them—voice, text, data, and more—including the telemetry from the driver's latest model electric car—must be satisfied by the wireless networks available on the roadway. Their needs include not only bandwidth: each of their devices (and all four will have at least two) require IP addresses for Internet access, even if their information does not directly involve the Internet, such as someone's telephone call.

WHAT COMES NEXT

Where do all these addresses come from? Not by the millions, but by the billions—potentially one or more for every person on earth.

That is the topic of the next chapter.

IPv6

OVERVIEW

We have already explored a major component of all modern networks and their infrastructures. This was:

- The need for almost everyone in the world to have multiple Internet connections to their home, office, car, and business in order to work, plan their lives, and entertain themselves. This requires much more than the simple 32-bit address space provided by IPv4, which is why we need IPv6.

WHAT YOU WILL LEARN

In this chapter, we will delve into aspects of IPv4, which is the version of IP addressing that is the next step beyond IPv4.

- The topics covered include:
- IPv4 and IPv6 comparison
- IPv4 and IPv6 address notation
- Drawbacks of IPv4
- Public and private addresses
- IPv6 protocols
- IPv4 and IPv6 headers

The main function of the network layer of the OSI-RM (Layer 3) or the TCP/IP network layer (the IP layer) is to hold the globally unique network address that makes every device in the world reachable by every other device that it is allowed to connect with. There are two major forms of network layer addresses used on the Internet today: IPv4 (the original addressing scheme of TCP/IP) and IPv6. IPv6 was once called "IPng" for "IP: The Next Generation" because the developers were supposedly fans of the TV show "Star Trek: The Next Generation."

Why is the successor to IPv4 not IPv5? The best answer is that there already was an IPv5 when IPng came along, so they called the new plan IPv6. (IPv5 was defined in RFC 1819 as the Streams 2 [ST2] protocol.) It often comes as a shock to people looking into IPv6 that the original specification is from December of 1995 (RFC 1883, now obsolete). (Internet standards are called RFCs or "Requests for Comments" for historical reasons; in almost all cases, no one is asking for an opinion on any of this today.)

With IPv4, often the most important person associated with a local area network in an office of almost any size was in charge of handing out IPv4 addresses. It is normal, even today, when a source mentions "IP addresses," it is understood to mean "IPv4" addresses. The added "v6" is used only when IPv6 is meant. This chapter always calls out IPv4 and IPv6 in full to prevent any misunderstanding, except when referencing the "IP layer" itself, as above.

The reason for the popularity of the person in charge of IPv4 addresses was that it was often difficult to obtain what are called *public IPv4 addresses*. Public addresses, in contrast to private IPv4 or IPv6 addresses, are the ones that are advertised by routers on the Internet and make the device that had one reachable (if allowed) by all other devices attached to the Internet.

IPV4 AND IPV6

TCP/IP had only been in widespread use for about ten years before it became obvious that there were issues with the IP layer, mainly in the protocols used in the network layer. Once the World Wide Web came along in the early 1990s, the Internet shifted from a place where you had to know the right commands to use line-by-line (`"telnet 10.123.45.6"`) to one where the Web page was sprawled out visually on a monitor, often in full color (well, in 256 colors). All you had to do was point and click with your mouse to follow a link or attach to another computer. With the Web, the Internet very quickly became a place where anyone could go and play, work, or just explore.

Every business, and then every person, had to have a Web site running on a server somewhere so that client computers could fetch information from them. In this case, the term information was not limited to text but included audio, video, maps, images, and every other kind of media that people could load onto a Web site.

By 1995, there was a plan to replace IPv4 with the "next generation" of IP. The two biggest issues with IPv4 were the potential exhaustion, and soon, of useful IPv4 addresses for all these clients and servers. That shortage was caused by the awkward structure of the original IPv4 address space, a system using classes. This legacy was changed but resulted in all kinds of backward and forward compatibility issues.

It is important to look at these two limitations in some detail in order to appreciate two things about networking infrastructure. First, it is better to be flexible than rigid. If it were easier to modify the IPv4 class structure, the pressure to come up with IPv6 would have been less. Second, technology changes rapidly in many cases. Things that were not considered during preliminary development often become roadblocks later on.

Both of these two limits are related, of course. Yet, it is always good to try and see if these two limitations might exist in any new technology when introduced to it for the first time.

Consider the second IPv4 problem: the classful address space. Then, this chapter will examine the continuing lack of useful IPv4 network addresses that the billions of people in the world would need to join the Internet.

Dotted Decimal Notation

IPv4 addresses are usually written in *dotted decimal* notation. Each 8-bit byte of the 32-bit IPv4 address is converted from binary (such as 0101) or hexadecimal (like FE34) to a decimal number between 0 (0000 0000 or 0x00) and 255 (1111 1111 or 0xFF). The four 8-bit-bytes of the IPv4 address are then written as four decimal numbers separated by dots: W.X.Y.Z, as with 192.168.11.27.

For example, 1010 1100 0001 0000 1100 1000 0000 0010 (0xAC 10 C8 02) becomes 172.16.200.2. Then, 1011 1111 1111 1111 0000 1110 0010 1100 (0xBF FF 0E 2C) becomes 191.255.14.44, and so on.

THE ISSUES WITH IPV4: CLASSFUL ADDRESSES

Useful IPv4 addresses were part of IPv4 from the start. IPv4 addresses were invented in a world where the best and brightest computer scientists saw a world where there were lots of little networks with not many systems on them (called Class C networks), fewer medium-sized networks with more systems (Class B), and a handful of really gigantic networks with a whole ton of systems on them (Class A), such as those run by Fortune 10 companies such as IBM, GE, Ford, GM, and the like.

The IPv4 address was 32 bits long, which was a considerable size for those days. Why is the number of bits important? That determines how many things you can count easily, such as the number of possible systems on a global network. It also determines the upper limit on easy memory location access.

Early 8-bit computers could count up to 256 things (0 to 255), or 2^8 (2 to the 8th power). Actually, it was a little more complex than that, because computers also used negative numbers (–127 to +127), but the idea is what is important there. In those days, memory was expensive and processors were slow, so programmers did what they could. The 16-bit chipsets could count up to 65,536, or 2^{16}. Intel only released their first 16-bit chip in 1980: the famous 8086 and then the 8088. The 16-bit processor did not move from PCs to video games until 1986. Even today, Windows operating systems have a folder named "Program Files (x86)" for applications that are built to that standard.

As chip size shrank and memory costs fell, the number of bits in an address grew. A 32-bit chip could handle counts up to a little over 4 billion (4,294,967,296). Therefore, that is the hard limit for IPv4 addresses: there could never be more than about 4 billion uniquely identifiable systems in the world. That would only cover about half the world's population today, not to mention all the "things" the Internet of Things (IoT) uses today. There are more processors in a single automobile today than there were in the world in 1950.

Most PCs today are 64-bit machines, which can address up to 18,446,744,073,709,551,616 systems. Usually written as 1.8446744e+19, this is an enormous number. Yet, even the 32-bit IPv4 address space with 4 billion systems still had problems with the awkward structure of the classes.

The problem with the "classful" IPv4 addressing scheme was that the Internet soon evolved into a series of interconnected networks where there were mainly large networks with many systems. The whole class system was very quickly obsolete. There were even two more classes that never could be used for individual systems: Class D addresses for multicast (sending to more than one destination) and Class E for experimental networks. The first bits of the IPv4 address were used to determine the network class, not to assign addresses to systems.

For example, those few Class A networks, 127 in total, had IPv4 addresses starting with 0 and therefore were assigned 50% of the entire 32-bit address space (about 2 billion systems in total). So, each Class A network could have 2^{24}, or 16,777,216, systems on it. Another 1 billion IPv4 addresses went to Class B networks (addresses starting with 10), with each of these networks having 2^{15}, or 65,535 systems. Class C networks, literally millions of them, could have only 256 system maximums of each (2^8). Class D and E used up 12.5% of the total address space and did not do anything very helpful overall.

Table 2.1 summarizes the sizes of these classes.

TABLE 2.1. The first bits of the first address byte determine the class, the number of useful addresses, and the percentage of the total address space devoted to that class.

First bits of IPv4 Address	Number of Useful Addresses	Percentage of Address Space
Class A: 0 (0 to 127)	2^{31} = 2,147,483,648 (about 2 billion)	50%
Class B: 10 (128 to 191)	2^{30} = 1,073,741,824 (about 1 billion)	25%
Class C: 110 (192 to 223)	2^{29} = 536,870,912 (about 500 million)	12.5%
Class D: 1110 (224-239) (multicast)	2^{28} = 268,435,456 (about 270 million)	6.25%
Class E: 1111 (240-255) (experimental)	2^{28} = 268,435,456 (about 270 million)	6.25%

Class D was designated for multicast, and Class E was reserved for experimental use. Already, 12.5% of the address space, approximately 500 million addresses, could not be allocated for clients or servers. Additionally, any IPv4 address starting with 127 (e.g., 127.2.3.4) was a loopback address used solely for testing purposes and never left the device. An entire Class A address was dedicated to packets that never left the source.

Figure 2.1 illustrates the variations in network sizes and number of bits for each class.

There were specific guidelines regarding what constituted a "useful" address, but the sheer numbers imposed strict upper limits on the number of potential networks in each class and the number of hosts on each network:

Class A: 128 networks with 16,777,216 (16 million) hosts (clients or servers) on each.
Class B: 65,536 networks with 65,536 hosts each.
Class C: 16,777,216 (16 million) networks with 128 hosts each.

To further complicate matters, IPv4 classes allowed a network to move the network/host boundary to the right, a process called *subnetting*. With subnetting, a

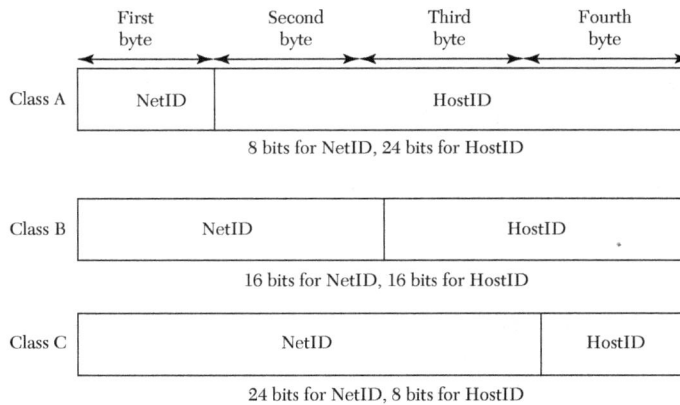

FIGURE 2.1. Network bits and host bits varied for each class of IPv4 network.

company with a Class A address (for example, IBM had IPv4 address 9.x.x.x), could split one large network with around 16 million hosts into two networks, each with 8 million hosts; or four networks, each with 4 million hosts; and so on.

The boundary between the network and host portions of the address was determined by the network mask or *netmask* applied to the address. If the netmask did not subnet the classful address, it was referred to as the *natural netmask* (or *default netmask*) of the class.

Table 2.2 shows how this natural netmasking functioned.

TABLE 2.2. Parsing IPv4 addresses with "natural" or default subnet masks.

Original Class	Default Mask	Network/ Host Bits	Example and Interpretation
A	255.0.0.0	8/24 (/8 prefix)	10.11.210.245 is host 0.11.210.245 on network 10.0.0.0 (10/8 in prefix notation).
B	255.255.0.0	16/16 (/16 prefix)	172.18.46.201 is host 0.0.46.201 on network 172.18.0.0 (172.18/16 in prefix notation).
C	255.255.255.0	24/8 (/24 prefix)	192.168.27.11 is host 0.0.0.11 on network 192.168.27.0 (192.168.27/24 in prefix notation).

The table shows two ways to write the network portion of an IPv4 address: for example, as 192.168.27.0 or as 192.168.27/24. On routers, a prefix notation such as /24 makes the first 24 of the 32-bit IPv4 address part of the network identifier.

Why are there two methods? Hosts are typically concerned with the host portion of the network address, and the masking applies to the start of the address to essentially turn the network part of the address off. Routers are typically concerned with the network portion of the address, and the /n notation tells the router essentially where it can stop caring about the bits.

So, through the use of classes, IPv4 crippled its use of the address space right from the start. IPv4 forecasts a world where there were a few huge networks (Class A), millions of small networks (Class C), and thousands of networks in between (Class B). Yet, once the Web came along, we live today in a world on millions of networks, and many of them are enormous.

THE ISSUES WITH IPV4: ADDRESS SPACE EXHAUSTION

The network layer was once called the "routing layer" because it had to determine, based on the source and destination addresses and little else, which of the links a system had available would take the packet the "next hop" closer to its destination. This "routing" process was initially so resource intensive that it gave rise to a system that did nothing more than perform these routing tasks. In the OSI-RM, these were intermediate systems (IS). Systems that were the user sources and destinations of packets were end systems (ES).

In TCP/IP, these devices are known as routers (the IS) and hosts (the ES). IP addresses, both for IPv4 and IPv6, have two portions: the network portion and the host portion. Together, they tell a router to forward a packet to *this* system on *that* network. Usually, a router needs only to look at the network portion (the starting portion) of the IP address, but even so, there are potentially millions of networks for a router to track.

Assigning IPv4 addresses intelligently can cut down on the size of the routing table needed, but the table still grows as the number of networks attached to the Internet explodes. Figure 2.2 shows the size of the Internet routing table since 1996, when the Web began to take off, according to an Internet organization called Asia-Pacific Network Information Center (APNIC).

Packets use IPv4 addresses at the network layer. These addresses have nothing to do with the hardware media access control (MAC) address on LANs, the addresses that the data link layer uses for frames. There is no real relationship between LAN media access control (MAC) addresses in the frame header and the IPv4 addresses used in the packet header; other than that given one, a system can find the other. In other words, an IPv4 address can be used to find the MAC layer address, and vice versa. There is a special exception for multicast addresses, but that does not change anything.

Internet BGP Routing Table Size

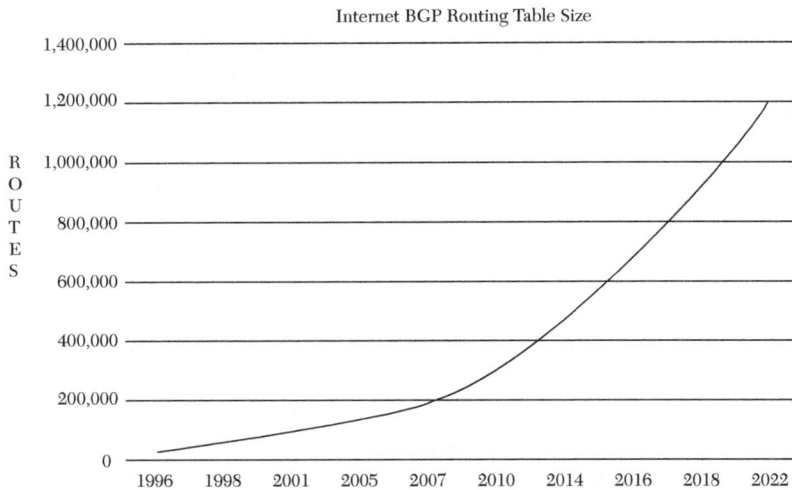

FIGURE 2.2. Internet routing table size according to APNIC.

Today's networks use *classless* IP addresses, which is the current way of inter-preting the 32-bit IPv4 address space. In classless addressing, the IPv4 network mask or prefix determines the boundary between the network and host portion of the IP address instead of the initial IP address bits, but only for the old classes A, B, and C.

Hosts really do not care about the differences between classful and classless IPv4 addresses. Routers, on the other hand, must. Because this book deals with networks as a whole, including routers, some understanding of both classful and classless IPv4 addressing is beneficial.

Hosts on the same LAN must have the same IP address prefix (the address network portion). This is because Internet routers route packets to next-hop links based on the network portion of the IP address. The whole IP address specifies the host on the network, and the network portion identifies the LAN itself. An IP address can be expressed in dotted decimal, binary (such as 0101), octal (base 8), or hexadecimal (hex, or base 16). While all are correct, it is most common to use *dotted decimal* notation for IPv4 and hexadecimal (hex) for IPv6. Some RFCs, such as those for HTTP, require dotted decimal for IPv4 ad-dresses.

Classless IPv4 addressing, on the other hand, as used on routers, does not derive a default subnet mask or default prefix length. The prefix length for class-less IPv4 addressing must be given (by the netmask or a /) to properly place the boundary between the NetID and HostID portions of the IPv4 address.

PUBLIC AND PRIVATE IP ADDRESSES

IP addresses, both IPv4 and IPv6, can be public or private. Public network address spaces are assigned by a central authority and should be unique. Private network addresses are very useful but are not guaranteed to be unique. Therefore, the use of private network address spaces has to be carefully managed because routers on the Internet would not work properly if a LAN showed up in two places at the same time. Nevertheless, the use of private address spaces in IP is popular for perceived security reasons. The security aspects are often overemphasized: The expansion of the locally available address space is the key reason for private address use. (If you have one IP address and three hosts, you have a problem without private addressing.) But private address spaces must be translated to public addresses whenever a packet makes its way onto the global public Internet.

Moreover, private IP addresses are not routable outside a local network, so a router is not allowed to advertise a route to a private address space onto the public Internet. Note that private addresses are just as routable as public ones within your own network or by mutual consent with another party. They are not generally routable on the global public Internet due to their lack of uniqueness and usual practices.

Almost all networks today rely on private network addresses to prevent public IPv4 address exhaustion, so these addresses are not just to test networks and labs any longer. Customer-edge routers often translate between a large pool of private (internal) and a smaller pool of public (external) addresses and insulate the local LAN from the outside world.

The dynamic host configuration protocol (DHCP) makes it possible to assign IP addresses to devices in a *dynamic* fashion. DHCP is the method many organizations use either for security reasons (to make it harder to find device IP addresses) or to assign a unique IP address to a device only when it needs to access the Internet. There are many more uses for dynamic IP address allocations on the Internet.

Private IPv4 Addresses

RFC 1918 established private address spaces for Classes A, B, and C to be used on private IP networks, and these are still respected in classless IP addressing. Books such as this one, where it is not desirable to use public IP addresses for examples, use RFC 1918 addresses throughout, much like using "555" telephone numbers in movies and on TV.

There are also IP address ranges set aside specifically for documentation, established in RFC 5737. These are 192.0.2.0/24 (TEST-NET), 198.51.100.0/24 (TEST-NET-2), and 203.0.113.0/24 (TEST-NET-3). There are even a few other "documentation" ranges for specialized applications.

There are three very important points that should always be kept in mind regarding private addresses. First, these addresses should never be announced by a routing protocol on a local router to the public Internet. Yet, these addresses are frequently assigned and used when they are isolated or translated to other addresses (using network address translation, or NAT). In summary,

- Private IP addresses are not routable outside the local network (they cannot be advertised on the public Internet).

- They are widely used on almost all networks today (even a small home network with DSL uses private IP addresses).

- Private addresses are usually translated with NAT at an edge router to map the private addresses used on a LAN to the public address space used by the ISP.

IPV6 PROTOCOLS

There is more to IPv6 than addressing, of course. IPv6 bundles several adjunct protocols that were completely separate in IPv4 into the main IPv6 operation. IPv6 does not need the address resolution protocol (ARP) to translate packet layer IPv4 addresses to link level (frame) addresses. Furthermore, IPv4's Internet control message protocol (ICMP) has been redone as ICMPv6.

With the assistance of ICMPv6, IPv6 can discover neighbors and routers through special neighbor discovery (ND) and router advertisement (RA) messages. This simplifies host configuration on LANs and lets devices find default routers on their own. ICMPv6 can automatically determine path maximum transmission unit (MTU) limitations and notify the sender if this is not respected (IPv6 routers cannot fragment packets, a major activity that slowed IPv4 routers down considerably).

IPv6 also does away with the IPv4 Internet group management protocol (IGMP) protocol for multicast group membership because the group membership function is bundled with ICMPv6.

KEY DIFFERENCES BETWEEN IPV4 AND IPV6

It is important to understand that IPv6 is much more than an extension of IPv4 addressing. IPv6, first defined in RFC 2460, is a completely new implementation of the network layer of the TCP/IP protocol stack, and it covers a lot more than a simple address space extension from 32 to 128 bits. IPv6 is more than a mechanism to increase IPv6's ability to allocate almost unlimited addresses to all the devices in the world for years to come.

IPv6 offers many improvements over IPv4:

- More efficient routing. IPv6 routers no longer fragment packets, an overhead-intensive process that slows a network down.

- Quality of service (QoS) is built-in. IPv4 has no way to distinguish delay-sensitive packets from bulk data transfers, requiring extensive workarounds. IPv6 can do this.

- Elimination of NAT to extend address spaces. IPv6 increases the IPv4 address size from 32 bits (about 4 billion) to 128 bits (enough for every molecule in the solar system).

- Network layer security has built-in IP security (IPsec). Security, always a challenge in IPv4, is an integral part of IPv6.

- Stateless address autoconfiguration for easier network administration. Many IPv4 installs were complicated by manual default router and address assignment—information that was not always available or inaccurate. IPv6 handles this in an automated fashion.

- Improved header structure with less processing overhead. Many of the fields in the IPv4 header were optional and used infrequently. IPv6 eliminates these, and the rest are handled differently.

Table 2.3 compares IPv4 and IPv6 operations.

TABLE 2.3. Some key IPv4 and IPv6 differences.

IPv4	IPv6
32-bit (4 byte) address supporting 4,294,967,296 addresses (although many were lost to special purposes, like 10.0.0.0 and 127.0.0.0).	128-bit (16-byte) address supporting 2^{128} (about 3.4×10^{38}) addresses.
NAT can be used to extend address limitations.	No NAT support (by design)

(Contd.)

IPv4	IPv6
IP addresses assigned to hosts by DHCP or static configuration.	IP addresses are self-assigned to hosts with stateless address auto-configuration, or DHCPv6.
IPSec support optional	IPSec support required
Options integrated in header fields	Options supported with extensions headers (simpler header format).

Even if you do not study the IPv4 and IPv6 packet header fields in detail, you can see the difference between the IPv4 header and the more streamlined IPv6 header. In the following sections, note the great reduction in header fields in the IPv6 packet that routers need to process or examine.

THE IPV4 HEADER

The fields of the IPv4 header are shown in Figure 2.3. The main things to remember are that there are a lot of fields, and many of them had to be looked at, processed, and changed as a packet made its way hop-by-hop through the network.

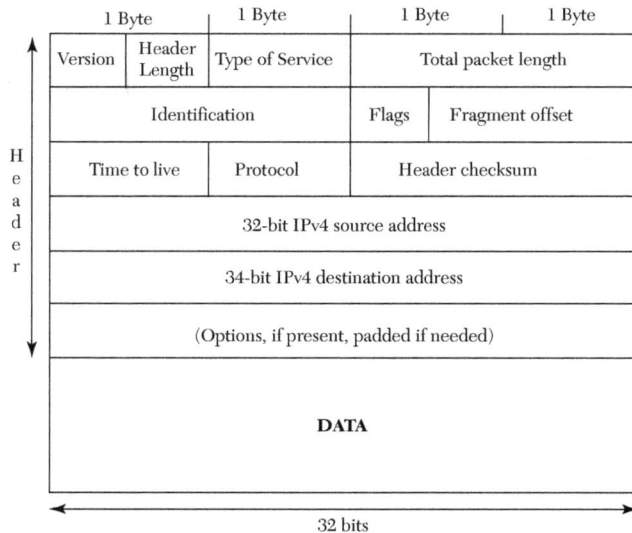

FIGURE 2.3. IPv4 header fields.

The following list presents more about the fields of the IPv4 header. There is a lot a router at home, in an office, or on the Internet backbone must do, very rapidly and very often, to find the proper next hop for the packet.

The main point is that processing an IPv4 header can be a very complicated business. Yet, back then, no one had any idea that these steps might become a burden.

- **Version:** This field sets the version of the IP protocol. As mentioned earlier, there are two versions of the IP protocol. The value of this field is set to 4 to indicate that the header belongs to the IPv4 protocol. The size of this field is 4 bits (already a waste: 4 bits can count 16 different IP protocols).

- **IHL (Internet Header Length):** The size of this field is 4 bits. Not all IPv4 headers are equal in length. The length of the header depends on how many options are added. An option tells intermediate devices how packets should be forwarded or processed. Many IPv4 options are rarely used. Depending on the specific requirement, nodes can add options.

  The length of the header is calculated in the number of 4-byte blocks. To calculate the length, the number of bytes is divided by 4. For example, if the header contains 20 bytes, the header length in the 4-byte blocks will be 5 (20/4). Similarly, if the value in this field is 10, then the length of the header will be $10 \times 4 = 40$ bytes.

  If an IPv4 option is not an integral multiple of 4 bytes in length, the remaining bytes are filled through padding options. The minimum size of the IPv4 header is 20 bytes. The maximum size of the header, including all options, is 60 bytes.

- **Type of service:** This field is used to set the desired service expected by the packet for delivery through routers across the network. RFC 791 defines services for this field. The most common services are precedence, delay, throughput, reliability, and cost characteristics. The size of this field is 8 bits. In IPv4, this feature has never been consistently used.

  RFC 2474 updates the definition of this field. It renames the original field name as the differentiated services (DS) field and defines the bits of this field into two separate groups. In the first group, it defines the first (high-order) 6 bits. In the second group, it defines the last (low-order) 2 bits.

  The first 6 bits are used to mark, unmark, and classify packets for forwarding and routing. Nodes can prioritize packets based on the requirements of applications. For example, nodes may prioritize data packets of real-time applications (such as voice over IP and video) over other applications (such as email and file storage). Prioritized data packets take precedence over normal data packets in congested areas of the network. This feature is commonly known as quality of service (QoS).

The last 2 bits are used for explicit congestion notification (ECN). The ECN allows an intermediate device to send a notification to the sender device if it is not able to forward the packet due to congestion. ECN is defined in RFC 3168.

- **Total Length:** This field specifies the total length of the packet (not just the header). This length includes the length of the header and the length of the payload. By subtracting the header length from the total length, routers can calculate the length of the payload. The size of this field is 16 bits. Since a 16-bit field cannot store a value more than 65535, the maximum length of an IP packet can be 65535 bytes.

- **Identification:** If the packet is large, the source node, router, or host can fragment the packet. If the packet is fragmented, then all fragments retain the identification value. The destination node uses this value to reassemble the original packet from fragments. The size of this field is 16 bits.

- **Flags:** This field is used to enable fragmentation. The size of this field is 3 bits. From these, only two bits are defined. The first bit indicates whether the packet can be fragmented or not. The second bit indicates whether more fragments follow the current fragment. Some protocols discourage or forbid resource-intensive fragmentation.

- **Fragment offset:** If there is fragmentation, this field is used to indicate the position of the fragment relative to the beginning of the payload. The size of this field is 13 bits.

- **Time-to-Live:** The size of this field is 8 bits. This field is used to decide when to discard undeliverable packets. The original specification defines this field as a time counter. Intermediate routers determine the length of time required in seconds to forward the packet and decrease this time accordingly.

  In the modern specification, the sending node sets the maximum number of links on which the packet can travel before being discarded. When the packet crosses a router, the router decrements the TTL value by 1. If the TTL value equals 0 before reaching the destination, the packet is discarded and an ICMP Time Exceeded message is sent to the source of the packet.

- **Protocol:** The size of this field is 8 bits. This field specifies the upper-layer protocol that will receive the payload of the packet on the destination node. For example, if this field contains a decimal value of 17, then the Internet layer of the destination node will transfer the payload to the UDP protocol.

- **Header checksum:** The size of this field is 16 bits. This field provides a checksum to detect bit errors for the header only. Since the payload contains its own checksum, the payload is not included in the checksum calculation. Intermediate routers that receive and forward the packet calculate and verify the checksum and discard the packet if checksum verification fails. Since a router decrements the TTL value by 1 before forwarding the packet, the header checksum value is recomputed at each hop between the source and destination nodes.

- **Source address:** The size of this field is 32 bits. This field stores the IPv4 address of the sending device.

- **Destination address:** The size of this field is also 32 bits. This field stores the IPv4 address of the destination device.

- **Options:** This field stores IPv4 options. The size of this field is a multiple of 32 bits. If an option is not 32 bits in length, it uses padding options in the remaining bits to make the header an integral number of 4-byte blocks.

THE IPV6 HEADER

In contrast with the IPv4 header, Figure 2.4 shows the fields of the IPv6 header. Note that the structure is much simpler, and that means the processing can be much faster than in IPv4.

IPv6 packets have their own frame ethertype value, 0x86dd, making it easy for receivers that must handle both IPv4 and IPv6 on the same interface to distinguish the frame content. The IPv6 header is comprised of the following fields:

- **Version:** A 4-bit field for the IP version number (0x06).

- **Traffic Class:** A 12-bit field that identifies the major class of the packet content (for example, voice or video packets). The default value is 0, meaning it is ordinary bulk data (such as for a file transfer) and requires no special handling.

- **Flow Label:** A 16-bit field used to label packets belonging to the same flow (those with the same values in several TCP/IP header parameters). The flow label is normally 0 (flows are detected in other ways).

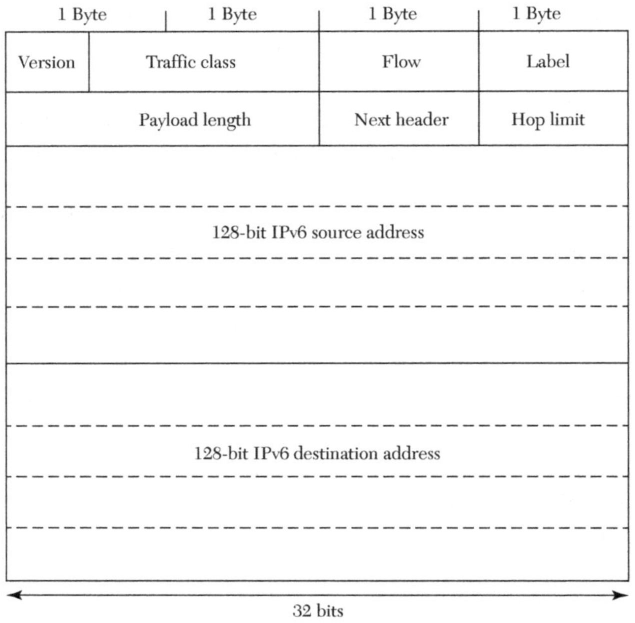

1 Byte	1 Byte	1 Byte	1 Byte
Version	Traffic class	Flow	Label
Payload length		Next header	Hop limit

128-bit IPv6 source address

128-bit IPv6 destination address

32 bits

FIGURE 2.4. The IPv6 header fields.

- **Payload Length:** A 16-bit field giving the length of the packet in bytes, excluding the IPv6 header.

- **Next Header:** An 8-bit field giving the type of header immediately following the IPv6 header. This field serves the same function as the Protocol field in IPv4.

- **Hop Limit:** An 8-bit field set by the source host and decremented by 1 at each router. Packets are discarded if Hop Limit is decremented to zero. This field serves the same purpose as the IPv4 Time To Live field. Generally, implementers choose the default to use, but values such as 64 or 128 are common.

Comparing the IPv4 and IPv6 Headers

Comparing the IPv4 and IPv6 headers, you can see the following:

- The number of fields has dropped from 12 (including options) in the IPv4 header to 8 in the IPv6 header.

- The number of fields that must be processed by an intermediate router has dropped from 6 to 4, making the forwarding of normal IPv6 packets more efficient.

- Seldom-used fields, such as fields supporting fragmentation and options in the IPv4 header, have been moved to extension headers in the IPv6 header.
- The size of the IPv6 header has doubled from 20 bytes for a minimum-sized IPv4 header to 40 bytes. Yet, the new IPv6 header contains source and destination addresses that are four times longer than IPv4 source and destination addresses.

Table 2.4 lists the individual differences between the IPv4 and IPv6 header fields.

TABLE 2.4. IPv4 header fields and their IPv6 equivalents.

IPv4 Header Field	IPv6 Header Field
Version	Same field but with a different version number.
Internet Header Length	Removed in IPv6. IPv6 does not include a header length field because the IPv6 header is always a fixed length of 40 bytes. Each extension header is either a fixed length or indicates its own length.
Type of Service	Replaced by the IPv6 Traffic Class field.
Total Length	Replaced by the IPv6 Payload Length field, which indicates only the size of the payload.
Identification Flags Fragment Offset	Removed in IPv6. Fragmentation information is not included in the IPv6 header. It is contained in a Fragment extension header.
Time-to-Live	Replaced by the IPv6 Hop Limit field.
Protocol	Replaced by the IPv6 Next Header field.
Header Checksum	Removed in IPv6. The link layer has a checksum that performs bit-level error detection for the entire IPv6 packet.
Source Address	The field is the same except that IPv6 addresses are 128 bits in length.
Destination Address	The field is the same except that IPv6 addresses are 128 bits in length.
Options	Removed in IPv6. IPv6 extension headers replace IPv4 options.

NOTE	*The one new field in the IPv6 header that is not included in the IPv4 header is the Flow Label field.*

As a result of the new IPv6 header, there is a reduction in the steps of router processing, which means the number of steps that a router must execute to determine how to forward a packet.

IPv4 Router Packet Forwarding

To forward a normal IPv4 packet, a router typically performs the following steps:

1. Verify the Header Checksum field by performing its own checksum calculation and comparing its result with the result stored in the IPv4 header. Although this step is required by RFC 1812, modern high-speed routers commonly skip it.

2. Verify the value of the Version field. Although this step is not required by RFC 791 or 1812, performing this step saves network bandwidth because a packet containing an invalid version number is not propagated across the IPv4 Internetwork only to be discarded by the destination node.

3. Decrement the value of the TTL field. If its new value is less than 1, send an ICMPv4 Time Exceeded-Time to Live Exceeded in Transit message to the source of the packet and then discard the packet. If not, place the new value in the TTL field.

4. Check for the presence of IPv4 header options. If present, process them.

5. Use the value of the Destination Address field and the contents of the local routing table to determine a forwarding interface and a next-hop IPv4 address. If a route is not found, send an ICMPv4 Destination Unreachable-Host Unreachable message to the source of the packet and discard the packet.

6. If the IPv4 MTU of the forwarding interface is less than the value of the Total Length field and the Don't Fragment (DF) flag is set to 0, perform IPv4 fragmentation. If the MTU of the forwarding interface is less than the value of the Total Length field and the DF flag is set to 1, send an ICMPv4 Destination Unreachable-Fragmentation Needed and DF Set the message to the source of the packet and discard the packet.

7. Recalculate the new header checksum and place its new value in the Header Checksum field.

8. Forward the packet by using the appropriate forwarding interface.

NOTE	*This is not a complete list and does not apply any specific implementation, nor does it form an authorized order in which to process IPv4 packets.*

IPv6 Router Packet Forwarding

To forward a normal IPv6 packet, a router typically performs the following steps:

1. Verify the value of the Version field. Although this step is not required by RFC 2460, performing it saves network bandwidth because a packet containing an

invalid version number is not propagated across the IPv6 Internetwork only to be discarded by the destination node.

2. Decrement the value of the Hop Limit field. If its new value is less than 1, send an ICMPv6 Time Exceeded-Hop Limit Exceeded in Transit message to the source of the packet and discard the packet. If not, place the new value in the Hop Limit field.

3. Check the Next Header field for a value of 0. If it is 0, process the Hop-by-Hop Options header.

4. Use the value of the Destination Address field and the contents of the local routing table to determine a forwarding interface and a next-hop IPv6 address. If a route is not found, send an ICMPv6 Destination Unreachable-No Route To Destination message to the source of the packet and then discard the packet.

5. If the link MTU of the forwarding interface is less than 40 plus the value of the payload length field, send an ICMPv6 packet too big message to the source of the packet and discard the packet.

6. Forward the packet by using the appropriate forwarding interface.

NOTE	*As with the IPv4 steps, this is not a complete list and does not apply to any specific implementation, nor does it form an authorized order in which to process IPv6 packets.*

Therefore, the process to forward an IPv6 packet is much simpler than for an IPv4 packet because it does not have to verify and recalculate a header checksum, perform fragmentation, or process options not intended for the router.

IPv6 Address Notation

Header fields are one thing, but users are not always concerned about the value of a certain header field. Headers on IP packets are important but often invisible. Yet, almost all users are familiar with IPv4 address notation, so it is a good idea to explore how IPv6 addresses are written down and spoken about.

IPv6 addresses are written very differently than IPv4 dotted decimal notation: there are now 128 bits in the IPv6 address. A new notation system was invented to represent this enormous address pool potential. So, in IPv6, the 128 bits in the IPv6 address:

- Are written as 8 16-bit hexadecimal blocks separated by colons (not case sensitive)

- Use abbreviations to simplify the notation

- Omit (optionally) leading zeroes

- Use double colons (::) to replace consecutive zeros (or leading or trailing zero strings), but never more than once per address

So, an address like:
2dfc:0000:0000:0000:0217:cbff:fe8c:0000

Can be written:
2dfc:0: 0:0:0217:cbff:fe8c:0

Or:
2dfc::0217:cbff:fe8c:0

But *not*:
2dfc::0217:cbff:fe8c::

Why? The double use of :: makes it unclear how many zeros were in each 0 string originally.

Most organizations today comply with RFC 5952 in the standard assignment and display rules for IPv6 addresses. These rules mean that:

- Devices must accept all methods of address entry (using ":" or not, for example)
- Leading zeros are always suppressed
- The double colon (::) is always used when applicable (if there are two 0 strings, the longer string always gets the ::)
- Hexadecimal characters in IPv6 addresses (a, b, c, d, e, f) must be represented in lower case.

IPv6 Prefix Notation

Routers do not often have to worry about complete ("host") addresses because their routing tables (and the forwarding tables they are based on) usually employ a prefix and examine only the number of bits that match the longest entry in the table. This is the "longest match" rule and makes sure that a 64-bit prefix (if present) is preferred over a 32-bit prefix when the first 32 bits of a packet's destination address are the same in both table entries (longest match wins).

Prefixes used for routing are defined in IPv6 by RFC 4291. So, the IPv6 address:

2bfc:0000:0000:0000:0217:cbff:fe8c:5c85/64
   ...Has a 64-bit prefix of **2bfc:0000:0000:0000:**

The rules and format for using literal IPv6 addresses in URLs are detailed in RFC 2732. Most organizations' devices comply with both RFC 4291 and RFC 2732.

IPv4 and IPv6 Address Usage Compared

The expanded address space is certainly one of the most distinctive features of IPv6. Yet, there is more to addressing than assigning an end device or network node (router or switch) an address. IPv6 eliminates some of the most awkward uses of IPv4 addresses and has some notable enhancements.

For example, the IPv4 address space was divided into "classes." IPv6 does away with the rigid class concept (it was already obsolete in IPv4) and uses subnetting (more on that below) to adjust network sizes with a given address space assignment.

Another oddity of IPv4 was the use of a class-type address space for multicast use (224.0.0.0/4). Devices needed both unicast and multicast addresses to receive multicast traffic. IPv6 uses a more integrated address space for multicast at FF00::/8.

IPv4 allows for "broadcast" addresses that force each and every device to stop and look at packets, even if they are useless to them (these were very popular in denial-of-service attacks). IPv6 does away with broadcast and uses multicast groups for everything.

IPv4 uses 0.0.0.0 as an unspecified address (for example, when a device does not yet know its IP address) and uses another whole class-type address (127.0.0.1) for loopback (testing). IPv6 uses :: and ::1 as unspecified and loopback addresses, respectively.

Finally, IPv4 uses globally unique public addresses for normal traffic and special "private" addresses that should not appear on the public Internet (such as 10.0.0.0/8). Instead, IPv6 uses globally unique unicast addresses and local addresses (FD00::/8).

Table 2.5 shows the major differences between IPv4 address types and their use in IPv6.

TABLE 2.5. IPv4 and IPv6 address differences.

IPv4	IPv6
Can be used in a classful manner	No such concept in IPv6 (uses subnetting)
Mulitcast address space at **224.0.0.0/4**	Multicast address space at **FF00::/8**
Has broadcast addresses for all devices	No such concept in IPv6 (uses multicast groups)

(Contd.)

IPv4	IPv6
Uses **0.0.0.0** as an unspecified address	Uses **::** as unspecified address
Uses **127.0.0.1** as loopback address	Uses **::1** as loopback address
Supports globally unique "public" addresses	Supports globally unique unicast addresses
Uses **10.0.0.0/8**, **172.16.0.0/16**, and **192.168.0.0/16** as "private" addresses	Uses **FD00::/8** as unique local addresses

IPv6 Address Allocation and Types

In the same way as IPv4, organizations and end users get IPv6 address allocations from their ISPs. The process is defined in RFC 6177.

Any subnet with a prefix of /64 or shorter (that is, less than 64 bits) is supported. In other words, an ISP should not be giving out addresses with /96 prefixes or any other value greater than /64.

Initial address assignments should allow for a site to establish multiple subnets. Subnetting in IPv6 is discussed a little later.

Users should allow a user or site to easily obtain additional IPv6 address space for additional subnets. Usually, a simple form request is all that is needed.

IPv6 defines three major types of addresses:

- Unicast addresses—Addresses used to send packets to one specific address.

- Multicast addresses—Addresses used to send to every member of a specific group. Group membership is either mandatory (a device *must* belong to certain multicast groups) or optional (a device can decide whether to join the multicast group or not).

- Anycast addresses—Addresses used to send to any *one* member of a specific group (such as the "closest" in terms of routing metrics). For example, a device can use the same anycast address to access a video stream located in the same country or halfway around the world. The routers and other network nodes decide which source is "closest."

Figure 2.5 shows the various types of IPv6 addresses and their relationships.

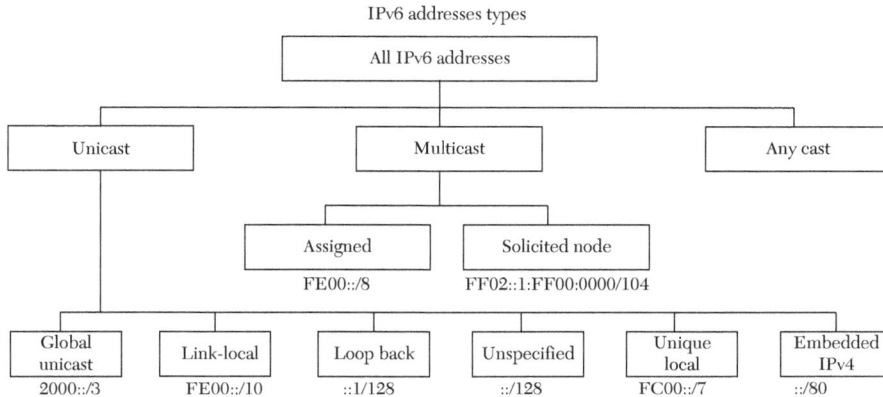

FIGURE 2.5. IPv6 Address types.

Notable IPv6 Addresses

Certain IPv6 addresses are seen over and over, and it is a good idea to know by their characteristic patterns (such as 0xFF80) what types of IPv6 addresses they represent. Note that it is common for end devices to have many IPv6 addresses and for routing tables to contain many entries reflecting these types of IPv6 addresses.

These are shown in Table 2.6.

TABLE 2.6. Some notable IPv6 addresses.

Node-scope Unicast (Should never be advertised publicly)	::1/128 is loopback (RFC 4291) ::/128 is unspecified (RFC 4291)
IPv4-mapped Addresses (Should never be advertised publicly)	::FFFF:0:0/96 (RFC 4291)
IPv4-compatible Addresses (Deprecated)	::<ipv4-address>/96 (RFC 4291)
Link-scoped Unicast (Should never be advertised publicly)	FE80::/10 (RFC 4291)
Unique local Addresses (Should never be advertised publicly)	FC00::/7 (RFC 4193)
Documentation prefix for user manuals, etc. (Should never be advertised publicly)	2001:DB8::/32 (RFC 3849)

(Contd.)

6to4 (Must be filtered, and some are not used)	2002::/16 (RFC 3056, but see RFC 3964)
Teredo (Advertised for Teredo service)	2001::/32 (RFC 4380)
6bone (experimental) (Currently unallocated per RFC 3701)	5F00::/8 (RFC 1897) 3FFE::/16 (RFC 2471)
ORCHID (not IP routable) (Should never be advertised publicly)	2001:10::/28 (RFC 4843)
Default route (see IANA registry)	For experimental purposes (RFC 4773)
Multicast (Must not appear in unicast routing tables)	FF00::/8 (RFC 4291)

IPv6 Host Addressing

IPv4 hosts are fairly easy to configure. Usually, the network interface has only one IPv4 address. When coupled with the default router address (if there is a way off the subnet), the host has everything it needs to decide where things go. Yet, IPv6 does much more.

In contrast to IPv4 hosts, IPv6 hosts (end devices) normally have multiple addresses on each interface. Yet, these multiple addresses greatly simplify the operation of the IPv6 network layer (finding network neighbors, routers, and so on).

- Unicast addresses
- Link-local address on each interface (unique local addresses, ULA, beginning with FC00::/7 can use www.sixxs.net/tools/grh/ula/ to generate and register site local prefixes based on RFC 4193)
- Additional unicast addresses for each interface (one is typically enough, but there can be multiple unique local or global addresses)
- Loopback address (::1)
- Multicast addresses
- FF01::1 is the interface-local scope all-nodes multicast address
- FF02::1 is the link-local scope all-nodes multicast address
- The solicited-node address for each assigned unicast address
- The multicast addresses of any groups the host has joined

Typically, IPv6 hosts are multi-homed logically. This means that they can receive packets sent to *at least* two interface addresses: the link-local address for traffic on the local link and a routable unique local or global address.

IPv6 Router Addressing

Remember, unicast IPv6 addresses are sent to one destination, and anycast IPv6 addresses send to any *one* member of a defined group. Routers in IPv6 have different requirements for unicast and anycast addresses. The physical interfaces on an IPv6 router are assigned the following IPv6 addresses:

- Unicast addresses
- Link-local address on each interface
- Additional unicast addresses for each interface (one is typically enough, but there can be multiple unique local or global addresses)
- Anycast addresses
- Subnet-Router anycast address for each subnet established
- Optionally, additional anycast addresses

All IPv6 router interfaces also listen for traffic on the following multicast addresses:

- FF01::1 is the interface-local scope all-nodes multicast address
- FF01::2 is the interface-local scope all-routers multicast address
- FF02::1 is the link-local scope all-nodes multicast address
- FF02::2 is the link-local scope all-routers multicast address
- FF05::2 is the site-local scope all-routers multicast address
- The solicited-node address for each assigned unicast address
- The multicast addresses of any groups the router has joined

IPV6 SUBNETTING

Subnetting is a way for users to take an assigned IP address space and partition it to meet their specific needs. For example, if an organization has two office locations, one large and one small, the IP address space can be subnetted so that the hosts get the addresses they need, and traffic can be efficiently handled internally without concerning the global public Internet. Subnetting today in IPv4 and IPv6 is done by prefixes, but again, IPv6 has its own rules.

As an example of how an IPv6 address would be subnetted, assume that the ISP has provided a 48-bit prefix to the user. Consider the address and prefix 2001:0867:5309/48, for instance. Because each four hexadecimal digits are

16 bits, and the last 64 bits are usually the interface identifier (the "host" portion of the address in IPv4), this leaves 16 bits for subnetting.

The 16 subnet bits allow for 2^{16} or 32768 subnets. In each subnet, all address possibilities are allowed except for all zeros, which are reserved in IPv6 for subnet router anycast messages. Assume the subnet bits, assigned locally, for a certain subnet are *9abc*.

This subnet would allow $2^{64} - 1$ addresses in the range:

2001:0867:5309:9abc 0000:0000:0000:0001 to 2001:0867:5309:9abc ffff:ffff:ffff:ffff

So, when subnetted, an IPv6 address consists of three parts:

- The global routing prefix (2001:0867:5309/48 in this example)
- The subnet identifier (9abc in this example)
- The interface identifier or "host address" (the remaining 64 bits in this example)

Things can get a little tricky when subnets are not established on the 16-bit boundaries. Yet, the principles of subnetting are almost the same as in IPv4.

IPv6 subnetting is easier than IPv4. It is also different. Want to divide or combine a subnet? All that is needed is to add or chop off digits and adjust the prefix length by a multiple of four. No longer is there a need to calculate subnet start/end addresses, usable addresses, the null route, or the broadcast address.

IPv4 had a subnet mask (dotted quad notation) that was later replaced by CIDR masking. IPv6 does not have a subnet mask but instead calls it a prefix length, often shortened to "Prefix." Prefix length and CIDR masking work similarly; the prefix length denotes how many bits of the address define the network in which it exists. Most commonly, the prefixes used with IPv6 are multiples of four.

Using prefix lengths in multiples of four makes it easier for humans to distinguish IPv6 subnets. All that is required to design a larger or smaller subnet is to adjust the prefix by multiples of four.

This is shown in Table 2.7, which lists the possible IPv6 subnet addresses, as well as how many IP addresses are contained inside of each subnet. Yet, technically, the subnet prefix lengths can be any number between 0 and 128.

TABLE 2.7. IPv6 subnet prefixes.

Prefix	Subnet Example	Total IP Addresses	# of /64 nets
4	x::	2^{124}	2^{60}
8	xx::	2^{120}	2^{56}

Prefix	Subnet Example	Total IP Addresses	# of /64 nets
12	xxx::	2^{116}	2^{52}
16	xxxx::	2^{112}	2^{48}
20	xxxx:x::	2^{108}	2^{44}
24	xxxx:xx::	2^{104}	2^{40}
28	xxxx:xxx::	2^{100}	2^{36}
32	xxxx:xxxx::	2^{96}	4,294,967,296
36	xxxx:xxxx:x::	2^{92}	268,435,456
40	xxxx:xxxx:xx::	2^{88}	16,777,216
44	xxxx:xxxx:xxx::	2^{84}	1,048,576
48	xxxx:xxxx:xxxx::	2^{80}	65,536
52	xxxx:xxxx:xxxx:x::	2^{76}	4,096
56	xxxx:xxxx:xxxx:xx::	2^{72}	256
60	xxxx:xxxx:xxxx:xxx::	2^{68}	16
64	xxxx:xxxx:xxxx:xxxx::	2^{64} (18,446,744,073,709,551,616)	1
68	xxxx:xxxx:xxxx:xxxx:x::	2^{60} (1,152,921,504,606,846,976)	0
72	xxxx:xxxx:xxxx:xxxx:xx::	2^{56} (72,057,594,037,927,936)	0
76	xxxx:xxxx:xxxx:xxxx:xxx::	2^{52} (4,503,599,627,370,496)	0
80	xxxx:xxxx:xxxx:xxxx:xxxx::	2^{48} (281,474,976,710,656)	0
84	xxxx:xxxx:xxxx:xxxx:xxxx:x::	2^{44} (17,592,186,044,416)	0
88	xxxx:xxxx:xxxx:xxxx:xxxx:xx::	2^{40} (1,099,511,627,776)	0
92	xxxx:xxxx:xxxx:xxxx:xxxx:xxx::	2^{36} (68,719,476,736)	0
96	xxxx:xxxx:xxxx:xxxx:xxxx:xxxx::	2^{32} (4,294,967,296)	0
100	xxxx:xxxx:xxxx:xxxx:xxxx:xxxx:x::	2^{28} (268,435,456)	0
104	xxxx:xxxx:xxxx:xxxx:xxxx:xxxx:xx::	2^{24} (16,777,216)	0
108	xxxx:xxxx:xxxx:xxxx:xxxx:xxxx:xxx::	2^{20} (1,048,576)	0
112	xxxx:xxxx:xxxx:xxxx:xxxx:xxxx:xxxx::	2^{16} (65,536)	0
116	xxxx:xxxx:xxxx:xxxx:xxxx:xxxx:xxxx:x::	2^{12} (4,096)	0
120	xxxx:xxxx:xxxx:xxxx:xxxx:xxxx:xxxx:xx::	2^{8} (256)	0
124	xxxx:xxxx:xxxx:xxxx:xxxx:xxxx:xxxx:xxx::	2^{4} (16)	0
128	xxxx:xxxx:xxxx:xxxx:xxxx:xxxx:xxxx:xxxx	2^{0} (1)	0

A /64 prefix subnet is the standard-size IPv6 subnet as defined by the IETF. It is the smallest subnet that can be used locally if auto-configuration is needed.

Typically, an ISP assigns a /64 or smaller subnet to establish service on the WAN. An additional network is routed for LAN use. The size of the allocation depends upon the ISP, but it is not uncommon to see end users receive at least a /64 and even up to a /48.

Special IPv6 Subnets

There are network subnets that are reserved for special use in IPv6. This is not a full list, which is easily found online. Here are six examples of IPv6 special networks and their addresses. These are shown along with the purpose in Table 2.7.

TABLE 2.8. Special IPv6 networks.

Network	Purpose
2001:db8::/32	Documentation prefix used for examples
::1	Localhost
fc00::/7	Unique local addresses (ULA)—also known as "Private" IPv6 addresses.
fe80::/10	Link local addresses, only valid inside a single broadcast domain.
ff00::0/8	Multicast addresses

IPv6 Neighbor Discovery

IPv4 hosts find each other on a local segment using ARP broadcast messages, but IPv6 hosts find each other by sending neighbor discovery protocol (NDP) messages. Like ARP, NDP works inside a given broadcast domain to find other hosts inside of a specific subnet.

By sending special ICMPv6 packets to reserved multicast addresses, NDP handles the tasks of neighbor discovery, router solicitations, and route redirects similar to IPv4's ICMP redirects.

Router Advertisements

IPv6 routers are located through their router advertisement (RA) messages instead of by DHCP. IPv6-enabled routers that support dynamic address assignment are expected to announce themselves on the network to all clients and respond to router solicitations.

Address Allocation

There are several ways to assign addresses to hosts on an IPv6 network. One way is the stateless address autoconfiguration (SLAAC). When an IPv6-aware DHCP server is not available, the automatic private IP addressing (APIPA) can perform auto-addressing. In APIPA, DHCP clients automatically configure an IP address and subnet mask.

DHCP6 Prefix Delegation

DHCP6 Prefix Delegation hands out a routed IPv6 subnet to a DHCP6 client. When on a WAN instead of a LAN, the interface can be set to receive a prefix over DHCP6. A router at the edge of a large network can provide prefix delegation to other routers inside the network.

Interworking Mechanisms

For a long time to come, IPv4 and IPv6 networks must coexist. RFC 2893 includes the following well-known interworking mechanisms for IPv6 and IPv4:

- **Dual IP Layer (dual stack):** Hosts and routers implement a complete suite for both IPv6 and IPv4.
- **Configured Tunneling of IPv6 over IPv4:** Point-to-point tunnels are used to encapsulate IPv6 packets with IPv4 headers to carry them over IPv4 routing networks.
- **Automatic Tunneling of IPv6 over IPv4:** Uses IPv4-compatible addresses to automatically tunnel IPv6 over IPv4 routing infrastructures.
- **IPv4 Multicast Tunneling:** A form of IPv6-over-IPv4 tunneling for multicast where the IPv4 tunnel endpoint address is determined using neighbor discovery, which, unlike configured tunneling, does not require address configuration and, unlike automatic tunneling, does not require the use of IPv4-compatible addresses.

WHAT COMES NEXT

It takes a lot of work to build and use a mobile and IPv6 network. So far, we have only covered how digital information is transferred within packets and frames between devices on the mobile platform (which could include trains, buses, or other forms of transportation) and the cell towers. How is all this data routed for phone calls, streamed media, or corporate network access?

Much of this *backhauling* work is done by high-capacity fiber optic links, often called IP-over-DWDM (dense wavelength division multiplexing) or packet optical networks. Fiber optical cables have been replacing older twisted pair or coaxial copper cables in telephones and all other types of networks for years.

Fiber optic cables enable data transmission across continents with minimal propagation delays, unlike satellites, which suffer from latency and are prone to outages. Today, fiber optics have extended from office parks and neighbor-hoods to homes.

The next chapter takes a closer look at packet optical networks.

Chapter 3

PACKET OPTICAL NETWORKS

OVERVIEW

Thus far, we have explored two major components of all modern wide-area networks (WANs). These are:

- The need for almost everyone in the world to have multiple Internet connections to their home, office, car, and business in order to do work, plan their lives, and entertain themselves. This requires much more than the simple 32-bit address space invented for IPv4. We need IPv6.

- IPv6 provides enough address space to give every molecule in the solar system its own IPv6 address. It also simplifies a lot of the added protocols than IPv4 required and does away with some that were seldom used or security risks (such as directed broadcasts).

WHAT YOU WILL LEARN

In this chapter, we will investigate the fiber-based packet optical networks that aggregate the traffic from regional mobile networks and take it back and forth, upstream and downstream, globally.
This includes:

- Fiber optic advantages over other media and the basics of fiber optics

- Wavelengths and frequencies for fiber optic communications
- Key components of optical fiber communication systems
- Packets and packet optical
- Wavelength division multiplexing (WDM) and dense WDM (DWDM) systems
- Optical transport network (OTN) standards
- The Reconfigurable Optical Add-Drop Multiplexer (ROADM)
- Colorless, directionless, contentionless, flex-grid (CDCF) packet optical networks

The explorations of mobile networks and TCP/IP were mainly chronological. There is a chronological element to packet optical networks as well, but the main investigations here will be the standardization for various aspects of the fiber-based optical network.

FIBER OPTIC DEVELOPMENT

The original global voice analog network, the *public switched telephone network* (PSTN), soon after its invention, used copper wires twisted into pairs to reduce crosstalk and to increase distance to carry conversations. They were elevated on poles to avoid damage from animals, road equipment, and standing water. Photographs of urban telephone poles in the late 1800s, especially in places like lower Manhattan in New York City where the telephone quickly became indispensable, show the crosstrees strung with hundreds of pairs of copper wire, each carrying an analog signal from the end user telephone to the central office, where connections were made through switches to other telephones.

When a harsh winter or hurricane came, like the famous Blizzard of 1888 in New York, the damage to these weighted-down poles was considerable. There are pictures of those down lines as well.

By the 1900s, urban areas began to bury their copper wires underground. These wires had to be protected against ground water, so the pairs were gathered into cables with layers of protection and often run inside canvas, and later plastic, conduits. Pairs were color-coded to distinguish them, and all telephone company employees as late as the 1970s, even if applying to be a computer programmer, had to take a color-pair test.

The few pairs of wires from each block multiplied to hundreds of pairs of wires as they got closer to the central office (CO). This was where the calls were switched, at first manually through an operator's switchboard, then automatically through huge machinery, and stayed connected for the duration of the conversation. (Many early switch machineries would not disconnecr a call until the caller hung up, and if a caller simply left the telephone off the hook, the other party could not use their telephone at all.)

In cities, the streets surrounding the central office could be populated by enormous 2700-pair cables, all ending the distribution pairs to individual landline telephones (which they all were) in the CO cable vault and then at the switch above. Not all 2700-pairs were used: the system had to account for future growth as telephone service transitioned from a business tool (doctors calling pharmacies, for example) to a residential luxury (fixed rates came during the 1930s United States Depression, when people had to know what their expenses would be month-to-month) to a near necessity after World War II.

One of the biggest advantages when fiber optic cables could carry many telephone conversations became apparent when a breakage of a massive twisted-pair cable happened.

In the summer of 1992, in White Plains, New York, workers resurfacing a bridge somehow managed to jackhammer through a 2700-pair cable. Within an hour, a large tent had been erected on the site, and automobile traffic was diverted. By nightfall, floodlights had been installed, and a crew worked around the clock for three days until all telephone service was restored. The costs, along with crew overtime, were enormous.

At the time, telephone companies were tightly regulated at the state level. So, it was not just a matter of "I have a purple and slate wire pair on this end. Anyone have a purple and slate pair over there?" Documentation came to the site in the form of massive binders of papers. Service had to be restored according to a particular customer hierarchy, as determined by the state regulators. In most places, hospitals got service back first, then the police and firehouses, then doctors, then pharmacies, and so on. Ordinary residential service was restored last. This finding of this information was often as time-consuming as the splicing to fix the copper pairs themselves.

However, once hundreds of conversations could be multiplexed onto fiber optical carrier systems, the service restoration task became trivial. In a few hours at most, a single strand of fiber could be fusion spliced, and all services carried in that cable restored all at once. This was a powerful incentive for the telcos to move everything onto optical fiber as soon as possible.

The process paid for itself in the form of reduced installation costs.

After all, the 2700-pair copper cable is 3.38 inches in diameter and weighs almost 7 pounds *per foot*. Weight prohibited running such heavy cables in ceilings or even across floor slabs with low load limits. Even when running outdoors, a 1,000-foot reel of 2700-pair cable weighs close to 4 US tons (8,000 US pounds). A normal four-person crew struggled to install a fraction of a mile per workday. Simply setting up the enormous trucks and pulleys consumed the better part of the day.

On the other hand, fiber crews work fast and with smaller crews and trucks. The savings paid for many miles of fiber optic cable. Even a 10,000-foot fiber reel weighs only a few hundred pounds. Smaller reels can be carried under a person's arm and weigh approximately 60 pounds. So, fiber optic cable can be installed above hung ceilings without worry and can be attached to a building floor slab without needing an engineering report to det`ermine if the building floor load factor may be exceeded.

Today, modern fibers carry many times the bandwidth of the 2700-pair cable. A service provider like a telephone company installs more bandwidth on fiber in a week than their entire network had on copper previously. In fact, few fiber cables even today operate at their maximum bandwidth and capacity. Change the transmitter and receivers at the ends of the link, add a new multiplexing method, and a carrier can easily increase the fiber bandwidth without running new cables.

This is a good place to pause and list all of the advantages that fiber optic cable has over the old, twisted pair wiring systems and other copper-based systems like coaxial cable (used for the original Ethernet LANs).

FIBER OPTIC ADVANTAGES

The full list of fiber optic advantages over twisted-pair or coaxial cable or wireless communications is impressive. Here is a more complete list:

1. Simpler and less expensive repairs
2. Fewer installation and repair costs
3. Smaller size and weight
4. Bandwidth upgrades on the same fiber
5. Longer distances than copper spans
6. Higher bandwidths than copper links
7. Reduced error rates
8. Immunity from electrical interference
9. Greater security

The first four on the list have already been covered. Even without the other five advantages, these few would justify replacing copper links with fiber. (As an aside, soon after the Web came along in the early 1990s, everyone needed more cables and wires for Internet access everywhere, all the time. Some observers claimed that the majority of the world's copper mined at the time went into telecommunications cabling.)

Here are a few words about the other five advantages:

- **Longer distances than copper spans:** Electrical signals sent over copper wires tend to attenuate (weaken) rapidly, especially at higher frequencies. Amplifiers are needed at intervals to boost the signal (which also introduces some distortion as noise gets amplified as well as the signal). Fiber optical cables require amplifiers too, but they can be spaced farther apart and are digital, so they can avoid amplifying noise.

- **Higher bandwidths than copper links:** For now, it is enough to note that the range of signals carried over fiber optical links is many times that of possible over copper cables. Additionally, a wider frequency range means more bandwidth.

- **Reduced error rates:** A rule of thumb was that a fiber link will perform at least 1,000 times better in terms of bit error rate (BER) than the copper link it replaces. With forward error correction (FEC), it could be a million times better (a thousand thousand). Which means that all the errors observed on the copper link yesterday now take approximately 3 years to accumulate. With FEC, yesterday's copper errors are spread over the next 3,000 years(!). With fiber networks, errors basically go away.

- **Immunity from electrical interference:** Many factories, especially with heavy tool and die machinery or long assembly lines, are very electrically noisy environments. Not only did some factory floors knock the signal right out of twisted pair copper wires, but they also prevented the efficient use of coaxial cable, which is more impervious to interference. Fiber optic cable, operating at optical wavelengths and frequencies, is completely immune to this interference (such interference can, however, upset the electrical senders and receivers that might be part of the fiber network; shielding is possible in these cases).

- **Greater network security:** Unlike wireless and copper network signals, which can be captured without ever physically compromising the system, fiber cables must be tampered with in order to tap them. This tapping is detectable by monitoring the signal loss in decibels on each span of the link. Any drop in signal strength means damage to the fiber cable, either because it has been kinked or someone has tapped into the fiber for nefarious purposes. Either way, repairs are in order.

FIBER OPTIC BASICS

There are lots of videos online of a laser following the path of a stream of water exiting a bucket. The light cannot escape the water because of the way that internal reflection works when light encounters two materials like air and water. The physics of light means that light reflects where there is a change of the *index of refraction* (or *refractive index*) of a material, as water to air.

This means that if an LED (a good light source) or laser (a better light source) illuminates one end of a fiber optic cable, the light follows the cable as it twists and turns through office ceilings or inside outdoor conduit. Attenuation is usually very minimal compared to other communications media, and, unless the fiber is kinked (for instance, by dropping the corner of a file cabinet on it), the receiver has an easy job of distinguishing 0 from 1 bit.

The fiber core itself is thinner than a human hair (120 versus 140 microns) and is surrounded by a layer of cladding that has a higher refractive index, keeping the light inside the core (most of the light, anyway). The fiber itself is typically made of very pure silica (there are fluoride fibers as well), so pure that if the ocean were made of fiber material, you could read a newspaper at the bottom of the ocean (with a powerful enough telescope).

The cladding buffer, done mainly to prevent exceeding the bend radius of the fiber or avoid kinks in the fiber that stop any signal in its tracks, makes the fiber easily visible to the unaided eye. The core and cladding are jacketed with plastic, then strengthened with nylon or Kevlar fibers, and jacketed again with a heavy coating, normally in pairs (one strand for sending, one for receiving). This layering helps to limit the bend radius of the fiber, which, kinked, can completely halt the light wave in its tracks.

The easiest way to send 0s and 1s over a basic fiber link is to simply turn the LED or laser off and on as rapidly as possible. Darkness in a time slot is a 0 bit and a certain level of illumination (often tunable at the receiver) is a 1 bit. For a long time, this primitive method, or "amplitude modulation," of light was the way fiber links worked. The receiver counted photons detected in a time period (light travels as a wave but is detected as a photon particle [wave packet]). If the number of photons exceeds threshold X, that is a 1 bit. Today, there are many more advanced ways to represent 0s and 1s, as on mobile networks.

Just like mobile networks, fiber optic networks changed over time. No one defined fiber optical "generations" as the standards organizations did for mobile networks, but some sources still cite "generations" for fiber optics. It might be better to think of them as "stages" of fiber optic links and networks.

Table 3.1 shows the informal stages, timeframes, typical bandwidth of a single fiber stand, and the characteristics of that stage of fiber optics.

TABLE 3.1. Fiber optic stages and characteristics.

Stage	Timeframe	Typical Bandwidth	Characteristics
1	1980-1982	45 Mbps	Single wavelengths, 850 nm lasers, MMF, and regenerators to boost signal
2	1982-1987	100 Mbps to 1.7 Gbps	Single wavelengths, 1310 nm lasers, SMF, and regenerators to boost signal
3	1987-1997	2.5 Gbps to 10 Gbps	Single wavelengths, 1550 nm lasers, SMF, regenerators to boost signal
4	1997-2011	40 Gbps to 3.2 Tbps	Multiple wavelengths (WDM/DWDM), SMF, EDFA, managed dispersion
5	2011-	8 Tbps to 50 Tbps	CDCF ROADM nodes, amplified DWDM

A few words are in order about the characteristics of each of these stages.

Around 1980, fibers thinner than a strand of human hair had a changing internal index of refraction to guide light waves in a helix around the core of the fiber. The fiber *core* was large, a type of fiber called multimode fiber (MMF) because there were several ways that these light helixes could travel without interference (similar to how two flashlight beams intersect without a problem). This meant the MMF fiber did not require lasers but could be lit by less expensive LEDs. When lasers were used for long-distance communications, they used what was called the "850 nm window," where attenuation (signal loss) was manageable. If a certain distance was exceeded, the optical signal had to be detected, converted to an electrical stream of bits again, and then resent on the next span of fiber. These devices were called "regenerators." They often failed in hard-to-reach places (underground or even under water). Speeds were similar to what the telcos used for digitizing analog television transmission at the time: the "T-3" rate of 45 Mbps. (Audio was sent separately, which is why live sports events sometimes lost the video while keeping the audio.)

By 1982, only two years later, single-mode fiber (SMF) with narrow cores that allowed only one wave propagation mode had to be lit by lasers. Another band became useful: 1350 nm lasers. The advantage was the ability to have longer spans before regenerators were needed and a boost in bandwidth up to 1.7 Gbps.

The third stage increased bandwidths to 10 Gbps and made the 1550 nm window useful and was fairly stable for approximately ten years, mainly because there was not much need for all the bandwidth. Even so, the arrival of the Web changed everything.

By the early 2000s, fiber transmission introduced widespread wavelength division multiplexing (WDM). This technology allowed the use of multiple wavelengths over the same fiber. Methods of cramming these wavelengths closer together gave dense WDM (DWDM). Regenerators requiring light-to-electrical conversions and back to light were no longer needed because special fibers known as Erbium-Doped Fiber Amplifiers (EDFAs) allowed direct strengthening of optical signals. (Erbium is a rare earth element, and doping is the process of intentionally adding impurities to a material.) The fibers also took care of *dispersion* (the "fuzzying" of optical pulses), another problem with long distance fibers.

The characteristics of fiber spans and links using CDCF ROADM nodes and amplified DWDM are explored in more detail later in this chapter. These nodes allow bit rates up to 50 Tbps, a good thing when Ethernet LANs now can run at 400 Gbps (almost half a Tbps).

Signaling methods have advanced as well. As mentioned, the simplest way to send 0s and 1s over a fiber link is to turn the laser on (a 1 bit) and off (a 0 bit). However, just as fiber speeds advanced, the methods of laser modulartion did as well. The drawback is that the achievable span distance shrinks as the modulation technique (its "constellation") becomes more advanced. The older methods of quadrature-phase shift keying (QPSK) allowed spans of approximately 4,000 km (2500 miles) but maxed out at about 12 Tbps bandwidth. The newer techniques used various types of quadrature-amplitude modulation (QAM) to increase bandwidth but got more expensive as the technique got more complex and the span distance became shorter. Notably, 8QAM spanned approximately 1800 km (1100 miles) and carried 12 Tbps, 16QAM 1000 km (620 miles) at 20 Tbps, 32QAM 400 km (250 miles) and 32 Tbps, and 64QAM 250 km (155 miles) at 38 Tbps.

This is a good lesson to learn about advanced technology (besides going faster at shorter span distances): there is always a trade-off to explore. At some point, the cost (expense) and benefit (savings) will be optimal, but it might take some work to figure that out.

WAVELENGTH WINDOWS

Fiber optic networks usually operate in a "wavelength window" where limiting effects such as attenuation and dispersion are at relative minimums. An example is the 850 nm window used by early fiber networks. These regions are more formally called *communication bands* and are defined by standards organizations and regulatory agencies. The bands are given letters that actually stand for something, as will be shown later.

These bands are shown in Figure 3.1. Note the attenuation "hump" at 1400 nm, something due to OH (hydroxyl) absorption at this wavelength. This loss can be compensated for by using low-OH fibers. Older fibers had a "water peak" attenuation bump in the 1500 nm range, but newer fibers used for DWDM do not have this.

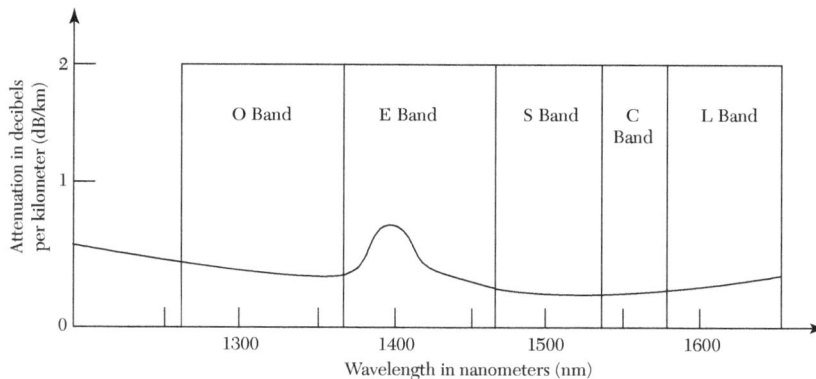

FIGURE 3.1. The optical fiber communications bands.

Initially, fiber optics used either lasers or LEDs operating in the 800-900 nm "window" (not shown in the figure) as transmitters. Receivers were based on silicon *photodiodes*. Early transmitters operated at the fixed wavelength and were *narrowband*, while receivers operated across a wide range of wavelengths and were thus *wideband*.

Today this window is only used for short-distance spans and often uses plastic optical fibers. This window is not easy to use with common modern fiber amplifiers, and the propagation losses due to attenuation are high.

The O-band window around 1300 nm was originally used for long-haul fiber networks. However, the fiber amplifiers used for 1300 nm (based on praseodymium-doped fiber) were not as good as the amplifiers used for the 1500 nm window. Today, EDFAs are the ones that people think of when talking about packet optical systems.

Some systems were prone to *nonlinearities* that hampered span distances. Engineers always try to keep things operating in the *linear range*, which means that doubling an input results in doubling an output. In the nonlinear range, doubling an input might drop the output to zero, or output nonsense.

The most widely used optical window today is in the 1500 to 1600 nm range, where EDFAs can be used effectively. Other transmission impairments can be countered with a special fiber known as *dispersion-shifted fiber* (DSF).

As noted in the figure, there are even higher wavelengths possible to be used. However, transmitters in the 2000 to 3000 nm range usually require special *fluoride fibers* and worry about *infrared absorption*. This would require wholesale changes to the transmitters, amplifiers, and the fiber itself—changes few are willing to consider. However, it is an area of active research.

The common fiber wavelengths are described in Table 3.2.

TABLE 3.2. Fiber optic wavelengths and bands.

Wavelengths	Characteristics	Band
1260-1360nm	The *Original* range of wavelengths used for long fiber spans	O Band
1360-1460nm	The *Extended* range of this initial window	E Band
1460-1530nm	The *Short* wavelength range	S Band
1530-1565nm	The *Conventional* wavelength range for the "erbium window"	C Band
1565-1625nm	The *Long* wavelength range	L Band
1625-1675nm	The *Ultralong* wavelength range	U Band

The search is always on for new and better fundamental fiber technologies. EDFAs work in the C or L bands, but other elements are being developed for other windows. S Band might be able to use thulium-doped fiber amplifiers, and, as mentioned, O Band might be well served by praseodymium-doped amplifiers with fluoride-based fibers. Bismuth might be useful for doping fibers in the O, E, and S bands, but these are still in the early stages.

KEY COMPONENTS FOR OPTICAL FIBER COMMUNICATIONS

Packet optical networks for long-range communication all use the same basic components. The most important pieces are:

- Optical transmitters—these are usually semiconductor lasers on a chip (for example, a vertical-cavity surface-emitting laser (VCSEL)). Today, many lasers are *tunable lasers*, which form the basis for wavelength-division multiplexing (WDM) and dense WDM (DWDM).

- Optical receiver—these are usually some form of photodiode (like an avalanche photodiode) that can count photons in a time slot. They operate over a wide range of wavelengths, which makes them easy to use for DWDM systems, as long as the multiplexed wavelength can be isolated with a Bragg grating or similar device.

- Optical fibers—almost always SMF today, even for rack-to-rack connections in a data center. The fibers are built with consideration for attenuation (loss of signal power), dispersion ("fuzzying" of a sent sharp pulse), and nonlinearities (where doubling input does not double the output).

- Modules to compensate for dispersion—you cannot avoid dispersion, but you can limit the effects.

- Amplifiers—These can be in the fiber, as with EDFAs or *Raman amplifiers*, or use semiconductors. Often a link will use an amplifier (preamplifier) before sending the signal to the receiver.

- Optical filters—in WDM and DWDM systems, filtering (selecting) one wavelength from a number of them is often done with a fiber Bragg grating. Signals are combined with an optical coupler.

- Optical switches and multiplexers—these are the reconfigurable add-drop multiplexers (ROADMs) that make packet optical networks possible. They deserve a section of their own at the end of this chapter.

In addition to these basic components, a packet optical network will also include devices for signal regeneration (which can function optically or convert the optical signal to an electronic one and back again), clock recovery (for establishing time slots and transmission frames), line errors and other monitoring equipment, and software to configure and control the whole system.

THE PACKETS IN PACKET OPTICAL

So far, this chapter has covered a lot about optical networks. However, where do the packets come in? What makes an optical network a *packet optical network*?

Consider a router in a corporate data center connected to another router on the Internet with a fiber optic link. Not too long ago, the router would take an IP packet inside an Ethernet frame from the subnet LAN in the data center and package it up in a Synchronous Optical Network (SONET) in North America and Synchronous Digital Hierarchy (SDH) in most of the rest of the world—the "synchronous" just means that the senders and receivers have access to timing signals that make it easier to determine where frames start and stop. These SONET/SDH transmission frames—do not confuse SONET/SDH frames with Ethernet frames because they are at different layers—are sent as a series of bits over the fiber optic cable.

However, once the SONET/SDH frame arrived at the Internet router, the first thing that the network interface card (NIC) or line card or other communications device did was convert the light to electronic signals again, then extract the Ethernet frame from the SONET/SDH frame. Finally, the IP packet was extracted from the Ethernet frame (in reality, the whole process was done with pointers) and routed as any other IP packet to the outbound link to the next hop.

Modern routers, switches, and other devices are equipped with line cards that can place IP packets directly onto optical transport links at the sender and extract the packets at the receiver. In packet optical networks, the packets leave the data center router in an optical transport "envelope," such as SONET/SDH or OTN, using a configured wavelength.

The advantages of direct optical network interfaces are many. The devices now have access to optical span performance parameters such as signal strength and noise, can gather trend information about corrected and uncorrected bit errors, and eliminate low-performance copper links at the ends of the span. Packet optical networks can record and analyze optical performance and even provide protection switching if the bit error rate (BER) exceeds a configured threshold.

Packet optical networks can do even more. For example, with ROADM network nodes, it is now possible to route a packet to a next-hop link on the Internet without converting the optical packet to an electronic version. This does not eliminate the need for electronic components, but it does make much of the node processing that much faster and more efficient.

More about ROADMs is covered later in this chapter.

PACKET OPTICAL MULTIPLEXING

As soon as a way to send communication signals over a medium is invented, efforts to make more efficient use of the medium are researched. This typically combines efforts to send as many different sources over the single medium and split them off again at the receiver. This *multiplexing* of signals is a constantly active area for engineers and theorists to explore.

In many cases, multiplexing involves the increase of the media's bandwidth to allow for multiple coarse signals to be carried out without interference. Alexander Graham Bell invented the telephone while trying to multiplex multiple sources of Morse code dots and dashes over a single telegraph wire. He accidentally increased the useful bandwidth—and the transmitter and receiver at each end—of the telegraph circuit so that an understandable portion of the full range of the human voice could be transmitted over it successfully. The analog telephone system struggled with high and low frequencies, but most of the power of the human voice came through—Bell's powerful voice, used in his research with hearing-impaired patients, helped a lot in early demonstrations.

Multiplexing can be performed electronically in a number of ways. The entire frequency range of the medium—approximately 4000 Hertz (cycles per second) in the case of the telephone—can be split into *channels*, with transmitters tuned to put their peak power out at a central frequency. Receivers can be tuned to pay attention to one of these channels and ignore the others. With frequency division multiplexing (FDM), a sender gets only a fraction of the whole bandwidth but can send whenever it likes.

Another common electronic multiplexing method is to divide time into a number of *time slots*. If there are four times slots per second, then four sources can share the media, and each can get the entire bandwidth of the media. With time division multiplexing (TDM), a sender gets the whole bandwidth, but only for a fraction of the time. Sender and receivers must agree where these time slots start and stop, so a considerable amount of effort is often needed to supply a timing signal, or clock, to the system.

However, for optical networks, a term other than FDM or TDM is used. Optical networks multiplex with wavelength division multiplexing (WDM). It is true that every frequency of any electromagnetic signal, light or electricity, also has a wavelength defined for it, so that waves with higher frequencies have shorter wavelengths and lower frequencies have longer wavelengths. For example, the important 1550-nm window used for DWDM is at a frequency of approximately 193 terahertz (THz), or 193,415 gigahertz (GHz). DWDM standards, somewhat confusingly, use wavelengths for some standards and frequencies for others. To convert a wavelength in nm to a Hertz frequency, divide 2.998×10^{17} by the wavelength in nm. Make sure the power of 10 of the result makes sense!

With optical networks, in WDM systems, each sender uses a wavelength in some form of FDM, and then each input is usually divided into time slots using TDM.

In modern systems like packet optical, the wavelengths used for multiplexing are much closer together than they have been in the past. So, it is common today to use dense WDM (DWDM) to talk about packet optical networks.

Various standards have been established for packet optical networks. There are standards for DWDM wavelengths in the FDM domain, the frame structures in the TDM domain for each input (the overall standard is OTN), and for the packet optical network node, the ROADM.

Today, many packet optical networks conform to the optical transport network (OTN) standard. The international standard for OTNs is G.709. This standard includes wavelength values for wavelength-division multiplexing (WDM), a method that allows a single physical fiber to carry multiple bit streams, all using different wavelengths. Systems that do not use DWDM are often called coarse WDM (CWDM) systems today.

SINGLE WAVELENGTH LIMITATIONS

Ethernet devices evolved from 10 Mbps to 1 Gbps to 10 Gbps and beyond. Fiber optical links also evolved to run at faster and faster speeds while still using just a single wavelength to send and receive. However, there are real limitations for optical networks using single-wavelength optical networks. These incentives led to the development of WDM and DWDM multiplexing.

The major limitations of single-wavelength optical networks are:

1. The requirement for receivers to deal with smaller and smaller serial bit intervals
2. The need for speed-specific repeaters
3. The requirement for expensive new fiber runs to increase capacity

Each of these is important enough to deserve a few words of explanation.

Smaller Serial Bit Intervals

As the number of bits per second on a serial link increases, the characteristic bit time or bit interval of each individual bit shrinks proportionately. At 1 kbps, each individual bit is represented by 1 thousandth of a second (1 millisecond, or 1 ms). On the link itself, bits might be grouped and represented by a single *baud* or change in line signaling condition, but this makes little difference to the serial receiver on the link. The serial port still deals with one thousand bits per second. Additionally, the original optical networks used modulation by simply varying the intensity of the light above or below the threshold of the receiver. This *intensity modulation* is essentially a one-bit-per-baud method of serial transmission.

At a line speed of 1 Mbps, one thousand times faster than 1 kbps, the characteristic serial bit time is down to 1 millionth of a second, or 1 microsecond (1 μsecond). This is only 1 thousandth as long as a millisecond, naturally. Transmitters and receivers have to generate and detect bits one after the other within 1 microsecond, or the link will drop bits and produce bit errors.

Gigabit Ethernet (GbE) produces and reacts to bits sent in only 1 billionth of a second, or 1 nanosecond (1 ns). 10 GbE bits last only 1/10th of a nanosecond (0.1 ns). Many optical devices operate at 40 Gbps and produce bit streams with characteristic bit intervals of only 0.025 ns. The time slots shrink even smaller as serial speeds increase.

The bit interval is important because of an impairment to all transmission systems known as *jitter*. Jitter is a term used for *timing variations on a transmission link*. Jitter is a time-domain impairment just as noise is a frequency-domain impairment in transmission systems. The two are related, and neither can be ignored in communications systems because both limit the effective speed of any communications link, electrical or optical. Jitter, like noise, can never be completely eliminated. At some point, jitter causes bits to arrive in the wrong time slot at the receiver. This makes it impossible for the link to function with an acceptable error rate.

A bit can be lost if jitter causes the bit interval to wander beyond the "edges" of the bit time at the receiver. A bit can be duplicated if jitter causes the bit interval to shrink smaller than anticipated by the receiver. Both cases will cause a bit error.

Enough jitter causes errors at low speeds as well as high speeds. Jitter effects always limit the effective line rate and time slot durations available for serial bit transmission. On optical networks, the only way to increase bit rates on links limited by jitter effects is to add WDM or DWDM.

Speed-specific Repeaters

Digital repeaters on an optical link perform "3R" signal regeneration: they restore, reshape, and retime a light pulse that represents a bit. Repeaters operate in the electrical domain (where all bits reside by definition), so the optical signal is converted to electrical, then turned into optical signals again, an "EOE" process for short. Digital repeaters are *code and timing sensitive*. To reshape a pulse, a repeater must know what line code is being used to represent the 0s and 1s. To retime the signal, the repeater must know the bit rate of the link to derive the bit interval. A repeater that works with a 10 Mbps link will not work if the transmitter and receiver are changed to operate at 100 Mbps.

A digital repeater will not function on a fiber optic link when there are multiple wavelengths present. The transmitter in a simple repeater, designed to be inexpensive and yet robust devices for field operation, can operate only at one wavelength. When WDM and DWDM are in use, it is necessary to use optical amplifiers instead of digital repeaters.

Expensive New Fiber Runs

When a single-wavelength fiber optic link has reached its upper limit for serial bit transmission, whether 1 Gbps, 10 Gbps, or 40 Gbps, there is no other way to increase the capacity on the link except to add new fiber. In some cases, this can be a simple process. Fiber is often run in conduits with lots of spare room for new fibers. However, this postpones the inevitable problem of what to do when the capacity of the conduit is exhausted, and no more fibers can be jammed into the conduit.

The cost of new fiber runs covers more than the cost of the new fiber. Trenches must be dug, conduit installed, the trench closed, fiber placed in the conduit, and new transmitters and receivers purchased and deployed. Undersea fiber is a special case and has its own concerns, among them the fact the sharks seem to enjoy biting the cables where they come ashore.

When using WDM or DWDM, a lot of the expense of running new fiber goes away. Sometimes it is possible to use the same fibers that are in use with single wavelength systems, but it is not always possible for older fiber runs. However, even if new fiber is required for WDM and DWDM, the new fiber can often replace or add to the older fiber without the need to run a new conduit. Even with the cost of new fiber factored in, WDM or DWDM requires the purchase and installation of new multi-wavelength transmitters, receivers, and optical amplifiers.

The major cost factor in WDM and DWDM installation is the cost of the transmitters and receivers, but these costs are coming down all the time.

CWDM AND DWDM

It took a while for simple point-to-point fiber optic links using CWDM to evolve into packet optical networks using DWDM. Four key developments were needed before DWDM systems became practical:

1. At the sender, the tunable laser diode operating in the C Band window at around 1550 nm

2. On the span, the in-fiber amplifier, such as the Erbium-Doped Fiber Amplifier (EDFA)
3. Between components, special fibers with certain dispersion and zero water peak characteristics
4. At the receiver, the in-fiber Bragg grating to isolate individual wavelengths

A full discussion of these components would provide a more complete understanding of fiber communications effects such as dispersion, attenuation, scattering, jitter, power limits, polarization effects, the odd self-interaction quantum effects of even a single ray of light, and so on. However, we have covered enough to understand the characteristics of CWDM and DWDN systems to compare them in a meaningful way.

All four of these DWDM components are shown in Figure 3.2.

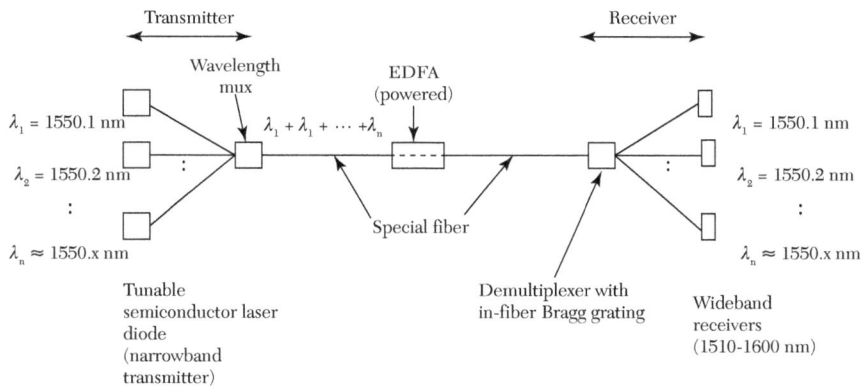

FIGURE 3.2. The components of a DWDM link.

Fiber spans with EDFAs, although they require electrical power, work on optical wavelengths directly. Without an EDFA, fiber spans of any considerable length need a repeater. Repeaters include conversion of the optical to electrical signals, regeneration of the original bits in the source signal, and then generation of an optical signal all over again.

The use of repeaters and EDFAs is shown in Figure 3.3.

When multiplexing is used, many individual wavelengths are combined and sent on the same physical fiber. Optical amplifiers (OAs), either repeaters or EDFAs, are used to allow the signal to be sent over longer span distances. At the other end of the link, another multiplexing device de-multiplexes the wavelengths and sends them to their individual destinations.

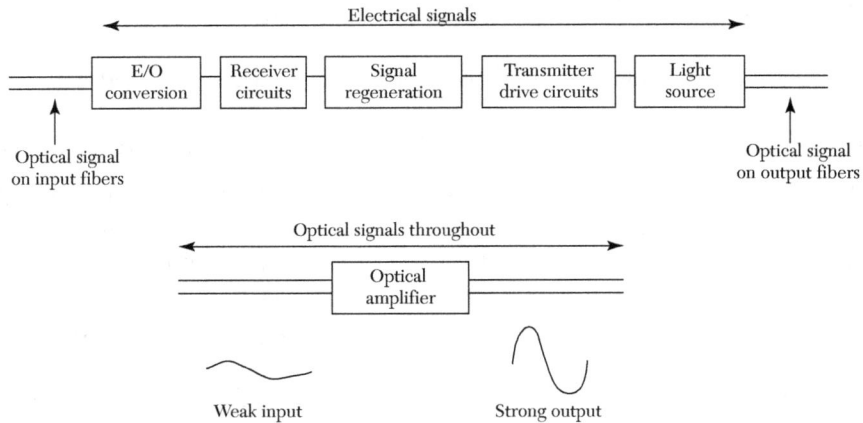

FIGURE 3.3. Use of repeaters and EDFAs.

This process is shown in Figure 3.4.

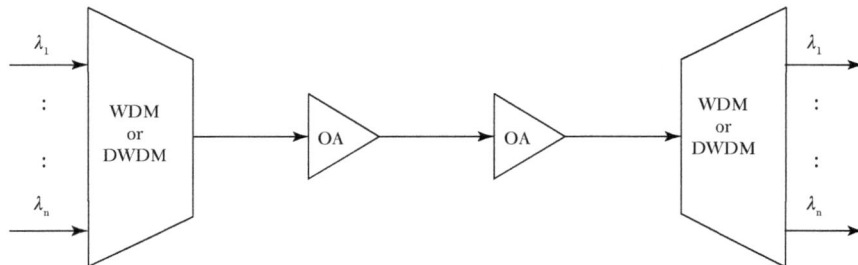

FIGURE 3.4. Multiplexing with WDM or DWDM

As mentioned, there are considerable differences between systems running CWDM and DWDM. Many books detail them all, but these are just summarized here.

The main features of CWDM and DWDM systems are shown in Table 3.3.

TABLE 3.3. CWDM versus DWDM.

Feature	CWDM	DWDM
Maximum wavelengths multiplexed	18 channels from 1271 nm to 1611 nm with 20 nm spacing	160 channels with 50 GHz spacing in the 1550 nm range (C-band spectrum)
Capacity	Lower	Higher

Feature	CWDM	DWDM
Characteristic Definition	Wavelengths	Wavelengths and frequencies
Cost	Low	High
Distance	Short range	Long haul (global)
Wavelength spacing	Broader	Narrower
Amplification	Not amplified directly: OEO repeaters used	Light amplifiers used (EDFA or Ramen amplifiers)
Spectrum utilization	Large chunks of spectrum	Small splices of spectrum used
Drift	Wavelengths used can drift	Precision, tunable lasers needed for each channel
Active wavelengths per fiber	Fewer than 8	More than 8

When speaking of DWDM especially, capabilities are expanding. It is always best to check the latest specifications.

The choice of CWDM versus DWDM is often clear, as the table shows. The main advantage of CWDM is cost. CWDM is optimized for cost, while DWDM is optimized for bandwidth utilization. DWDM offsets the cost of running new fiber by increasing costs for new devices feeding and being fed by the fiber. Considering the cost of running new undersea fibers from, for example, North America to Africa, this trade-off makes perfect sense. DWDM provides high scalability, low and consistent latency, and unparalleled distance, but at a steep cost. CWDM, on the other hand, is less complex to configure and operate, saving more in the long run.

In summary, DWDM provides greater capacity and a higher number of channels to use, but at a cost that might be prohibitive. CWDM is more cost-effective in metropolitan or campus networks where distance is not a major concern, leaving DWDM for long-haul networks run by major carriers.

DWDM DETAILS

It is always good to remember that the fiber optic cables used on spans are always deployed in pairs: one fiber to send and one fiber to receive. You cannot really shine a light down the same fiber from both directions. All the components described are used in only one direction; a complete matching setup is used to make sure communications are two-way. By convention, the fibers are described as East and West, although nothing geographical is implied by the use of these terms, as shown in Figure 3.5.

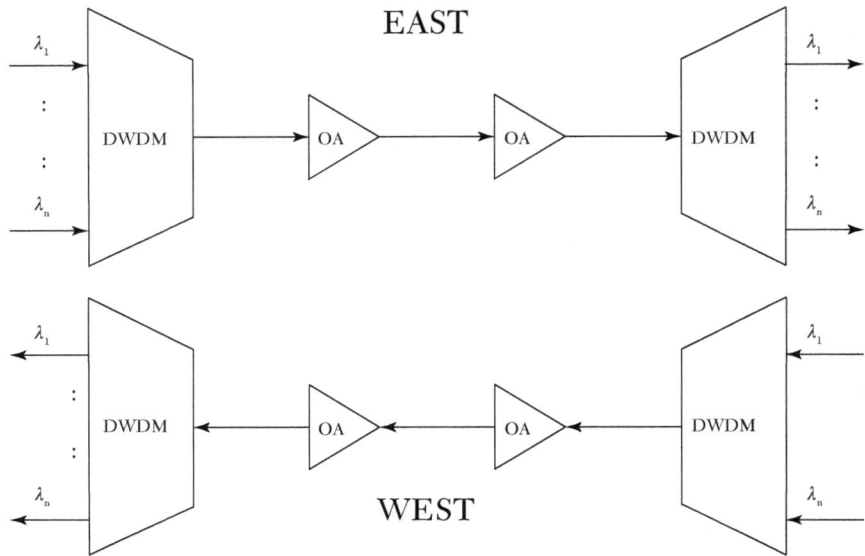

FIGURE 3.5. East and West DWDM fiber spans.

As with many high-level pictures of technology, a lot that happens inside simple boxes labeled as components like "DWDM" conceals a lot of detail.

The way that receivers de-multiplex DWDM wavelengths is by using special devices such as Bragg gratings or Ramen filters. Bragg gratings are short segments of transparent optical fiber with a periodic variation of refractive indexes, so that certain wavelengths are reflected and separated from the combined multiplexed signal.

This is easier to illustrate than to explain. The way that a DWDM receiver separates the combined signal is to use a wavelength splitter to send all the multiplexed wavelengths on all the possible output fibers. Each output fiber uses a Bragg grating (in this example) to split off the individual wavelengths that were multiplexed at the sender.

This allows wideband receivers, perhaps in the 1500–1600 nm range, to be used on all output fibers, keeping expenses under control. This process is shown in Figure 3.6.

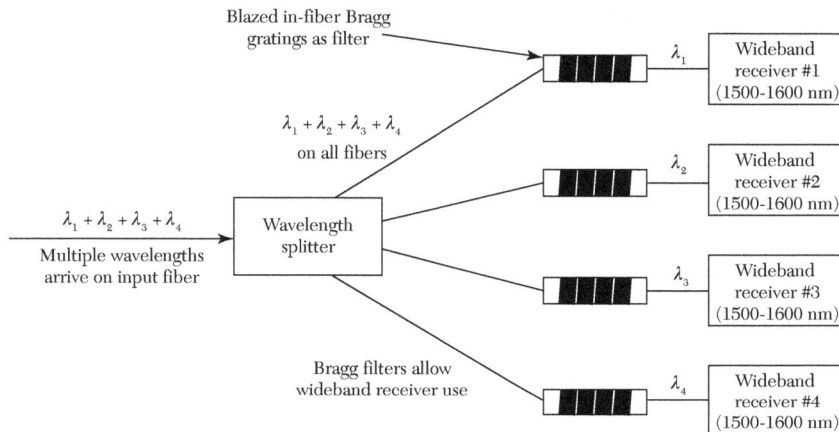

FIGURE 3.6. Bragg gratings and DWDM.

OTN AND GFP

Today, DWDM is standardized for international use as part of the Optical Transport Network (OTN) defined as G.709 by the International Telecommunications Union (ITU). Operation of these advanced fiber optical networks is tied to the use of forward error correction (FEC) codes to enable higher-speed connections over extended distances.

FECs are part of a new set of standards that are a key component of the overall architecture of a packet optical network using DWDM. The distinguishing characteristic of a packet optical network is that in many cases, but not all, the optical interfaces are not in separate pieces of equipment but implemented on simple line cards that are placed in the router or switch like any other physical interface.

Why are FECs needed? Because with this increased DWDM bit-carrying capacity comes an increased risk. A failed or marginally operating link can threaten not only the loss of one stream of bits but many bit streams that flow on the same physical link. A failed link carrying many gigabits of information can be catastrophic for a network unless some method to compensate for these losses is used. These methods include not only FECs but also fast traffic reroute.

One other aspect of packet optical networks is important to keep in mind. First, these networks are in a very real sense optimized for the transport of IP packets. This is not literal in the sense that IP packets are favored over other types of traffic—optical networks are intended to be versatile. It is nonetheless true that most voice and video today are carried inside IP packets, and optical networks acknowledge that dominance.

However, IP packets are usually sent over these packet optical networks inside Ethernet frames. Ethernet has become more or less the *de facto* standard for interface input and output, and packet optical networks are not an exception. A lot of hardware and software exists to generate and interpret Ethernet frames, and so it makes sense to use this capability rather than invent yet another Layer 2 frame format (Layer 2 frames are not the same as transmission frames).

The ITU issues standards (technically, "recommendations," but they have the force of international law) for all aspects of telecommunications. The main standard for packet optical networks is G.709, which defines a standard OTN. There are also closely related standards such as G.707 for submarine fiber optical cables and G.975, which contains recommendations for FEC code use in DWDM submarine optical systems. However, the FEC codes in G.975 can be used in other places as well.

If a local communications carrier does not offer fiber links that conform to OTN standards, they could always run or lease their own dark fiber that has no other signals on it. However, in many cases, this is not possible.

Fortunately, the Internet Engineering Task Force (IETF) has standardized RFC 6363, which defines how FEC can be used with a stream of IP packets, whether the carrier employs packet optical network technologies or not.

FEC AND OTN

It is usually possible to use almost any FEC you like, as long as sender and receiver agree. OTN standards (often just called "G.709") allow various types of digital wrappers to operate at tunable wavelengths. The rules of OTN are much more permissive than they were in older optical standards like SONET or SDH.

This flexibility means that if you want to send IP packets over an OTN link, go right ahead. Send Ethernet frames? No problem. SONET/SDH? Yes, even those frames and rates have been adopted for OTN use.

The four main Optical Transport Unit (OTU) levels (and sublevels) of the OTN digital hierarchy are shown in Table 3.4.

TABLE 3.4. The OTN digital hierarchy.

G.709 OTN Level	Line Rate	Content
OTU1	2.666 Gbps	OC-48/STM-16 (2.488 Gbps)

G.709 OTN Level	Line Rate	Content
OTU2	10.709 Gbps	OC-192/STM-64 or as a physical layer for 10GBase-W (10G Ethernet WAN)
OTU2e	11.09 Gbps	10G Ethernet LANs from a switch or router at 10.3 Gbps (G.Sup43)
OTU2f	11.32 Gbps	10G fibre channel
OTU3	43.018 Gbps	OC-768/STM-256 or 40G Ethernet
OTU3e2	44.58 Gbps	Multiplex of up to four OTU2e signals
OTU4	112 Gbps	100G Ethernet

When it comes to OTN itself, there are four key aspects of the OTN standards:

Protocol Transparency—OTN can carry all types of payload data, including IP packets, Ethernet frames, and SONET/SDH frames. OTN line rates are 7% higher than their corresponding payload line rates. The additional bits are used for additional overhead and to accommodate many different types of FEC methods.

Asynchronous Timing—OTN maps payloads into digital wrappers in an asynchronous manner. This means that the OTN clock generating the frames can run freely and not be locked to the client signal clock. Timing mismatches are handled by allowing the payload to "float" in the OTN wrapper. As an option, the payload clock can be used to generate the timing for the OTN frames.

Management—OTN allows monitoring and management of both link segments and end-to-end. Segments can overlap (a span can be a member of more than one management segment), and the architecture allows up to six monitoring segments at any point. This means that if a link from Network A passes through Network B, the operator of both networks has access to relevant monitoring and management information.

FEC—OTN does not add FEC onto a basic architecture but builds FEC consideration into its very fabric. Very high data rates over very long distances are subject to significant noise and large error bursts. These links could not function without FEC. OTN uses a standard called *RS (255, 239)* FEC code built right into the OTN frame outside of the frame payload area in a special section called the *FEC area* and so is considered to be an *out-band FEC* instead of in-band. In other words, the FEC is outside of the payload but still inside the OTN frame. Each 255-byte block contains 16 FEC bytes generated from 239 data bytes. The

RS code designation means that OTN can correct up to 8 bytes of errors in a data block and detect up to 16 bytes of error in a block. More sophisticated interleaving can improve this at the cost of more processing and buffering delay.

OTN is a layered hierarchy that reaches from the optical fiber at the bottom to the payloads (called *clients* in OTN) that are carried inside the wrapper. These payloads can be IP packets, Ethernet frames, SONET/SDH transmission frames, and other types. It is not necessary to detail these layers, but it will be a good idea to take a quick look at the OTN frame structure.

The overall structure of the OTN frame is shown in Figure 3.7.

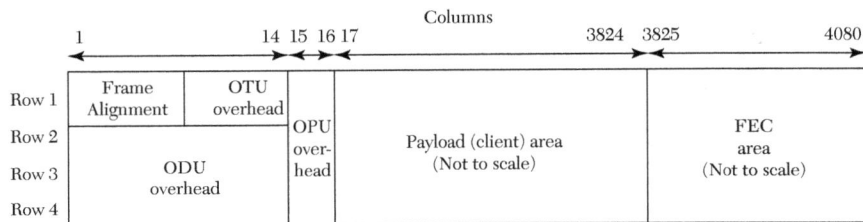

FIGURE 3.7. The OTN Frame Structure.

OTN frames have 4 rows and 4080 columns of bytes (octets). Frames are sent starting with row 1, column 1, left to right, to row 4, column 4080. Each row consists not of bytes as in SONET/SDH but of 16 interleaved FEC "blocks" of 255 bytes ($16 \times 255 = 4080$). Each 255-octet block consists of 238 bytes of payload, 1 octet of overhead, and 16 bytes of redundant FEC bytes. The FEC bytes are carried in a special *FEC area* in the frame, columns 3825 to 4080 (16 FEC bytes $\times$ 16 blocks = 256 columns).

The 16 blocks in each row are interleaved so that each block can correct up to 8 bytes (64 bits) in error, and burst errors can be corrected up to 128 bytes long. All in all, the frame structure in OTN is optimized for FEC and expects FEC to be used, not added on. The FECs used in OTN can be more than one type, depending on whether the optical span is a submarine cable or in some other environment. Naturally, both ends of the link must agree on the FEC method used.

There is OTU and optical data unit (ODU) overhead in the first 14 columns of each row, followed by two columns of optical payload unit overhead that are used to fit the payload client signals into the OTN frame. The first six bytes of each OTN frame are used for frame alignment, followed by eight bytes of OTU overhead.

Generic Framing Procedure

OTN frames allow many different types of client payloads inside the frame by using an intermediate structure called the Generic Framing Procedure (GFP) frame. This allows many potential client signals, such as IP packets or Ethernet frames, to be placed inside the OTN frame. Now, IP packets can be carried in OTN by loading them first into Asynchronous Transfer Mode (ATM) cells or SONET/SDH frames, but many IP packets end up in OTN frames inside Ethernet over GFP frames. Many interfaces use Ethernet already, so it is easy to adapt these interfaces to OTN using DWDM, but this is not mandatory. The main requirement is that the equipment on the other end of the span be compatible with whatever method is used by the sender.

GFP frames fall into two main categories: client frames and control frames. Client frames carry the payloads (and some types of payload control information), and control frames carry things like idle frames, which are used to fill the link when no IP packet or Ethernet frame is available, and other link management information.

Unlike OTN frames, the GFP frame has a simple, linear structure. The first two bytes are the payload length identifier (PLI), and the next two bytes are a cyclical redundancy check (CRC-16) to protect the PLI. The payload area that follows can be up to 65,535 bytes long and end with an optional 4-byte frame check sequence (FCS). The payload area includes a payload header that indicates the structure of a payload (ethernet frame, SONET/SDH, and so on), followed by the client signal information. The general structure of the GFP is shown in Figure 3.8.

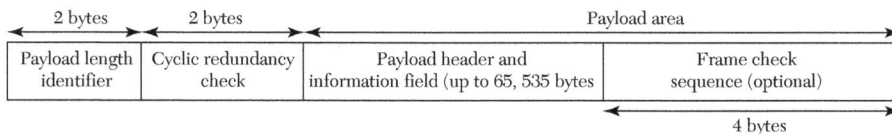

FIGURE 3.8. The GFP Frame Structure.

THE ROADM

The last key component of the packet optical network is the reconfigurable optical add-drop multiplexer (ROADM). The ROADM is as basic to the packet optical transport network as the router is to the Internet.

ROADM *nodes* are collections of rack and cable that keep the optical signal in the optical domain without ever having to convert data bits into electrical signals.

Without getting into very detailed operational internals, ROADM nodes operate in a similar way to a router:

- An Internet router is a device that looks at input streams of IP packets and separates them to route them onto their next hop output links. Configuration is usually done through a routing protocol, but manual configuration of *static* routes is also possible.

- A ROADM node is a device that looks at input fibers with multiple wavelengths and separates them to drop them onto configured output fibers, even as the node adds configured wavelengths from other input fibers. Configuration is usually done manually, but some devices try to automate at least some of the configuration process.

How a wavelength is dropped from a DWDM stream of wavelengths using a Bragg grating and shunted onto a drop fiber is shown in Figure 3.9.

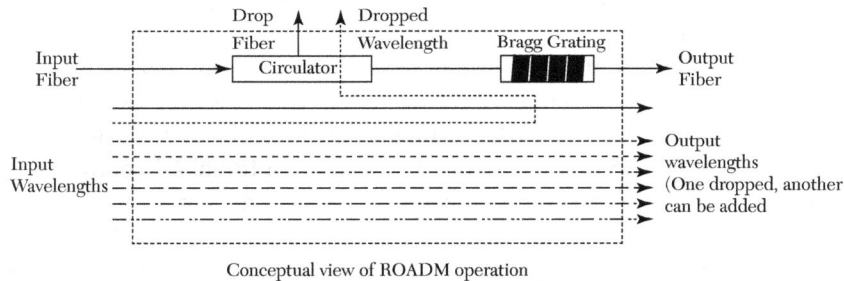

Conceptual view of ROADM operation

FIGURE 3.9. How a ROADM drops a wavelength.

Although not shown, this ROADM now has room to add an input stream of bits using the wavelength that has been dropped from the aggregate.

ROADM vendors speak of other features like *degrees* and how they scale as the network grows, but they really all do essentially the same thing: drop some wavelengths here and add some wavelengths to go there.

The most important feature of ROADMs is whether or not they support a collection of features known by the acronym CDCF, which stands for:

- Colorless
- Directionless
- Contentionless
- FlexGrid

These terms can be very confusing, so this chapter closes with a look at how these four terms fit together.

CDCF DEFINITIONS

The packet optical ROADM node characteristics of colorless-directionless-contentionless-flexgrid (CDCF) are easily confused because the terms are presented in the historical order in which they were popularized instead of the more natural order of their features. A more natural order is *Colorless-FlexGrid, Directionless-Contentionless*. It is even more accurate to present two of the features as sub-features of the two main features, like this:

- Colorless
  - FlexGrid
- Directionless
  - Contentionless

This organization of the terms reinforces the idea that any FlexGrid ROADM node must first be colorless, and any contentionless ROADM node must first be directionless. Let us look at each of the characteristics in detail, but in the order presented in the bullet list above rather than the order in the acronym.

Colorless (CDCF)

The colorless property of a ROADM node is the ability of the ROADM node to have multiplexer ports (not the line cards that drive output wavelength but the multiplexer ports themselves) in which the *channel center frequency* (or wavelength; they are the same thing) are initially unassigned. This flexibility can be achieved with a very broadband multiplexer or a programmable/tunable multiplexer.

In other words, the channels are basically "colorless" and have no preassigned wavelengths. The operational center frequency of the port is determined through provisioning (the carrier word for configuration).

The important points are that colorless operation is a property of the multiplexer ports, not the line cards, and that the center wavelengths used on the multiplexed port channels must be provisioned.

FlexGrid (CDCF)

It might seem odd to talk about the last property immediately after the first. However, it makes sense to do so because FlexGrid is closely related to the "color" or wavelength of the channel. In FlexGrid operation, the ROADM node not only provisions the channel center frequency or wavelength for the muiltiplexer port but also provisions the *width* of the channel. This capability is important because the channel width can now be optimized to match the spectral width of the channel. For example, a channel that previously operated in a 50 GHz window can now be run in a 37.5 GHz window.

As with colorless operation, this flexibility can be achieved with a very broadband multiplexer or a programmable/tunable multiplexer.

The operational width and center frequency of the port are determined through provisioning.

The important point here is that FlexGrid ports are all colorless, but all colorless ports are not necessarily FlexGrid ports.

Directionless (CDCF)

The directionless property is *not* something that a single ROADM node element, such as a stand-alone ROADM rack with 20 ports, can have. After all, there is only *one* direction (or destination path) for the line port on a single ROADM node element. The idea of the multiplexer port being "directionless" is meaningless: the port traffic can only go in one line direction, input or output.

However, in more complex ROADM node configurations, the term "directionless" refers to the ability of the ROADM node to have a multiplexer port that is initially *unassigned* to a line port direction. Obviously, it would take at least two line ports to offer any choice of line direction, but the choices are not limited to two as long as there are multiple degrees to the ROADM node.

In its simplest form, a directionless configuration consists of two ROADM node elements connected to each other and to a common add/drop device that they share.

Directionless operation can be achieved with a broadcast or direction-switchable multiplexer. The line port direction used is determined through provisioning.

Contentionless (CDCF)

The contentionless property of a ROADM node is a sub-characteristic of directionless operation. Contentionless operation is the ability of the ROADM node to have a multiplexer port that is *non-blocking* to any other multiplexing port. For example, many devices do not allow the same wavelength used within a group of multiplexer device ports because of the way that their internal optical design functions. This architecture creates blocking within the group and therefore is *not* contentionless (it is a contending architecture).

The point is that if the multiplexer is designed to provide a fully non-blocking solution, then the solution is contentionless (as well as directionless, because there are no preassigned multiplexer ports-to-line cards provisioned initially).

In summary, the packet optical ROADM node terms Colorless-Direction-less-Contentionless-FlexGrid (CDCF) can be confusing. The terms in the acronym CDCF are listed in historical order rather than the natural order of their features. It is more accurate to present two of the features as sub-items of the other two, like this:

- Colorless
  - FlexGrid
- Directionless
  - Contentionless

WHAT COMES NEXT

This chapter introduced packet optical networks that are used to backhaul (or fronthaul) mobile data from the mobile platform and back again. However, where is all this data going to and coming from?

The next chapter talks about cloud data centers.

Chapter 4

CLOUD COMPUTING AND DATA CENTERS

OVERVIEW

Up to this point, we have explored three major components of all modern wide-area networks (WANs), which are:

- The need for almost everyone in the world to have multiple Internet connections to their home, office, car, and business to work, plan their lives, and entertain themselves. This requires much more than the simple 32-bit address space invented for IPv4. Therefore, the need for IPv6.

- IPv6 provides enough address space to give every molecule in the solar system its own IPv6 address. It also simplifies a lot of the added protocols that IPv4 required and does away with some that were seldom used or security risks (like directed broadcasts).

- Packet optical networks based on new fibers and techniques like WDM make fiber links more effective for backhauling data to the cloud data center and delivering streams of data to mobile (and fixed) endpoints.

WHAT YOU WILL LEARN

This chapter delves into how data has become as valuable as it is today and the evolution of modern cloud-computing data centers based on virtual machines.

It explains how you can type in an Internet query about something like "baby carriages" in the morning and then see ads for other baby-related products all afternoon, topped off by previews for baby-related shows and movies when you stream after dinner.

Topics covered in this chapter include:

- The rise of the data center and computer networks
- Cloud computing
- Hardware and software advances
- Virtual machines
- Distributed networks and protocols
- Network function virtualization (NFV)

THE FIRST "DATA CENTERS"

In the late 1960s and early 1970s, computers—mainly IBM™ mainframes—became commonplace in public utilities to calculate and print monthly bills for customers. (Prior to 1962, monthly telephone bills at New York Telephone® were manually typed by a clerk on a typewriter using pre-printed forms.) There were two reasons for the rise of corporate computing in public utilities such as water, natural gas, electric, and telephone companies.

First of all, public utilities had plenty of money to spend. As regulated entities, guaranteed a profit, they could pass along capital expenses (CapEx) on new equipment by raising rates, which was usually a given in the post-war prosperity period of the United States. Second, they had a pressing need to save on the expense of billing each and every one of their often millions of customers each month, even customers paying a fixed rate for service whose bill this month was exactly the same as last month. Computerized billing, which inserted a punched card into every printed bill, saved money in the long run because an army of clerks was no longer needed to type bills.

Large companies, such as New York Telephone, could never bill every customer on the same day each month. Instead, they split the thirty or thirty-one days up into ten "billing cycles" like the 10th or 13th, which made the task manageable, even with a giant IBM mainframe pumping out bills twenty-four hours a day. Computers were so expensive and required air-conditioned rooms in an era when most offices were still cooled in the summer by opening windows and turning on big fans. So, the computer department had day, evening, and night shifts to keep things rolling smoothly.

There was no separation of computing power and data in those days. Most customers' billing data was held on reels of computer tape, stored in the back room in massive racks, and numbering up to 10,000 reels of 2400-foot 9-track magnetic tape. The whole building was the "data center," or, in the case of New York Telephone, the "processing center."

But in the 1980s, much of the data transitioned to magnetic disk drives, often with higher capacity and greater reliability (no worry above broken tapes) than the older magnetic tape drives, now relegated mainly for backup purposes.

In 1965, the United States government began to consider building the first data center to store more than 742 million tax returns and 175 million sets of fingerprints. They decided to do this by transferring those records onto magnetic computer tape that had to be stored in a single climate-controlled location. The project was dropped but is generally accepted as the beginning of the large-scale data storage era.

Some of the largest databases before the arrival of the Internet and World Wide Web were assembled by the insurance companies of the United States. The insurance industry, with the need to track income and payouts and compute and maintain all types of probabilistic actuarial tables, had a high need to maintain tight security as well. No one wanted their hard-earned data copied by a rival firm. In some cases, visitors were required to state that they were US citizens. Access to the room where the disk drives churned and supplied the mainframes with data was sometimes controlled, in those pre-video days, by weighing visitors in a kind of double-door booth to make sure their card-key access was not being shared by another person.

Even then, data was worth a lot. Databases with two hundred "spindles" (the term used to describe the drives that removeable disk drives spun on) were not unheard of. Governments maintain very large collections of data for mapping, budgeting, tax purposes and even espionage.

Yet all of these early data center applications shared one feature in common: all of the data was housed at or near where the computer hardware and software applications processed the data to achieve the results needed.

Where does the information that the massive data centers maintained by the large global technical companies come from?

They came, like so many other aspects of modern life, from the rise of the Internet, the World Wide Web, and client-server computing.

REMOTE ACCESS TO THE DATA CENTER

Remote access to a centralized computer's data was possible before the rise of the Internet, of course. Back then, network protocols were mainly proprietary and "closed," meaning that they only worked with the manufacturer's computer equipment, were controlled by the manufacturer, and not all of the operational details were published. Therefore, if you sent "Message A" to another vendor's computer, you were never quite sure if what you got back was valid in all cases at all times.

Nevertheless, early computer networks and protocols like the international program airline reservation system (IPARS) and the (eventually) IBM-computer-based semi-automated business research environment (SABRE) system for American Airlines became popular in the 1960s. Back then, reserving seats for long flights was a nightmare. Planes did not fly non-strop coast-to-coast as a rule, so passengers got on and off (for example) in Philadelphia, Kansas City, Denver, and San Francisco. Overbooking was common, and it took computers to figure it all out.

The SABRE/IPARS system was so popular that by 1976, it was a tool used by travel agents to book flights on most airlines. Even after the rise of the Internet and TCP/IP, IPARS was an important part of computer networks. In 1998, RFC 2351 on "Mapping of Airline Reservation, Ticketing, and Messaging Traffic over IP" showed programmers how to add reservations to Internet traffic.

Early networks used "dumb terminals" like the IBM 3270 family of devices that displayed 80 columns and 25 lines of fixed-pitch Courier font showing as green phosphor characters on a dull black background and were used to access remote data on a mainframe. They were "dumb" devices in that they were hardwired to a simple send and receive task and had no independent processing power. A Windows computer still often displays that layout and color scheme when the command line interface (CLI) is invoked.

In the 1970s, the largest computer vendor in the United States was IBM. There were other computer equipment vendors, seven of them in all, but most made smaller computers called "minicomputers." The mainframe business was left to IBM. In fact, the computer industry in the USA at the time was often called "IBM and the Seven Dwarfs." IBM even controlled the character set used on these terminals, so the minicomputer vendors used an open standard called the American Standard Code for Information Interchange (ASCII, pronounced Ass-Key) on their "dumb ASCII terminals."

The network architecture of IBM computers was systems network architecture (SNA). In most large corporations at the time, clerks or other "knowledge workers" whose job depended on fetching and using information from corporate mainframe data sat in front of IBM 3270-type dumb terminals and spent their day using the SNA network to answer customer queries, sell goods and services, or formulate marketing plans.

SNA networking was not really client-server networking, mainly because of the extremely limited capabilities of the client user device, the dumb terminal. However, there were components in an SNA network that ran programs and did quite a bit of independent processing, although they had nothing like the capabilities that similar devices have today. A simple smartphone has more processing power than an IBM mainframe did in 1964.

An SNA network in the 1970s and 1980s, which remained popular until the Web came long, had many of the components that are familiar from a TCP/IP network like the global public Internet. One big difference is the speed on the wide-area network links, which usually ran over regular analog telephone lines using modems at 9600 bits per second (9.6 kbps).

The user terminals were attached to a controller device such as the IBM 3274 that told the terminals when they could send their request messages to the mainframe and distributed replies as they came back, sometimes as quickly as six seconds or less. Six seconds was a common response time threshold in order to keep user attention focused on the task. Today, of course, data centers strive to deliver sub-second response times to their users.

The SNA controller was linked by telephone lines to the mainframe location but not directly to the mainframe. Even a mainframe did not have enough processing power in those days to access data from the hundreds of controllers in remote locations and the thousand or so terminals that were all involved in SNA sessions all day. So, the network was coordinated at the data center end by a series of front-end processors (FEPs), a term that was also used for the Internet.

The FEPs were cabled directly to mainframe communication channels (often called "bus and tag" cabling). The tape drive and disk drives that held the data that users were after were cabled that way as well, although many disk or tape drives could be serviced by one channel.

Today, the SNA architecture is vaguely familiar to people who know the structure of the Internet. The terminals have been replaced by client apps running on laptops, tablets, or smartphones connected wirelessly to LAN switches or hubs. Banks or insurance companies concerned about data theft still often used docked laptops or other devices and wired connections. The hubs in turn connect to routers in the home office or remote corporate space, and these used wide-area links or digital subscriber lines (DSLs) to reach the data center server locations, which can be many and located almost anywhere in the world.

The old SNA architecture and the modern Internet-based Web data center architecture are compared in Figure 4.1. In the Internet data center, the router is typically mounted on top of a server rack and called (unsurprisingly) the top of rack (TOR) router. Sometimes, the more things change, the more they stay the same, especially architecturally.

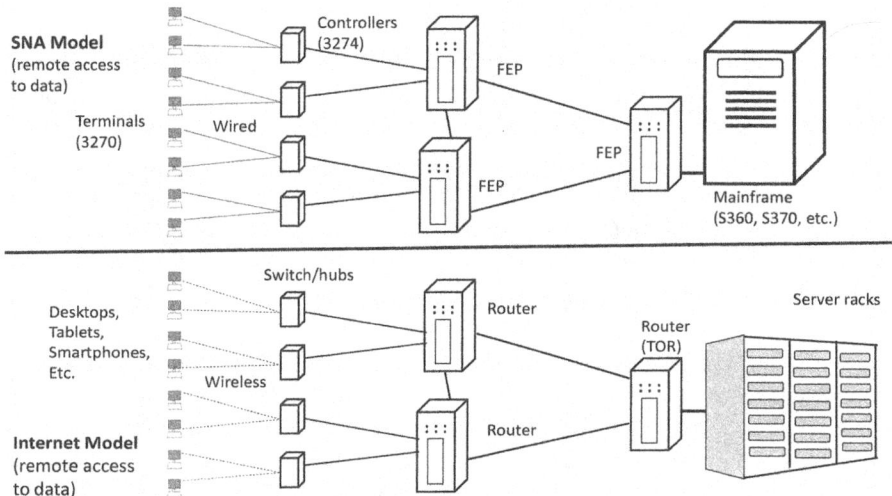

FIGURE 4.1. The SNA model and the Internet model for remote data access.

THE DATA CENTER DISTRIBUTES ITSELF

Although there are structural similarities between an SNA network of the 1970s and a TCP/IP-based network of the late 1980s and early 1990s, much had changed. Device processing power moved from the network center toward the edge. Terminals, especially once the PC came along in the 1980s, became "intelligent"—able to run their own applications to enhance requests sent to the data center and massage replies before presenting the results to the user. The routers, switches, and hubs, often housed under the same cover in cases like home DSL, got more sophisticated as well, running all kinds of different protocols and options as configurable software rather than being hard-wired into the device fabric.

This phase of data center networking was called *distributed processing*. In order to make all of these pieces of software seem as if they were all running in a coordinated fashion, it became possible to write programs on one computer that invoked a subprogram or procedure on another remote computer attached to the network. A request with data was sent over the network to another device, the remote program ran, and the response (or error) was relayed across the network to the originating device.

This aspect of distributed computing was called a *remote procedure call* (RPC). In a distributed network, there is no need to have all data concentrated in a central location. With the PC and other devices acting as the users' window into the network, those devices could maintain shopping carts—we will see how later—compute discounts, apply coupons, and more without bothering the data center at all. If a customer wanted a particular product in red, the network would find it in the inventory of a store that could be located anywhere in the world. Not only could the network ship it to a local store or direct to the customer, but the system would register the sale from daily, weekly, or other sales reports and could automatically order a replacement from a supplier. The new red product could be shipped closer to a place where data shows that the red color is particularly popular right now.

Distributed computing led to many changes in the way that application programs were built and run. Previously, application programs were monolithic blocks of code that fetched a record from a file on the network, processed it, and then put the modified record back, perhaps updating other data at the same time. Then the program moved on to the next record. However, once the data in a distributed network grew to a certain point, a new way to write and run "apps" became important. Today, these apps are sent to the data, rather than trying to move huge databases around the internet. Apps are "scattered" out to data centers, where they process data wherever they find it, and then "gather" the results to present to the user.

This is a good place to consider how RPCs work in more detail because they are the foundational concept behind such data center application program interface (API) structures as representational state transfer (REST), simple object access protocol (SOAP), or even APIs using JavaScript Object Notation (JSON) when the apps are employing Javascript. Although they all seem very different, all of these API methods are founded on the essentials of RPCs.

The basic operation of an RPC is shown in Figure 4.2. The heart of RPC operation is the presence of an RPC *stub* on the client and server. An RPC stub is a specially coded, compiled, and linked run-time program component that allows the client and server applications to think that the function, procedure, or subroutine they are running remains local, even though the client and server are connected only over the Internet.

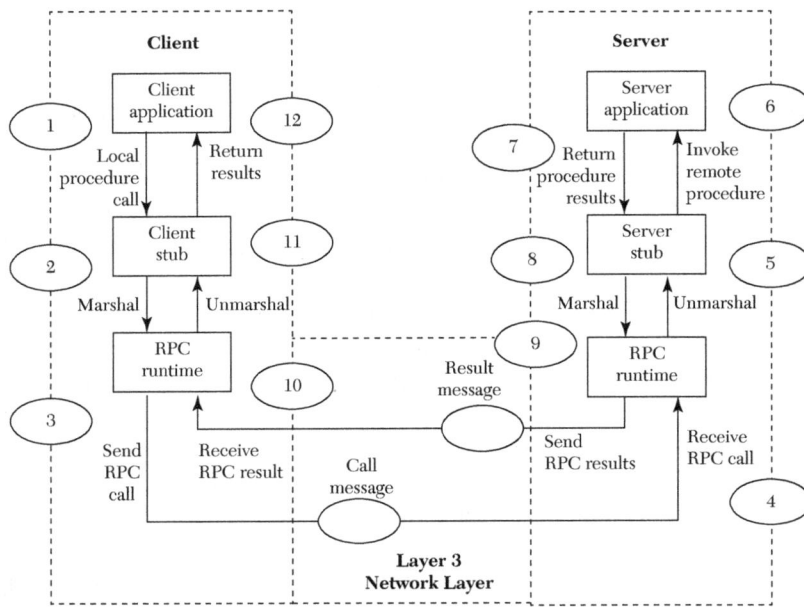

FIGURE 4.2. Remote procedure call operation.

The RPC process works as follows:

1. The client application makes a local procedure call to a subroutine exactly the same as the program did before. The function can be as simple as sorting files into alphabetical order or as complicated as configuring a load balancer for a set of servers in a remote data center. The key is that the subroutine call is intercepted by the RPC client stub.

2. The client stub performs what is called *mashalling*. This is the act of assembling all of the information that would be passed to the local procedure, such as the data to be sorted or the load balancer parameters to use at the server side.

3. The RPC runtime module packages the information up into an IP packet and sends the RPC call out over the Internet. Layer 3 is the connectionless network layer, and RPCs generally do not deal with the overhead needed to create a TCP connection.

4. The RPC runtime module of the remote server receives the packet and passes the data up the server stub.

5. The server stub "unmarshals" the data to present it to the subroutine the same way that it would if the subroutine were still on the client computer.

6. The server application is in many cases little more than a collection of all the procedures and subroutines that the customer's programs ran before RPC. In any case, the remote procedure is run, and the result, often just a code like "0" for successful operation, but it could be the sorted list, is returned to the client application.

7. As on the outbound side, the return results are intercepted by the server stub.

8. The server stub marshals the return data into the required format.

9. The server RPC runtime module sends the RPC results back across the Internet in another packet.

10. The client RPC runtime module receives the results packet.

11. The client stub "unmarshals" the result to present to the calling client application.

12. The client application has the data it needs to continue. If the network is fast enough, there is no sign that the procedure invoked is local or halfway around the world.

Today, RPC is more understood as a kind of model for cloud computing and client-server operation. If there is a need to run an application in one place and have it perform some other task in another location, the RPC model is a good way to understand how that happens.

The twin ideas of distributed computing with smarter clients and network components and the use of RPCs are the foundations on which modern "cloud computing" and data center virtualization are built.

THE ROAD TO CLOUD COMPUTING

The original network "cloud" was invented by the giant telephone company AT&T™ when they were trying to sell their version of the international standard public packet-switching service known as X.25. At the time, most large organizations built corporate-sized networks using leased lines from telephone companies to link routers and switches (the "network nodes"), which they owned and operated in their facilities. It was a private network from top to bottom, but leasing long-distance links could be very expensive. It was very secure: only their data flowed on it and through it. However, they were also responsible for their troubleshooting and, in the case of leased lines, had to call in a broken link to the telco they had leased the link from.

With the X.25 service of AT&T, you just leased a short local link to the nearest network node at each network location. The X.25 network had powerful network nodes and high-speed links that allowed them to carry traffic from many customers over these shared facilities.

But why would customers give up the complete control and security of a private network for the shared nodes and links of a public service like X.25? If things went wrong, could some of their data end up in the hands of a competitor? Cost savings were one reason to use a public service, but banks, insurance companies, and other organizations often had plenty of money to spend on their network. Another plus was that it was up to the service provider to report and fix any failed network nodes or links, and AT&T often had alternate paths through the network ready to go.

But would customers readily give up their private networks for a public service? At the time, the great fear was, "No." Another thing that customers had to consider was the transition from a fully-owned private network as a capital expense (CapEx) to an asset on the accounting books to a network service paid for as an operational expense (OpEx). This debate still matters today.

Back then, AT&T did a smart thing: they hid the details of the public X.25 network inside a "cloud" icon. This amorphous cloud concealed the uncomfortable truth that the X.25 network consisted of network nodes and links, just like the private network the service replaced, but with the data from lots of other customers mixed in.

By 1994, the cloud symbol was applied to the Internet and Web, and the rest is history.

CLOUD COMPUTING

In a sense, the "cloud" symbol that did so well to hide the details of the X.25 public network also served to hide the details of the public data centers of the early 21st century that slowly but surely replaced the private data centers of the late 20th century. By now it should be clear that a data center, even if running on a distributed network without a completely centralized database, is still a place where applications run on ever-smaller but more and more powerful computers process data out there on the network record-by-record or "chunk-by-chunk" and process it.

What was needed to make a data center into a cloud computer data center? What did cloud computing add to the data center?

Terms that are often heard today are cloud computing, cloud native, and cloud enabled. Here is what each of them means:

- *Cloud computing* (often just "the cloud") is the software-based infrastructure of an external data center accessed over a network. The cloud is made available to users on a pay-as-you-go basis. Because there is no need to own and maintain servers, cloud computing often saves customers money. Cloud providers usually offer a range of services for database, storage, application, and other types of capabilities. We will look at offerings like software as a service (SaaS) later in this chapter.

- *Cloud-native* is an approach where all new applications and services are structured and built with the intention of running in a cloud computing environment. The application is intended to be run in a cloud environment from design to implementation to use. Cloud-native environments have their own set of terms, like *microservices* (small pieces of code that fetch, sort, format, and otherwise massage data), *containers* (semi-independent applications that can swap in and out of cloud servers), and *orchestrators* (software that handles containers and needed data),

- *Cloud-enabled* applications are older applications that originally ran in a proprietary data center environment but have been adapted for a cloud computing environment. These are usually legacy client-server applications where the server functions have been ported to the cloud servers. The client can typically run in a browser window and retains all of the capabilities of the legacy application, although they do not have the flexibility that cloud-native applications have.

There is a set of common features that cloud-native applications must have if they are to be called such. They were formulated in 2015 by the Cloud Native Computing Foundation (CNCF).

According to the CNCF guidelines, cloud-native computing means an environment where the following apply:

- **Immutable infrastructure:** The servers that host cloud-native applications are never changed once deployed. They have a fixed amount of processing power and memory. If the application needs more processing power, the application is seamlessly moved to a new server with higher performance and memory characteristics. There are no manual upgrades applied to the server racks once installed.

- **Microservices:** These small and independent software components are chained together loosely to perform as an application collectively. The microservices communicate with each other and pass data to accomplish their tasks. Application developers make changes to the overall application, not by rewriting it but by making changes to the microservices it consists of. Once formulated, a microservice can be used in other contexts or exist in several copies, so one failure does not halt the entire application.

- **Application program interface (API) communication:** An API is the way that software programs exchange information. APIs weave the microservices together so that the loosely coupled microservices work as if they were a single entity. The details of the API detail what data can be passed to the microservice and what data can be passed back as the result. APIs do not as much tell the microservice what to do as tell the microservice where it fits in the chain of steps to a final result.

- **Service Mesh:** The service mesh is the cloud software layer that handles communications among various microservices. Developers use the service mesh to add functions to the cloud application without the need to write new code.

- **Containers:** No other concept defines cloud computing better than the concept of a container. Consider a legacy PC with an operating system (perhaps Linux) to handle file I/O and user interactions and an office suite to handle word processing, spreadsheets, and more. A container can isolate only those operating system features and document editing features in the form of microservices and package them up in a container that runs independently on a cloud server. The container can be deployed on-premises, on a cloud provider's network, or in a hybrid environment with both. The container has everything needed, such as resource files, code libraries, scripts, and anything else needed so that the application does not have to worry about the underlying hardware or operating system.

    The use of containers has been the most visible benefit of cloud computing for customers. The main benefits of containers are:

- Containers can scale the cloud resources that the application requires very efficiently. Because they are independent of hardware and a particular operating system, a container can make use of all the processing power and memory it has at its disposal.

- Containers can "boot" much faster than an entire operating system because they encapsulate only a portion of the entire operating system and application. This makes a big difference when scaling applications to larger cloud environments.

- Containers use fewer computing resources than a full deployment of (for example) a Linux operating system and an office suite on a customer's server.

VIRTUALIZATION

It has already been noted that a simple smartphone today has more processing power than an IBM mainframe did in 1964. There are many more examples like that. A simple "singing" birthday card has more processing power than the entire world did in 1950. A video game console has more processing power than a Cray Supercomputer did in 1976, and the Cray cost $4 million.

Hardware and Software Evolution

All these things are true due to Moore's Law about hardware. Moore's Law, named after Intel co-founder Gordon Moore, states that the processing power of an integrated circuit doubles over a short time frame. The details vary, and this "rule" is often declared dead, but this is the reason that hardware today is able to run multiple virtual versions of an entire computer's software—applications and operating systems—inside a simple server box.

The gains made by software, on the other hand, have never been as rapid or radical, and software seems to have settled on ease of formulation over speed of execution and memory requirements, although using AI to write code might alter that equation.

Early computers used "bare metal programming" and manual switches on the front panel of the computer to enter the 0s and 1s directly into the device's memory. Eventually, programmers could write in semi-understandable assembly language that was run through a process to yield the bare metal instructions the computer actually ran.

For example, the assembly language for one type of computer could require the programmer to write LOAD REGA ACC, which meant for the computer to move the contents of "Register A" (a memory location) to the "Accumulator" (memory used for mathematical manipulations). The assembler took these instructions and translated (assembled) LOAD to 0010011, REGA to 10001, and ACC to 00011. This gives sixteen bits because this example uses a 16-bit computer, meaning the natural unit for program directions and memory locations is a group of 16 bits (sometimes called the "word" of the computer).

Writing long programs in assembly language was a chore. Programmers had to know the instruction set of the computer, how many registers they had to use, and what the other pieces were called and how they were addressed.

Then a genius who worked on the computer code for nuclear submarines, a Naval officer named Grace Hopper, came up with a way to allow programmers to write programs without knowing anything about computers at all. Her work led to the invention of the common business-oriented language (COBOL) that was *compiled* into the machine-level instructions that type of computer required. As long as the COBOL compiler worked for that particular brand of computer, the programmer could just know COBOL and let the compiler worry about the details.

COBOL was said to compile each statement into at least five assembly lines of code. Overnight, programmers became five times as productive as they had been before, and without any knowledge of the type of computers their programs would run on. COBOL introduced the idea of *high-level languages* to computing.

Today, we have a large number of possible high-level languages programmers can use for modern computing. COBOL yielded to C language (there were A and B languages, but they did not work well) and then to GO language (made for networking), even as a whole host of specialized languages grew up around the modern data center. Aside from a few important tweaks to prevent programmers from clobbering memory locations they should not reference, computer languages have languished as hardware capabilities ran rings around everything else.

These increased hardware capabilities, coupled with the ease of writing applications with the new high-level languages, led directly to the concept of cloud computing and the cloud data center.

The rapid advancement of hardware capacity and power over more conservative software advances led to a situation where the hardware of the modern computer has literally swallowed the previous generations of computers whole. It seems odd to speak of it this way, but this is one way to think about the process of *virtualization*.

Virtualization and the Cloud Data Center

Most people today are familiar with the "virtual" term due to *virtual reality*, where you don a special helmet or goggles and are transported to a fantasy world or different planet. The immersion in this world is so complete that it seems real. Yet it is not.

It is best to remember that when you read or hear the word "virtual," the next word is a lie. Virtual reality is not reality. With this in mind, no one would want to receive a virtual paycheck.

Cloud data centers today offer capacity on physical servers, and each of these servers can typically offer to support many *virtual machines*, or VMs. Naturally, these "machines" or computers inside the servers are not real in any sense. They are really just simulations of another computer and operating system, right down to the file system operations and formats supported. This is possible by running the code so efficiently that, like donning the helmet or goggles, it seems that users are directly experiencing the physical computer running Linux or some other operating system. After all, the command lines and windows look the same, the applications are still office suites or performing other tasks, and the output is identical.

Virtualization has been so successful that cloud computing standards include a component for network function virtualization (NFV). NFV means that the functions provided by individual network hardware components can be supplied by having the VMs run software that accomplishes the same task. VMs can be connected by NFV switches or routers. VMs can access or have client computers anywhere in the world access the VM through software gateways.

Other examples of NFV components are load balancers and firewalls among VMs. An overall *hypervisor* or *software-defined networking* controller lets network engineers program features for each segment of this virtual network, as well as offering automated network provisioning.

The nice thing about virtualization is that a customer can make a modest investment in cloud computing and take advantage of its virtualization features to run everything they did on their own, and even more. Today, the "even more" is often a cluster of high-powered graphical processing units (GPUs), which are increasingly necessary for any decent AI applications or bitcoin mining.

GPUs were originally developed, as the name implies, from the graphical processing needs of computer animation and artwork. Consider a highly realistic depiction of a red apple. There is a shine to the skin, a certain reflectivity, and colors vary across the curved surface as the illumination varies. Shadows should fall only where they must and could be muted or sharp. Artists could do this with pens and inks and paints, but computers struggled to perform the complex mathematics of reflection and shading, especially at large scales.

For computerized animation films, things were even worse. It was not one picture that needed computation, but twenty-four of them for every second of the film. The network was a limitation as recently as the late 1980s as well. Most places still used 10 Mbps Ethernet and 32-bit computers. An animator started the day by fetching from the server the last frame they stopped working on the day before. Then they went for a cup of coffee. Because it would often take a few minutes for the image to form on the screen, pixel-by-pixel, line-by-line. Then the animator would make a small movement of an arm, leg, or expression, calculate the changes in shading and reflections, and store the new frame back on the server, then work on the new frame. By now, it was almost time for lunch.

GPUs were invented to offload the heavy graphical tasks from the computer and have them take place on an intelligent board with its own processor and memory. Once the GPU was churning away, the user could move on to other tasks.

Today, GPU clusters are one of the main attractions of the service offered by cloud data centers.

Public, Private, and Hybrid Clouds

Clouds can come in a variety of forms. The type you hear about the most is the public cloud, where a major cloud service provider fills a gigantic warehouse space with server racks and storage, where every customer's data is stored in their own defined area.

Organizations nervous about potential data leaks, which happened in traditional public data centers, can build a totally private cloud. Private clouds have all of the characteristics of public clouds, but only the organization's data is present. Naturally, the organization must supply the floor space and other resources needed for the private cloud. Even then, there are still VCNs to isolate departmental data, data that can be shared if the rules are set up correctly.

A popular option is the hybrid cloud. A hybrid cloud has some servers and storage on the customer's premises as a private cloud, but it is connected to a public cloud as well. This hybrid model can keep really sensitive organizational data isolated from the public side of the cloud.

There is also the idea of a "cloud within a cloud," but there is no formal name for this (yet). In this case, a cloud service provider can supply a public cloud for a certain customer, but the customer can then host *another* cloud "inside" the public cloud. Because everything can be virtual, starting with the cloud itself, there is nothing revolutionary about this arrangement. It is just software being software.

A related concept is a cloud-oriented hardware rack that is its own small cloud data center, complete with GPUs and storage modules. It can be deployed to move data closer to the edge of the network, where the clients are, or as an "air gapped" device in a customer's own data center, separate, perhaps for security reasons, from the other cloud applications.

CLOUD DATA CENTER SERVICES

Customers do not go to a cloud data center provider and buy "cloud." They buy services, and cloud service providers generally differentiate their services by what part of the feature stack the customer is still responsible for and what part the cloud provider is taking on. Until recently, there were three services that almost everyone agreed upon in terms of what the cloud did and did not provide. The foundational three services were:

- Platform as a Service (PaaS)
- Infrastructure as a Service (IaaS)
- Software as a Service (SaaS)

In the constant quest for cloud service providers to differentiate and promote their own services over others, there are usually more than just these three services offered. Common ones are desktop as a service (DaaS), containers as a service (CaaS), and more. The Web site lists fifty-one distinct "as a service" offerings, but many on the list are variations on a basic capability.

Because they are so important for understanding cloud data center services, this is a good place to talk about the differences in the three major service types: SaaS, PaaS, and IaaS.

Essentially, when you buy cloud services, you as the customer still have to do the most with IaaS, and you do next to nothing with SaaS. PaaS is somewhere in the middle, but far above IaaS.

Here is why.

It is nice to think about these three services as a kind of nested cloud, with each outer cloud being a superset of the ones inside. This is shown in Figure 4.3.

SaaS essentially provides everything that the customer needs to perform a certain task. The biggest difference between SaaS and the "pre-cloud" environment is that the customer does not own any of the hardware or software that the application uses. The service is supplied on a flat rate or metered basis and resides "in the cloud."

Examples are applications like Salesforce, Slack, Zoom, or Dropbox. Access is usually through a browser window or smartphone app. Customers can also arrange to port their own custom applications to the cloud for others to use, which is how the other SaaS apps got these in the first place.

PaaS requires users to supply their own application programs to run on the cloud, either written in-house or purchased and licensed separately. What the users get is a "platform" to run these applications on, such as a form of Linux, Ubuntu, or Windows. Users can also access Docker if the app is a container and

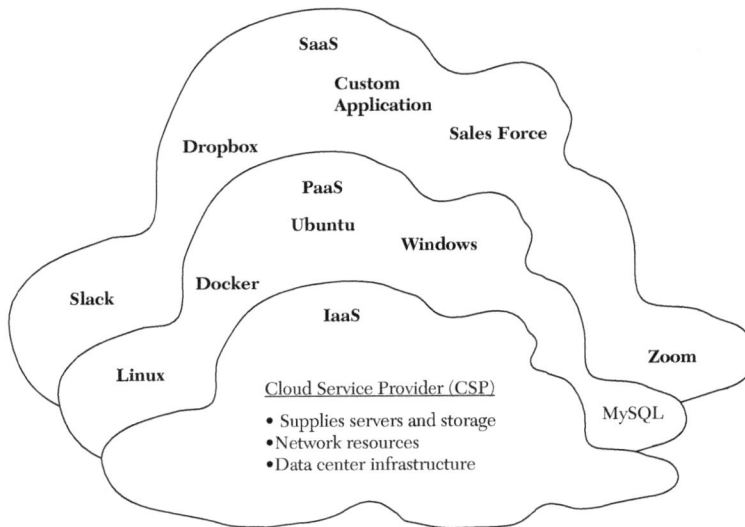

FIGURE 4.3. SaaS, PaaS, and IaaS as nested clouds.

MySQL for database access, among other possibilities, as long as it is offered by the cloud service provider (CSP).

IaaS is the most basic cloud service and gives the customer the most flexibility, along with the most responsibility. The CSP offers the customer physical servers and storage, network resources to keep everything connected among the VMs and servers and TOR routers, and the cloud data center infrastructure itself to keep the servers cooled and powered and the lights on.

All else, from CPUs and GPUs, memory and cores, application APIs for development, and the management environment, must be supplied by and rented from the CSP.

This cloud nesting is more than just conceptual. It is true in the sense that the layers that make up a modern computer (different than the OSI-RM or TCP/IP layers) are included in the outer cloud. The service therefore defines the layer that the user can access to customize the service for their specific needs.

The basic layers that cloud computing models use most often, from the user at the top to the power cord at the bottom, are:

- **Applications:** The programs that users run to perform their job every day.
- **Development and Management Tools:** Applications often need modifications, and the overall efficiency and performance of the data center device need to be tracked.

- **Operating Systems:** Applications are built to run on Linux, Windows, or some other form of OS.
- **Servers and Storage:** The many VMs still have to run on a physical machine somewhere, and the data they generate and use has to be kept somewhere.
- **Network Resources:** All of these servers and storage devices and switches and routers have to communicate among themselves and with the outside world over the Internet. The GPU clusters are in the mix too.
- **Data Center Structure:** These are those huge buildings that house all of this equipment. There is a real fear that 50% of all the world's electricity might be needed for these cloud data centers in the near future. Many provide their own power through solar or other means.

In order to make a case for added services like DaaS and CaaS, cloud providers add layers, such as a "runtime" or "middleware" layer. Yet these layers add little to the basic understanding of what these "as a service" offerings bring to the table.

Cloud Services and Automobiles

A company called RubyGarage has a blog that explores a nice way of explaining the differences between the three main cloud services and an on-premises "pre-cloud" data center system with servers and storage. They consider the various "as a service" offerings as different ways of getting somewhere using surface transposition.

In the on-premises model, you own and operate an automobile. You have total control over the content of the vehicle and where it goes, but you also supply the fuel, perform your own maintenance, and troubleshoot it yourself when things go wrong. You can hire others to do these things, but it is all under your control. You as owner are responsible for its maintenance, and any driving "upgrades" mean buying a new car.

SaaS is like riding a bus. It still gets you where you want to go, but you have no control over the route, the color of the bus, or anything else concerning the operation and maintenance of the vehicle. You share the ride with the other passengers, who are the other users of the software application.

PaaS is like hiring a taxi or other car service. You are not driving the taxi, but you can still tell the driver where you want to go. You can relax while the cab company worries about buying fuel, maintenance, and diagnosing issues.

IaaS is like leasing a car instead of owning it. You get to drive it wherever you like, but it is not totally under your control. You can report issues like a broken taillight or complain about trash left under the driver's seat, but aside from going places, the car service provider controls all that. If you want to upgrade, you have to lease another car.

An analogy like cloud services and cars can only be pushed so far. Yet the six basic layers of data center resources can represent the three major cloud services as well. The differences are where in this stack the break occurs between what the customer can access, manage, and provide and what the cloud service provider manages and provides. These differences are shown in Figure 4.4.

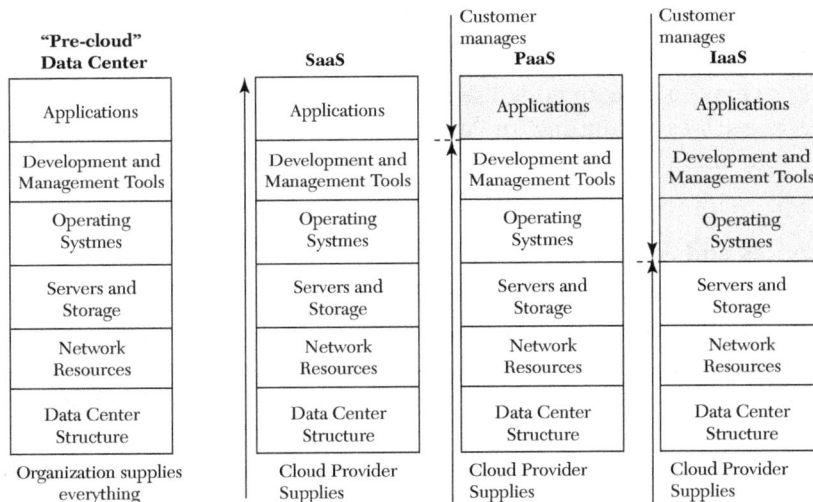

"Pre-cloud" Data Center	SaaS	Customer manages PaaS	Customer manages IaaS
Applications	Applications	Applications	Applications
Development and Management Tools	Development and Management Tools	Development and Management Tools	Development and Management Tools
Operating Systmes	Operating Systmes	Operating Systmes	Operating Systmes
Servers and Storage	Servers and Storage	Servers and Storage	Servers and Storage
Network Resources	Network Resources	Network Resources	Network Resources
Data Center Structure	Data Center Structure	Data Center Structure	Data Center Structure
Organization supplies everything	Cloud Provider Supplies	Cloud Provider Supplies	Cloud Provider Supplies

FIGURE 4.4. SaaS, PaaS, and IaaS as resource stacks.

In the figure, the leftmost column shows the resource stack for the "pre-cloud" data center, one owned and operated by a particular company or organization. All six of the layers are completely the responsibility of the organization, with the partial exception of leased data links and network equipment that might be under warrantee or a service contract.

SaaS is the next column, and here, for this particular application, the cloud service provider supplies everything, from the application to the data center air handling and data security.

SaaS is the easiest transition to the cloud for end users. However, these users have no ability to add or customize the application features offered as part of the

SaaS agreement. Connectivity with the Internet is a prerequisite for the application to function at all.

The big change comes with PaaS, where the hosted application is now under the control of the organization. There is a layer customers can access to develop and manage these cloud applications. However, as before, the rest of the resources are what the cloud provider supplies to that particular user.

PaaS is a good fit for software developers, who can concentrate on application features and leave the rest of the cloud features to the service provider. However, not every aspect of all customer applications can always be cloud-enabled. Also, the customer is dependent on the service provider's support for responsiveness and reliability when issues arise.

IaaS gives most of the control over cloud resources to the customer. They basically get a kind of basic hardware server and storage arrangement from the service provider. The customer gets to deploy a range of operating system types, with more choices for the number of cores, memory, storage space, and GPUs used in the VCN. However, IaaS is the most attractive for organizations that have a fully staffed IT department but one that is willing to forego some control for the ability to concentrate on applications and the features they need to run the best. Because the environment is virtual, it is easy enough to add cores, memory, GPU clusters, and other features to an application that is growing more and more popular with users.

IaaS users generally establish a VCN in a region of the globe with a range of public or private IP addresses to use and then create non-overlapping IP subnets with these VCNs. The subnets then host one or more virtual machines (VMs) consisting of operating systems, data storage options, and user-created applications. The customer also has the choice of what communications to allow between these VMs and the Internet, as well as the type of IP address translation to use, if needed. Firewalls and load balancers, among other features, are often part of the IaaS offering as well.

IaaS is not without its drawbacks. Any shared resource environment raises issues for data security, so firewall and router configuration become very important. If the cloud provider has an outage due to electrical failure or flooding, the customer's data becomes inaccessible. There are new methods for reporting and fixing issues that involve the service provider that need to be understood.

DATA CENTER AND CLOUD COMPUTING DIFFERENCES

Table 4.1 shows the main differences between a pre-cloud data center and a modern cloud-computing data center.

TABLE 4.1. Pre-cloud data center and cloud computing data center compared.

Characteristic	Pre-Cloud Data Center	Cloud Computing Data Center
Ownership	Owned and operated by the organization	Services provided by third-party CSP companies
Location	Physically tied to a geographic location	Virtual networking, accessible worldwide over the Internet
Control	Full control over the infrastructure	Less control, but maintenance included in service pricing
Cost	Upfront capital expenditure (CapEx)	Pay-as-you-go, operating expense (OpEx)
Scalability	Limited by the physical space	Virtually unlimited scalability by regions
Maintenance	Responsibility of the organization	Responsibility of the CSP
Disaster Recovery	Recovery plan executed by organization	Often includes automatic backups and failover capabilities at added cost

Here is a bit more about the differences in each characteristic listed:

Ownership: Ownership is nice for control, but in many cases, spare capacity lies idle during slack times or slow periods. For example, the telephone network in the United States was built to handle the five busiest calling days of the year: Mother's Day, New Year's, Christmas, the day after Thanksgiving, and Valentine's Day. The rest of the time, 80% of the system is idle. Paying only for resources consumed can be a big cost savings.

Location: Large corporations can afford to have major data centers on each continent where they market goods, but many organizations have only one of two data centers globally. Response times can be long. The CSPs are some of the largest companies in the world and have data centers all around the world. Response times are usually very fast.

Control: Control means staffing and the related expenses for security and troubleshooting. Much of this often considerable effort can be offloaded "to the cloud." However, the precise features vary depending on the type of service provided.

Cost: Capital expenditures are major purchases that a company makes that are used over the long term, such as buildings, machinery, and vehicles. Operating expenses, on the other hand, are the day-to-day expenses that a company incurs to keep its business running, such as employee salaries, rent, utilities, and property taxes. One key difference is that in most countries, capital expenditures cannot be deducted from organizational income for tax purposes, but operating expenses can.

Scalability: One of the biggest challenges before the cloud was making sure that there was room for data center growth as the organization grew and their apps became more popular. Extreme events like politically sensitive reports could crash servers or even portions of the Internet. With a cloud service, the popular app can just be ported to a new server rack.

Maintenance: Pre-cloud organizations had to have on-staff employees who could troubleshoot and repair or replace every type of server, client, wireless hub, switch, or router in the network and data center. With cloud providers, almost all of this burden is no longer the responsibility of the customer.

Disaster Recovery: One of the most attractive features of cloud services is the reliability offered by the massive redundancy and capabilities of these gigantic companies. Even keeping adequate and up-to-date backups could be a challenge for pre-cloud data centers.

TRACKERS AND COOKIES

As time goes by, cloud data centers get larger and larger and store more and more data. Estimates in 2021 placed the global total at 1,327 exabytes of data, or 1.3 zettabytes. (See Appendix 1 for an idea of just how big these numbers are.) To store a zettabyte, one billion storage devices holding one terabyte each would be required.

What does all this data represent?

One guess would be that it represents data that the Internet and Web have accumulated about its users. In other words, *us*. However, there are only about 8 billion people in the world. Using the one billion terabyte drives equation cited above, each and every person in the world would have more than 125 gigabytes of data devoted to facts about themselves.

There must be more going on, and there is.

Data centers store more than information about people. It has been estimated that no more than 8% of the world's supply of money is in the form of cold, hard cash like coins and banknotes. The rest, all 92%, is as a form of data stored by accounts referenced by a series of numbers in the world's data centers, protected by passwords, but accessible by anyone who knows how.

Moreover, the data associated with our persons is not merely factual information like date of birth, health history, assets, and so on. The Internet tracks our every move, each search, every purchase, all messages, all in the name of improving our "online experience." This data is mined for marketing purposes by companies eager to sell you something. The data is purchased from companies that make their profits by tracking every mouse click and keystroke.

More will be covered about this activity in the last two chapters of this book. This chapter closes with a more detailed look at how cookies and tracking are used to enhance our online experiences, usually without our being aware of it.

Cookies and trackers are an enormous topic. The Wikipedia entry for "HTTP Cookies" is longer in words and pages than this chapter, although ten of its twenty-eight pages are references to source material. That entry forms a good foundation for an entire book on the topic. Here are some highlights of cookie use for this chapter.

Cookies

Programmers were always fond of putting undocumented little snippets into the code they wrote to make life easier when the program was executed. They were initially popular in Unix-based systems, where programmers used them to convey password authentication or as a token to unlock certain functions. They were called "cookies," one old story goes, because they were a kind of "sweet treat" for programmers tasked with modifying or maintaining the program. They are just text files or strings of text that are passed around subroutines during a run of the program.

Because they were invisible to users, they were called "magic cookies" in many cases. The concept was also common in network protocols, known in that context as a "magic number." In many file formats, the first few bytes serve to identify the file type. For example, JPEG files all start with the hex value FF D8 (xffd8).

Eventually, the term "cookie" came to cover all kinds of small files that Web sites and other servers would pass to clients at the start (or end) of a session. If the server is a Web site, the cookie is technically an *HTTP cookie*, but most people today assume that a cookie is an HTTP cookie unless told otherwise.

Once users started buying things over the Internet when the Web came along in the early 1990s, cookies became a crucial part of the experience. Early Web sites took a lot of processing power to run. For example, the first Web server for Pace University in New York ran on a Sun SPARCstation that cost $20,000 (in 1992 dollars) because you could not just throw TCP/IP and a Web server on an ordinary Windows PC and expect them to run reliably.

So early online merchants did not want to store shopping cart information for every browsing customer on the Web server. TCP/IP had no true session layer like the OSI-RM that stored the history of an interaction between client and server. If the connectivity between client and server were severed, it was totally up to the applications to decide what the state of the session was once the user reconnected. So, cookies were pushed from server to client to store shopping cart information, or to show that the user was currently logged in, or where in a large file download the client had stopped storing data, and so on. The server could fetch this cookie information and pick up where it had left off before the failure.

Cookies that are used in tracking store the cookie text on the client and relay it to the server when told. The server in turn shares the cookie's information with cookie tracking companies. These tracker companies, who often get their information from *other* tracker organizations, use the data gathered to determine characteristics of the user's activity through demographic profiling or by triggering other profile mechanisms.

Types of Cookies

Cookies have evolved to fill all kinds of niches and serve all kinds of purposes. There are authentication cookies that are used to keep users logged in as they browse from page to page. A risk is that hackers might obtain the cookie and use it to access the user's data with exploits known as *cross-site scripting* and *cross-site request forgery* (CSRF). Tracking cookies are used to compile lists of a user's browsing history. Many countries now require "informed consent" from users before using tracking cookies, but few users likely take time to consider the consequences of granting that power to others.

Here is a list of the most common types of cookies and their uses. Keep in mind that these cookies are distinguished not by a major difference in structure but mainly by the presence of certain flags in the cookie text.

- **Session Cookie:** These cookies only exist while a user browses a Web site. Also known as *in-memory cookies* or *transient cookies*, these cookies are deleted or expire when the Web browser is closed.

- **Persistent Cookie:** These cookies expire at a specific date or length of time set by the originator. The cookie's information is sent to the Web server every time the user visits or when the user links to a related site, such as clicking on an advertisement. These cookies also store login information, so if a user goes to a Web site using a different browser or computer, they are often surprised that they have to log in again when they did not before. Persistent cookies form the basis for tracking cookies that store our history over a long period of time.

- **Secure Cookie:** This type of cookie is used for encrypted connections using the HTTPS protocol. They are never used with "regular" HTTP, and these cookies are therefore more secure and less vulnerable to cookie theft.

- **HTTP-Only Cookie:** These client cookies cannot be accessed by APIs such as JavaScript, which eliminates the risk of cookie theft by way of cross-site scripting (XSS). The risk of cross-site request forgeries and cross-site tracing (XST) remains, however.

- **Same-site Cookie:** These cookies are used to make sure browsers only send cookie information to the Web site domains that granted them in order to prevent the CSRF cookie attack. A "lax" option is more permissive, and a value of "none" (no restrictions) is valid. This was a controversial move, and software companies still debate the proper default setting and other values to support.

- **Supercookie:** This term is used in different contexts, but most often refers to a type of cookie that covers a whole high-level Internet domain like ".com" or ".co" or ".us" instead of more focused domains like "example.com." They are widely perceived as very risky, and many Web browsers simply reject these types of supercookies. Otherwise, hackers can set a supercookie for the whole "com" domain and then request information for "example.com," even if the supercookie site had nothing to do with the "example.com" Web site. Fake logins and altered user information can result. There are lists of these high-level domains that browsers can use to filter out supercookies.

- **Zombie Cookie:** This type of cookie is placed by a Web site server not only in the generally used location on the browser but in an odd place where it is unlikely to be found. If the "regular" cookie is deleted, the missing cookie is recreated from the data stored in the zombie cookie location. All instances of the cookie must be deleted to get rid of the cookie.

Today, many Web sites employ a "cookie wall" that appears when a user accesses a Web site. The cookie wall informs the user that cookies are used on the site and asks the user to accept the cookies. If the user rejects the use of the cookies, the Web site is simply not accessible to the user.

Tracking with Web Beacons

Cookies can tell those who gather data for data centers where users are going online. Nonetheless, they cannot be used to tell what ads on a page or in an email that users are clicking on. For that information, more sophisticated tracking is needed, such as that offered by *Web beacons.* They are also referred to as Web bugs, tracking bugs, page tags, tracking pixels, and more.

Web beacons are used by third parties to monitor user activity at a Web site as a part of *Web analytics* or *page tagging.* They are called *Javascript tags* when implemented with JavaScript. Web beacons can be tied to cookies to create a form of user tracking that is not disclosed to the user.

The original Web beacons were an unobtrusive or all-but-invisible addition to an email or Web page. They could be used to tell when an email has been read or forwarded or track activity concerning a Web page, such as if it has been copied to another Web site. They could be as small as a single pixel, but the same color as the background and therefore invisible.

However, once the user opens the Web page or email, the browser has to send a request to the server for the "image" to load. This request is noted by the server and passed along to the tracking server, along with any other information about the user or computer used that can be determined this way.

This original Web beacon concept is shown in Figure 4.5.

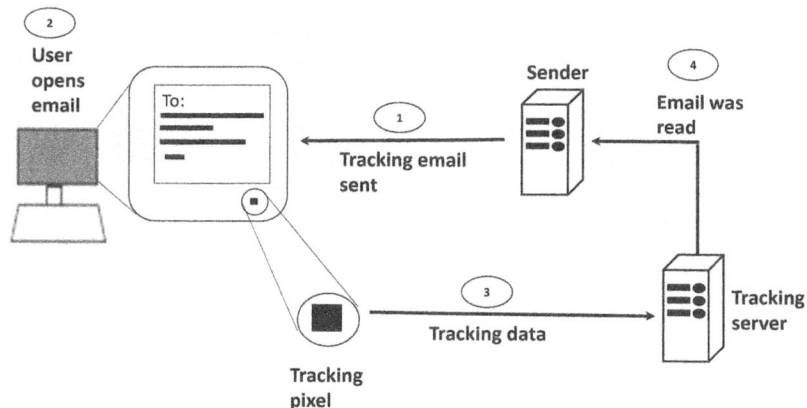

FIGURE 4.5. The original Web beacon in use.

Today, Web beacons are an accepted part of data gathering. Graphics, banners, buttons (such as "like" buttons on social media sites), and more can be used as Web beacons. Most uses are relatively benign, but when coupled with spam and phishing emails, their use is more problematic. Email marketers and more sinister players can buy an email list and blast emails to all of them. The Web beacons in them can be used to tell which email addresses are still valid and which emails are opened by the recipients. The beacon lets them know which emails make it through the spam filters and that the content of the email was at least displayed on the screen, if not read.

Most users accept that the world of data tracking is here to stay. Some predicted this new world long ago. A song by the group Best Kissers in the World was released around the same time as the World Wide Web in 1993. The lyrics noted that marketers wanted to "be with you wherever you go" to "talk to you night and day" and to "know who you know." This was a radical idea back then. There was more to the lyrics: they wanted to be "inside your room when you close the door." They wanted, most of all, to be "inside your head when it explodes."

What Comes Next

Not all of the data that is stored in these massive data centers comes from us or is about us. Much of it is generated by devices such as automobiles and trucks that have embedded processors built into them as they are manufactured. In fact, the entire manufacturing process generates and is controlled by robots and other smart machines.

The twin aspects of dealing with this non-human data are called the Internet of Things (IoT) and machine-to-machine (M2M) communications. The way things are arranged in a factory today is nothing short of revolutionary.

The next chapter explores these aspects of data and information.

Chapter 5

IoT AND M2M

OVERVIEW

Up to this point, we have explored four major components of all modern networks, which include:

- The need for almost everyone worldwide to have multiple Internet connections to their home, office, car, and business to work, plan their lives, and entertain themselves. This requires much more than the simple 32-bit address space invented for IPv4. We need IPv6.

- IPv6 provides enough address space to give every molecule in the solar system its own IPv6 address. It also simplifies a lot of the added protocols that IPv4 required and does away with some that were seldom used or security risks (like directed broadcasts).

- Packet optical networks based on new fibers and techniques like WDM that make fiber links more effective for backhauling data to cloud data centers and delivering streams of data to mobile (and fixed) endpoints.

- The cloud data center is where all the information flowing to and from users congregates to be analyzed, stored, and used as the basis for future actions. The cloud data center, public or private, is also the location where much of modern AI processing takes place. However, not all the information and data originate from users. Much of it comes from the machines themselves, including the embedded processors in modern vehicles.

WHAT YOU WILL LEARN

This chapter explores some of the major aspects of Internet of Things (IoT) and machine-to-machine (M2M) communications. The chapter focuses on the Industry 4.0 standard and the use of specialized high-speed fiber optical access networks, such as passive optical networks (PONs). Like every other chapter in this book, a tighter focus is needed due to the sprawling nature of the entire field, although all the major terms and concepts for further exploration are presented.

The topics covered include:

- How IoT is different than M2M
- Industrial revolutions and Industry 4.0
- Optical access networks
- High-speed optical access for Industry 4.0
- Edge Computing

Similar to previous chapters, there is a chronological aspect to IoT and M2M. However, the primary focus here will be on the standardization of various aspects of Industry 4.0 network standards and passive optical networks (PONs).

IOT AND M2M

There is significant overlap between IoT and M2M definitions and uses. The way that these terms are used in this chapter are outlined in Table 5.1.

TABLE 5.1. IoT and M2M characteristics.

Characteristic	IoT	M2M
Protocols Used	IP networks used, but with many protocol options	Point-to-point communications embedded in device hardware
Network Type	Data usually delivered to the Internet cloud	Can use cellular or wired networks
Internet Use	Devices usually require an active Internet connection	Devices do not usually require active connection
Device Integration	Unlimited integration options for hardware and software	Limited integration options due to need for embedding

As is typical for such broad terms, the use of the word "usually" shows that many uses for IoT and M2M are defined solely by the ingenuity of developers and the widespread adaptation of various use cases.

Both IoT and M2M refer to devices communicating directly without human intervention, either as the sender or recipient of data. However, there are meaningful differences between the two concepts, even though the line between the two becomes blurred more and more. Generally, IoT functions on a grander scale, using software stacks to manage and automate communications among multiple devices. On the other hand, M2M applications are more isolated and limited in their device-to-device communication.

Simply put, IoT involves using the Internet to add machines to the type of devices that the Internet supports, such as automobiles, and M2M is about point-to-point machine-to-machine communications, as on a factory assembly line. There is a lot to IoT. Examples of IoT types of applications include temperature sensors, smart home meters for water, gas, and electricity, vehicle telemetry, truck fleet tracking, wearable technology, and automated supply chain management. In contrast, M2M is usually more restrictive. An example M2M application includes a network controlling welding machines as a related conveyor system supplies the parts to be welded. The robots that scuttle around modern warehouses and pluck products from shelves to ship to purchasers are usually M2M network examples.

Sensors are devices that come up over and over in industrial applications. Some sensory abilities are built into all modern smartphones. These include acceleration and tilt sensing, position and proximity sensing (as with GPS), temperature, sound and vibration detection, light intensity sensing, and more. Industrial environments may include sensors for determining the intensity of electrical or magnetic fields, fluid levels, leak flow, and forces such as pressure, load, or torque. They can detect the presence and concentration of certain chemicals or gases, humidity and moisture, among other things.

It is possible for a device to employ both IoT and M2M technologies to perform its main functions. Bottom line: do not be surprised to find something listed as IoT in one source and M2M in another. Terms are used by people, and language serves to express ever-changing ideas.

In this chapter, IoT is typically used to refer to residential applications, like the "smart home," while M2M is used to describe a factory or industrial environment.

The benefits of IoT and M2M technologies are many. They include:

- Cost savings due to increased operational efficiency
- Better and new data to improve decision-making
- Personnel productivity gains
- Better tracking of assets and resources throughout the organization

- Revenue growth from quicker expansion and new products and services
- Automated business and office processes like supply procurement

Many service industries have already taken this automation and M2M process to an extreme. Instead of talking to a human, customers are often left with no alternative but to run automated remote tests and diagnostics that do not help. Or they can chat online with an automated response system that seems to repeatedly suggest cycling power or resetting equipment in the hopes of finding a cure. Even human customer representatives must follow a strict troubleshooting checklist before even admitting that the customer might actually have a problem with their equipment, which suggests the default situation is that the customer is too ignorant to use it properly.

INDUSTRIAL REVOLUTIONS

Both IoT and M2M are part of a broader movement known today as Industry 4.0. Industry 4.0 is a term for what many in the field of technology call the *Fourth Industrial Revolution*. This latest revolution in the way industry operates evolved from the previous three revolutions, all of which transformed the way people in developed nations live and work.

At each stage, individual worker and national industrial productivity, value, and output rose to levels that were inconceivable before the revolution kicked in. This is shown in Figure 5.1, although both the horizontal timeline and the vertical productivity measure are not to scale.

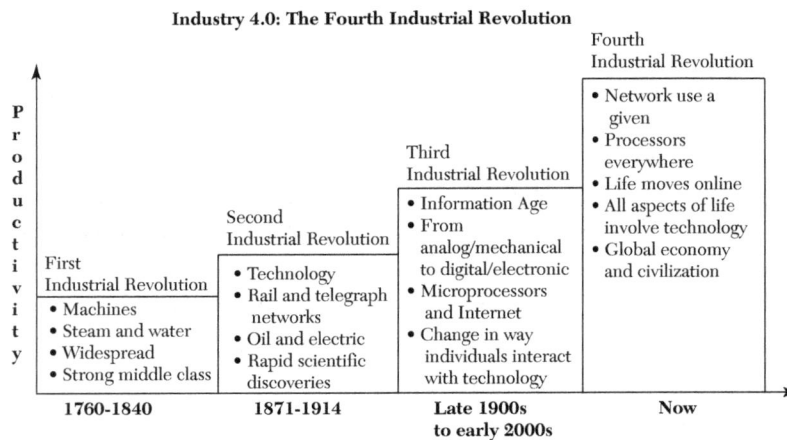

Industry 4.0: The Fourth Industrial Revolution

			Fourth Industrial Revolution
Productivity		Third Industrial Revolution	• Network use a given • Processors everywhere • Life moves online • All aspects of life involve technology • Global economy and civilization
	Second Industrial Revolution	• Information Age • From analog/mechanical to digital/electronic • Microprocessors and Internet • Change in way individuals interact with technology	
First Industrial Revolution • Machines • Steam and water • Widespread • Strong middle class	• Technology • Rail and telegraph networks • Oil and electric • Rapid scientific discoveries		
1760-1840	1871-1914	Late 1900s to early 2000s	Now

FIGURE 5.1 Industry 4.0: the fourth industrial revolution.

It is worth reviewing some of the factors affected by these revolutions. Not only do these rapid changes share certain features in common, but there is considerable discussion now about whether the historic changes in these fields are a net positive or a net negative for the planet.

The First Industrial Revolution

Between 1760 and 1840, the first industrial revolution featured machines replacing manual labor to perform tasks like spinning yarn and weaving cloth. Instead of working at home, people began to go to places outside the home where they worked, places that came to be called factories. Machines, or "jennies," as these early "engines" were called, could do more work than a single person and did not tire or get sick. While it took years for these "gins"—another word for engines—to become as good as an individual craftsperson, the savings for producers were immediate and significant.

It took time for society to adjust to the workday world. In the United States, early textile mills in the Northeast had to surround factories with moats and walls to keep workers from wandering off and friends from dropping by to visit. Farmers were used to making their own schedules once animals and crops were taken care of, but machines required constant attention. Eventually, loud whistles told workers—few of whom owned watches—when it was time to go to work and leave to go home.

At the same time, brute muscle power was enhanced and sometimes replaced by steam and water power, although water wheels to grind grain were known since antiquity. Steam power, once used mainly to clear mines of water, emerged in the form of railroads, starting in 1830. These monster locomotive engines were so novel and beyond any comparable experience that people were run over before they could clear the tracks in front of locomotives running at up to thirty miles per hour (44 feet per second), or forty-eight kilometers per hour (approximately 12 meters per second).

This initial industrial revolution was enormously widespread, at least in the developed nations of Europe. Once railroad tracks appeared in northern England, they soon began to appear on the continent, although the rapid expansion of national railroad networks would have to wait until the next industrial revolution.

The factory system, which had drawbacks in terms of worker freedom, did lead to the appearance of a strong middle class between rich land and business owners and the poor peasants.

The Second Industrial Revolution

Technology was a feature of the second industrial revolution, which the IEEE dates to between 1871 and 1914. This period spanned between the end of the Franco-Prussian War and the start of World War I, a time of peace when efforts could turn to exploration and scientific discovery.

Although invented earlier, railroads expanded at an unbelievable rate during this period. As usual, one technology influenced others. Railroads became natural paths for the new telegraph lines to follow. The rail networks moved goods, and the telegraph networks moved information. The telephone enabled people to talk to each other over vast distances, although the inventor, Alexander Graham Bell, never had a telephone in his office because he could not understand why people would stop talking to another person to answer the telephone.

Power, once supplied almost exclusively by coal, now uses oil and related petroleum products to create steam and drive internal combustion engines in automobiles. Hydroelectric power and a grid system of distribution brought electricity to the factory and then the home.

As for rapid scientific discoveries, this was a time when major scientific and engineering advances seemed to come along every other month. Thomas Edison in the United States exemplified this period of rapid advancement, mainly by exploiting new discoveries in mathematics and materials science. He pioneered the patenting and marketing of every small advance in techniques, paving the way for not only improvements but legal challenges over intellectual property as well.

The Third Industrial Revolution

Often called the "Information Age," the period from about 1950 to the first years of the 2000s was the time that computers basically took over the civilized world. There are more computers in a modern car than there were in the world in 1950, and the ideas behind IoT and M2M were formed then.

The world quickly transformed from a place of analog devices (think of a wall clock with a sweep second hand) and mechanical wind-up toy innards to a world where everything is digital zeroes and ones and uses some form of electronics inside. Solid-state electronics like the transistor replaced bulky and hot vacuum tubes that often failed at the worst possible time.

Once the transistor began to shrink, microprocessors became possible, which shrunk a whole room of computer equipment down to a handheld device. The processor in a modern cell phone is more powerful than an IBM mainframe was in the 1960s. Starting around the time of Woodstock in the summer of 1969, the

Internet grew from an experimental network encouraged by the military in the USA to the global public network we use to work and play every day.

This combination of computers and networks changed the way that individuals interacted with technology. For example, there were once workers called *travel agents* who you would call to make arrangements for a business trip or family vacation. These travel agents would know who to call to make reservations for hotels and airlines, for rental cars, and other types of things you might need. Now most people do all this for themselves over the Internet.

The Fourth Industrial Revolution

Today, network use is a given, and there are processors everywhere, right down to the wristband you can wear to the gym to show heart rate and calories burned.

It sometimes seems that life itself has moved online. People post photos and videos from their vacations—while they are on vacation—so that others can stare at them on their cell phones. Take a photo at a concert, and it is likely to reveal everyone else in the shot doing the same thing. Memory is preserved, but enjoyment is perhaps postponed as well.

All aspects of our lives today involve technology. Once appliances and automobiles could be fixed when problems arose, but today these units are sealed and isolated. Things today are not repaired but discarded or recycled.

In spite of attempts to create tariff barriers, today's economy is a global economy, just like the Internet. Parts of large databases can be stored across continents, and therefore which nation's laws apply when they do can be a puzzle. Civilization is becoming global as well, although some aspects like music are more globalized than entrenched traditions like religion.

Overall, it seems to many obvious that the benefits of modern health care, lifestyles, technologies, and so forth allow people to live better lives than peasants squatting in huts weaving or laboring in fields for twelve to fourteen hours a day just to survive. Yes, there are massive differences between countries and between rich and poor, but abandoning technology does not seem like a good way to address these evident inequalities.

INDUSTRY 4.0

The road to the Industry 4.0 concept began in 2013, when scientists in Germany introduced the idea as a high-technical strategy. The next year, 2014, the Industrial Internet Consortium (IIC) was founded in the United States to promote interoperability standards and accelerate movement toward what they called the Industry Internet.

These efforts came together in 2015 when the leaders at the World Economic Forum introduced the idea of Industry 4.0. Before the global pandemic came along to complicate things, many countries had formed their own initiatives to promote the spread of technology in industrial settings:

- In 2015, China started a plan they called Internet Plus.
- In 2016, Australia established the Prime Minister's Industry 4.0 Task Force.
- In 2017, Korea started the I-Korea strategic plan.
- In 2019, the government in the UK published a policy paper calling for Industry 4.0.
- That same year, the USA formed a new agency to promote Industry 4.0 and coordinate its different parts.
- Also in 2019, South Africa appointed a Presidential Commission to investigate Industry 4.0.

Industrial Networks

An industrial network is one that allows the connection of industrial assets and enables the transfer of data within the industrial environment. We can loosely define "industrial assets" as robots, motors, sensors, cameras, and other devices used in the creation of a factory product. The industrial environment can be an individual factory, group of factories, a campus of manufacturing and supply buildings, or even a campus that also includes industrial resources next to corporate offices. The definition here is intended to be inclusive rather than restrictive. The key is that these networks are involved in the creation of some good or product to be sold.

Industrial networks function in environments that are much harsher than office networks. They are usually subject to wider variations of temperature, environmental contamination and hazards, electromagnetic interference, and acoustic noise.

All industrial networks were designed to support industrial device and system interconnections, mainly for control and monitoring purposes. Industrial networks are intended to reduce product cycle churn, increase data acquisition, and enhance worker safety.

What Industry 4.0 adds to these traditional industrial networks is higher speeds, longer ranges, and other features that were limitations beforehand. Some of these major changes are shown in Table 5.2.

TABLE 5.2. Industry 4.0 enhanced features.

Connectivity Feature	Traditional Industrial Networks	Industry 4.0 Networks	Comment
Speed	Less than 1 Gbps	1-10 Gbps and beyond	Higher speeds are needed for real-time monitoring and control
Volume of Data	Up to 10s Kbytes per second	Up to a Gbyte per second	Video support requires high volumes
Range	Less than 100 meters	Up to 10s of kilometers	Can reach multiple campuses
Transmission Media	Category 5 (Cat5) plus twisted pair	Fiber optic cable, wireless	Copper cable can degrade over time
Data Sources	On-site or one-purpose systems	Many types of devices and systems	More types can be added
Traffic Types	Device control and data acquisition	Adds interactive real-time multimedia support and diagnostics	More and more devices will include video feeds
Network technology and protocols	Ethernet, bus protocols like Modbus and other FieldBuses	Adds to these IoT and wireless technology and protocols	Multiple technology and support is a requirement

Fieldbuses are industrial standards for bidirectional serial networks that operate at Layer 1 and Layer 2 (physical and data link layers) of the OSI-RM. Some fieldbuses offer services all the way up to the Application Layer (Layer 7). Examples beside FieldBus include the FOUNDATION fieldbus, DeviceNet, ControlNet, Modbus, and PROFIBUS.

One major point about these common industrial network fieldbus devices is that, in addition to the usual Ethernet connection, these devices include an additional network interface. Because Ethernet today is usually built into the CPU motherboard itself, no additional hardware is needed to use an Ethernet interface. However, the inclusion of "extra" hardware for Industry 4.0 support increases cost and complexity.

The generalized and overall architecture of an Industry 4.0 network is shown in Figure 5.2.

It should be noted that this is not an "official" image of the architecture. It is designed to educate rather than illustrate and includes features often shown in separate diagrams. One of these key points is that industrial networks do not have to be entirely separate from corporate information systems or cloud data center networks. In fact, there are good reasons to allow access to enterprise

Generalized Industrial Network Architecture

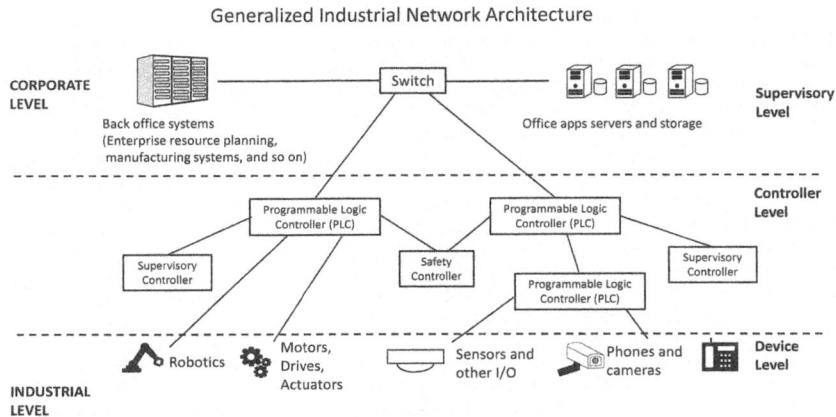

FIGURE 5.2. Generalized overall architecture of Industry 4.0 networks.

resource planning (ERP) systems and other applications. The device labeled "Switch" in the figure could be a router or gateway of some kind, but should include solid firewall functions to prevent the accessing of industrial components by unauthorized users or hackers.

The left margin of the figure shows the corporate level at the top and the industrial device level at the bottom. The point at which the upper corporate function becomes the lower industrial function is not defined here and up to the network architect.

The right margin of the figure shows the levels of the network. Here the key in the middle level: the controller level. These controller devices bridge the gap between the upper supervisory level of the corporation or enterprise and the devices being controlled. Note that in addition to the directly connected programmable logic controllers (PLCs) that connect the device to the supervisory software in the network, there are other controllers that offload some of the processing burden from the PLCs and do not have to check every instruction and reading at all times. However, when necessary, these low-level supervisory and safety controllers can take action and prevent accidents.

Finally, consider the wide range of devices under the Industry 4.0 umbrella, devices that often required separate networks to support in the past. Now many different things are brought under the Industry 4.0 standards: robotic arms and whole warehouse robot units, the motors and drives and actuators that make up an assembly line (including welding machines when needed), sensors for temperature and other needed environmental variables such as humidity, as well as the telephones and cameras used for communication on the factory floor. There is no limitation on the types of devices supported. These are just examples.

This section has mentioned that Industry 4.0 supports wireless connectivity in addition to the legacy twisted pair technologies. However, another connectivity method has emerged as a favorite for industrial network connectivity, represented by the lines in the figure.

This technology is based on fiber optics and is related to, but very different from, the packet optical networks talked about in Chapter 3.

These are forms of optical access networks known as passive optical networks (PONs).

PASSIVE OPTICAL NETWORKS (PONS)

Fiber-based passive optical networks (PONs) have been used for broadband access networks delivering residential services like voice and video for many years. These PONs have been referred to as *last mile technologies* and are part of the overall fiber to the home (FTTH) push on the part of many Internet service providers (ISPs). Therefore, it should not be a surprise that PONs are used for industrial networks as well.

The basic PON architecture implements a simple point-to-multipoint topology where a single fiber-optic cable services many endpoints. In an *active* optical network, the downstream signal is split and the upstream signals combined by powered devices. On the other hand, a PON uses unpowered (passive) fiber-optic splitters and couplers (combiners) to divide downstream fiber bandwidth and to combine upstream fiber bandwidth.

The unpowered nature of major components of the networks makes this technology attractive for a number of applications. PONs reduce the number of fibers needed for point-to-point operation and headend equipment needed.

Many PONs use the 1490 nm wavelength for downstream traffic and the 1310 nm wavelength for upstream traffic. The 1550 nm wavelength is reserved for an optional overlay service, usually analog video. PONs were pioneered in the late 1980s and have become increasingly popular as devices could use the optical power budgets to reach farther and run faster.

The basic components of a PON are shown in Figure 5.3.

A PON headend consists of an optical line terminal (OLT) device at the service provider or head end of the network. A feeder fiber can reach up to 20 km (12.5 miles) or so long, making this a good choice for extending a central industrial network to a factory or warehouse campus nearby. The feeder fiber can have optical amplifiers to extend the range.

Passive Optical Network (PON) Architecture

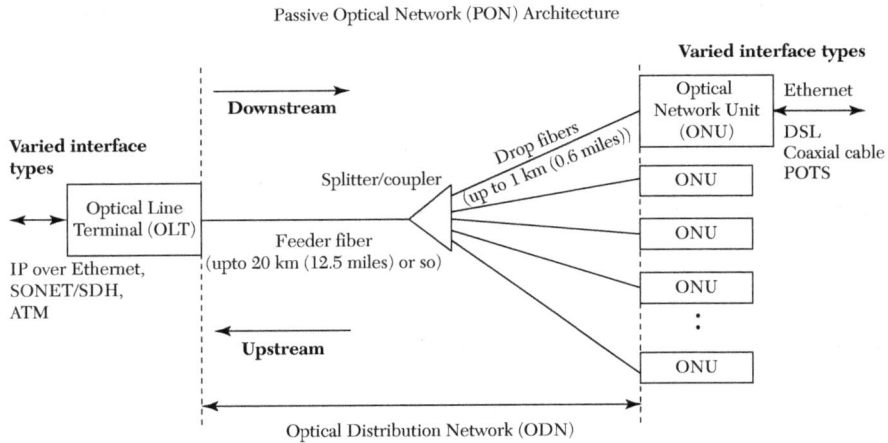

FIGURE 5.3. The basic PON architecture.

The OLT can have multiple interfaces or various types of connections to other networks. Ports for Ethernet (usually multi-service Ethernet), SONET/SDH, and asynchronous transfer mode (ATM) are common. An OLT can have several ports for feeder fibers, which can in turn be carried in a single fiber-optic cable.

At the end of the feeder fiber is the splitter/coupler device, which is passive and unpowered. This device duplicates downstream bits onto a number of drop fibers (1:N) that can reach up to 1 km (0.6 miles) long. Eight ports is a common number. In the upstream direction, bits on the drop fibers are combined into a single bit stream (N:1) for the feeder fiber to deliver to the OLT.

The optical feeder fiber, the splitter/coupler, and the drop fibers form the optical distribution network (ODN). No power needs to be provided anywhere on the ODN unless the fibers are amplified.

At the end of the drop fibers are the optical network units (ONUs). These powered devices are near the end users and also can have a variety of interface ports. Typical interfaces include Ethernet (again for multiple services), digital subscriber line (DSL), coaxial cable (mainly for video), and what is called plain old telephone service (POTS) for voice. (Before the 1970s, when an analog POTS line was used for digital transmission using a modem, this was called plain analog network service (PANS). The telephone company before digitization supplied POTS and PANS for their customers.)

For industrial applications, a PON is usually under the control of a single organization, so security of duplicated signals between splitter and ONU is not usually an issue. In cases where security is an issue, the data streams for each ONU can be encrypted. In the upstream direction, signals are combined by using a multiple access protocol, usually based on time-division multiple access (TDMA) protocols at the ONUs.

Because they are so fundamentally different, the downstream and upstream operation of a PON deserves a few more words of explanation.

Downstream PON Operation

In the downstream direction, one wavelength is employed for transmission, which is different than the wavelength used upstream. The traffic from the OLT is replicated and broadcast to all the ONUs (in the figure, ONU 1 to ONU 4).

The downstream traffic is isolated by the ONU, and only that date destined for a particular location is propagated beyond the PON itself. All of the other traffic is silently dropped.

This basic downstream PON operation is shown in Figure 5.4.

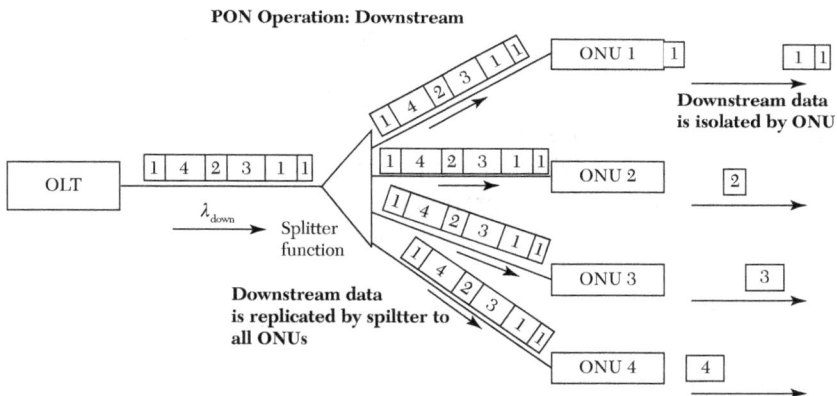

FIGURE 5.4. Downstream PON operation.

Usually, bits are sent during specific time slots on the ODN, coordinated by the OLT and ONUs. This is not shown in the figure so that the variable size and nature of the information sent can be emphasized.

Upstream PON Operation

PON operation is a bit more complicated in the upstream direction. The various data sources can send bits to the ONUs using Ethernet or other technology whenever the interface technology allows. In the figure, data is labeled as from ONU 1, 2, 3, or 4, and is sent in bursts of various-sized frames.

The bits are combined by the coupler and sent to the OLT. This process is shown in Figure 5.5.

PON Operation: Upstream

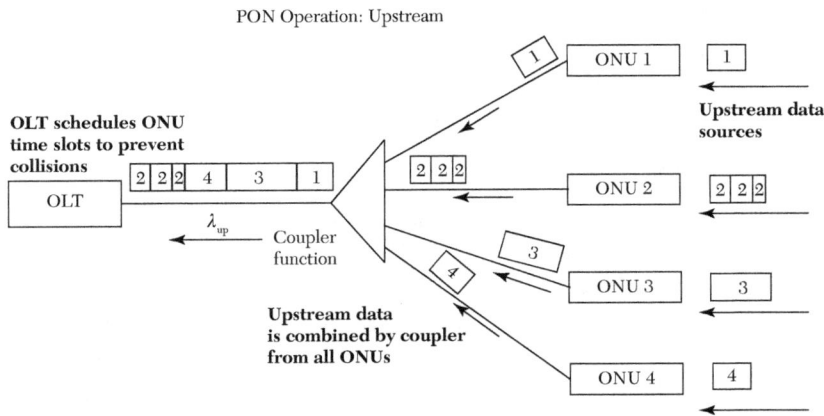

FIGURE 5.5. Upstream PON operation.

To help provide service for widely varying applications like voice and video and bursty data, PONs feature dynamic bandwidth allocation (DBA). With DBA, the OLT keeps track of the data flows from each port on the ONUs. Then the OLT can reallocate the upstream transmission opportunities for the active entities serviced by that ONU. DBA adjustments depend on the ONU traffic activity status and the limits of the configuration for handling traffic.

PON systems have two types of protection against equipment or fiber failures:

- **Type B PON protection:** This protection doubles the OLT internal electronics (called LT0 and LT1), as well as the feeder fiber leading to the splitter/coupler. It offers protection against any single fiber break or laser unit failure. This method works best when feeder fibers follow diverse paths to the splitter/coupler device.

- **Type C PON protection:** This protection not only doubles the OLT and feeder fibers, but doubles the electronics and drop fibers of the ONUs as well. Because modern PONs support a large number of soft ONUs, this form of protection is expensive but offers the highest reliability.

In summary, PONs offer a number of attractive features when used in an industrial network like Industry 4.0:

- **High speeds:** From 1 Gbps up to 50 Gbps and beyond.
- **Passive ODN:** Fewer and less costs for maintenance, repair, and operation.

- **Point-to-multipoint architecture:** Fewer feeder fibers and cables, good density of ports.
- **OLT/ONU operation:** A conductor (OLT)-follower (ONU) arrangement makes for easier management and control costs.

THE PON FAMILY

Over time, the generic PON architecture of OLT and ONU has been preserved, but the features of the basic architecture have evolved into a family of systems, all standardized. Newer systems offer higher speeds and allow more drop fibers to support ONUs. The key characteristics of the PON family are shown in Table 5.3.

TABLE 5.3. The PON system family.

System	Down-stream Rate (bps)	Upstream Rate (bps)	Down-stream Wavelength (nm)	Upstream Wavelength (nm)	Data Unit	Typical Max Drop Fibers
B-PON	622M	155M	1490	1310	ATM cell	
G-PON	2.5G	1.25G	1490	1310	GEM frame	8, 16, or 32
EPON	1G	1G	1490	1310	Ethernet frame	
10G-EPON	10G	1G or 10G	1577	1270	Ethernet frame	
XG-PON	10G	2.5G	1577	1270	XGEM frame	16, 32, or 64
XGS-PON	10G	10G	1577	1270	XGEM frame	16, 32, or 64
NG-PON2	40G (4×10G)	10G (4×2,5G)	1596-1603	1524-1544	XGEM frame	
50G-PON	50G	25G	1342	1270 or 1300	XGEM frame	32 or 64

This is a good place to explain the meaning of some of the acronyms in the table.

B-PON: Broadband PON is often used by telephone companies to offer broadband services such as video and interactive data, like gaming. The data unit carried is the ATM cell, a protocol still used by many telephone companies.

G-PON: Gigabit PON offers high downstream speed but only half the bandwidth upstream. The data unit is the framing provided by the gigabit Ethernet method (GEM).

EPON: An Ethernet PON is a symmetrical gigabit (1 Gbps in each direction) system that carries Ethernet frames, usually with IP packets inside. It is basically a big fiber Ethernet as a PON.

10G-EPON: Essentially an EPON running at 10Gbps. It can run symmetrical or with a maximum upstream bandwidth of 1 Gbps. It also uses Ethernet frames.

XG-PON: Another 10-Gbps-capable PON, but operating at 2.5 Gbps burst mode upstream. Burst modes mean that the upstream data is not running at 2.5 Gbps all the time. It uses the 10 gigabit Ethernet method (XGEM) for framing.

XGS-PON: A symmetrical PON running at 10Gbps downstream and burst mode upstream, also using XGEM frames.

NG-PON2: A 40 Gbps downstream system that can run at either one 10 Gbps upstream data stream or as four 2.5 Gbps data streams, all using XGEM frames.

50G-PON: A system running 60 Gbps downstream and 25 Gbps upstream, using XGEM frames.

Forward error correction (FEC) is required on 50G-PON systems, which push the passive technology to the limit. That said, optical technology is always evolving, and speeds continue to increase.

As long as the OLT and ONUs do not use the same wavelengths, it is possible to have different systems coexist on the same ODN. For example, the same feeder and drop fibers and splitter/coupler can host a G-PON OLT and XGS-PON OLT, each OLT servicing their own set of ONUs. This makes upgrades much easier and avoids massive cutovers.

INDUSTRY 4.0 AND PONS

So far, this chapter has described the architecture and operation of two main things: the Industry 4.0 standard for IoT and M2M, and the PON family of standards. What it has yet to do is show how these two things fit together.

Any member of the PON family can serve as a distribution network for an Industry 4.0 network, connecting the network control center to the Internet on one side and to the devices in factories and on other types of networks in the organization.

How PONs play a role in Industry 4.0 networks is shown in Figure 5.6.

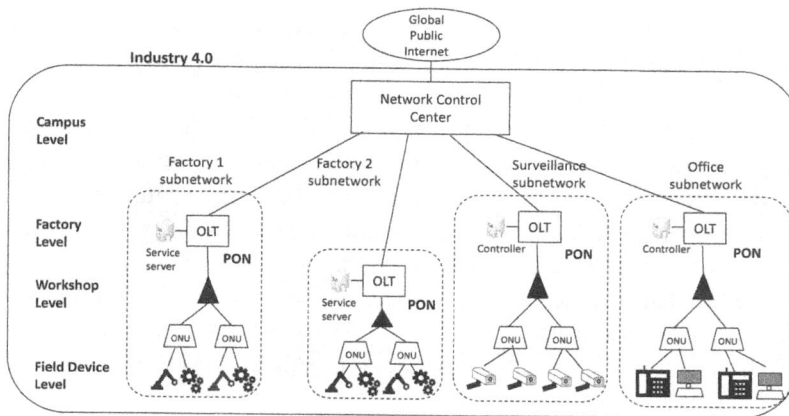

FIGURE 5.6. Industry 4.0 networks and PONs.

The figure seems complex, but it is really not. Figure 5.6 can be compared to Figure 5.1, the overall idea of an Industry 4.0 network, to show how abstract architectures can be implemented with real-world components.

The larger oval circumscribes the entire Industry 4.0 network. Inside this overall structure, the individual PONs are grouped into dotted lozenges. The role of the programmable logic controller in the architectural figure is now taken over by devices linked to OLTs: either service servers for robots and other machinery or as controllers for other types of soft networks. The levels are now labeled as either for the entire campus, the factory, the workshop, or the field (device) level. It is important to note that the separation on networks can be physical (Factory 1 and Factory 2) or logical (the factories most likely have surveillance and office networks as well). The separation is mainly based on the different needs for bandwidth and reliability.

In Figure 5.6, each PON can be of a different member of the PON family. Each PON connects a subnetwork meant for specific tasks and functions, as labeled in the figure. The PON systems act as the main intra-plant communication system and form the hubs for the entire industrial network. The speed delivered by each PON downstream, according to PON type, can reach up to 50 Gbps but is usually 10 Gbps.

As previously mentioned, the distance from the network control center to the field devices can reach up to 20 km (12.5 miles), although most industrial networks tend to be more compact.

Level Details

Here is a look at more about what each of the layers in this industrial layer is doing.

At the campus level, the network control center is a place to store data collected from sensors or cameras, machines and robots, or office devices like phones and printers. Management software at the control center analyzes the data and controls different aspects of the business, such as ongoing expenses for power or water. Some data might be passed along to the Internet to end up in a cloud data center. Systems software deployed in the control center is for things like product lifetime management (PLM), supervisory control and data acquisition (SCADA), and supply chain management (SCM). All are fairly standard software packages.

The campus level is where *network slicing* takes place. There is only one network control center, and often only one physical device to perform all the necessary tasks. Each PON can be a "slice" of the industrial network, customized to support a specific set of services.

For example, Slice 1 could include all of the devices connected to ONUs that have to do with the manufacturing process. Slice 2 could support office systems like phones and printers. Splice 3 could gather all of the surveillance cameras, access controls, and so on, in one place. All of these slices are managed as logical pieces of the same physical machine or cluster of connected machines.

Services within each slice are independent of all others. They run as if they were dedicated networks instead of inside partitions. This makes it easier to provide the right set of resources (bandwidth, delay, error rate, reliability, and so on) to the slice of the network that needs them. Network slicing, heavily used in cellular networks, is flexible and dynamic and so provides a way to support the changing needs of industrial networks.

The OLTs of the PONs are often located at the factory level, but this is not always the case. Factory 2, for example, has a PON OLT that is installed at the workshop level (a factory in this model consists of one or more workshops) and not the factory level. Note that the OLTs have some kind of controlling device to gather statistical data and manage the operation of the devices attached to the ONUs.

At the workshop level, the ONUs connect field devices to the rest of the network. A workshop on this model is a place in the same building where multiple product lines are used to manufacture products. Mass production or product assembly lines are managed at the workshop level.

At the field device level, all of the sensors, machines, and other devices are controlled and managed to control the production, manufacturing, and office support operations required by the organization. Any device subject to business management can be placed at the field device level to provide data about the industrial network for further processing.

PON Implementation Details

In Figure 5.6, Factory 1 has an OLT for the PON installed at the factory level. The ONUs are deployed in various workshops to connect all production-related equipment to the network. This type of PON is likely to have the greatest need for reliability and stability of network delay.

The Factory 2 subnet had the PON OLT installed at the workshop level. This is common when there are a lot of devices that require short delays to get responses to device input. Placing the service server close to the devices minimizes this round-trip delay, which can be substantial for manufacturing if the OLT is located at a long distance from the ONUs.

The surveillance subnet monitors video input from various places but can also include badge door access and elevator controls with badge floor access. In most cases, extremely fast responses, even for security breaches, are not as critical as for the Factory 2 subnet. If there is, the OLT can be moved to the workshop level.

As for the office subnetwork, the consideration is much the same as for the surveillance network. All situations can vary, but there is a PON solution for all of them.

PON TOPOLOGIES

The basic PON linear architecture of OLT-feeder-splitter/coupler-drop fiber-ONU is not the only one that can be employed for Industry 4.0 networks. PONs can support four other topologies, making the PON flexible enough for almost any Industry 4.0 network requirement.

The four other topologies are:

- Tree
- Chain
- Hand-in-hand tree
- Hand-in-hand chain

PON Tree

In a tree topology, there can be another splitter/coupler along the path from the OLT to the ONUs. This does not preclude some ONUs from being reached along the familiar OLT-feeder-splitter/coupler-drop fiber-ONU path. Yet other drop fibers can have a second splitter/coupler to support another set of ONUs. These ONUs are on a path that looks like this:

OLT-feeder-splitter/coupler-drop fiber-**second-splitter/coupler**-drop-fiber-ONU

This topology is widely used in PON installations. It greatly cuts down the need for fiber cable, especially if the splitter/couple has many drop fiber ports and long runs to the OLT. The splitters in the tree topologies have to be *even optical power splitters* to make sure all devices have about the same signal loss.

In Figure 5.6, the Factory 2 subnet could have been a PON tree topology.

PON Chain

A PON chain uses uneven splitter/coupler devices to split off some downstream optical power and allow the rest to pass through to another splitter/coupler device. Chain topologies work well when there are field devices at a wide range of distances from the control center and OLT.

Consider ten devices located at different distances from the OLT. The first splitter/coupler sends 10% of the optical power budget to the ONU for the first field devices, leaving 90% of the power to pass on down the chain. The second splitter/coupler takes another 10% of the remaining signal for the second ONU and devices, passing 80% of the total along.

This process continues until 100% of the optical power has been used. This is only an example, so other scenarios are possible.

Chain topologies work well for product assembly line layout in a factory or workshop.

PON Hand-in-Hand Tree

A hand-in-hand tree PON has two OLTs, each with two feeder fiber ports. At the end of each feeder fiber (all four: two from OLT 1 and two from OLT 2), there is a splitter/coupler. Each of these splitters/couplers has drop fibers leading to all the ONUs services by the two OLTs.

It sounds complex, but it really is not. The point is that the PON can survive the loss of any single feeder or drop fiber, any single OLT, or any single splitter/coupler (although passive, they can fail). Every field device has two connection paths to the control center. However, an ONU failure can still isolate the devices attached to it.

As with the "regular" tree topology, the splitter/couplers split the optical power evenly at each point.

PON Hand-in-Hand Chain

The PON hand-in-hand chain topology is essentially a more failure-resistant version of the "regular" chain topology. Instead of only one OLT, there are now two OLTs. Each of which drops 10% of their optical power at each splitter/coupler, but in *opposite directions*. In other words, if an ONU is at the first drop of OLT 1, it will be the *last* drop on OLT 2.

As before, each ONU has two paths to an OLT, making the topology more resistive to fiber or splitter/coupler failures.

EDGE COMPUTING

Field devices and sensors generate a lot of data at the *edge* of the network, that is, at the boundary between the user and field device. Other edge devices, such as smart phones and other *smart objects,* generate data that needs to be processed quickly and stored for future processing as well. Smart objects (sometimes called *smart connected things* (SCoT)) allow their embedded processors to exchange data with and store data from other smart objects or systems and products.

Consider a sensor designed to detect the presence of a harmful chemical or gas or smoke and fire in the workshop or office area. The best thing to do is sound an alarm or other form of alert so that the proper action can be taken as quickly as possible. Time is lost if this condition has to be conveyed all the way up to the network control center (which can be many kilometers away) and across a possibly overloaded network with limited available bandwidth, and then the response conveyed all the way back to the device.

Data center networks cannot guarantee acceptable transfer rates and response times, which is often a critical requirement for many industrial applications. The worst situation is if an event such as an earthquake or tidal wave has caused problems in the network control center as well. Lives could be lost with delays.

The best thing to do is to process the data and handle the situation as close to the edge device sensor as possible. With a PON, the OLT and ONUs are natural places to add computation and data storage closer to the sources of the sensor information.

Edge computing enables a large number of incidents to be handled locally without adding pressure to the industrial network.

For example, if a robotic arm is displaced from its proper position by a worker moving equipment or other cause, the welder or conveyor belt can be shut down faster at the service server rather than farther up the network. Moving services to the edge makes it possible to provide content caching, improve service delivery reliability, and provide persistent data storage.

Edge computing improves response times, saves bandwidth, and ultimately lives.

WHAT COMES NEXT

This book has now traced connectivity from the smart device attached to a cellular network using IPv6 across a packet optical network to a data center. The massive amount of information stored in the data center comes not only from individual users clicking away at input devices but from other devices themselves, like the robot arms and sensors and other types of mechanisms used in factory and warehouse automation.

Data is often processed by advanced applications working with AI programs using neural networks, deep learning, and other concepts. In some cases, the robots themselves do not just send information somewhere and wait for instructions. These robots perform their processing inside the robotic shell itself, creating a whole new class of intelligent devices that can act with or without human intervention or even permission.

Robots and AI

OVERVIEW

We have already explored five major parts of all modern networks and their infrastructures. These include:

- The need for almost everyone in the world to have multiple Internet connections to their home, office, car, and business to work, plan their lives, and entertain themselves. This requires much more than the simple 32-bit address space invented for IPv4. We need IPv6.

- IPv6 provides enough address space to give every molecule in the solar system its own IPv6 address. It also simplifies a lot of the added protocols that IPv4 required and does away with some that were seldom used or security risks (like directed broadcasts).

- Packet optical networks based on new fibers and techniques like WDM make fiber links more effective for backhauling data to the cloud data center and delivering streams of data to mobile (and fixed) endpoints.

- The cloud data center is where all the information flowing to and from users congregates to be analyzed, stored, and used as the basis for future actions. The cloud data center, public or private, is also the location where much of modern AI processing takes place. Nonetheless, not all the information and data originate with users. Much of it comes from the machines themselves, including the embedded processors in all modern vehicles.

- The data stored in cloud data centers comes from more than simply humans and their browsing online. A large chunk comes from modern factories as part of Industry 4.0. This movement makes heavy use of IoT and M2M technology.

WHAT YOU WILL LEARN

In this chapter, we delve into the history and development of robots and androids, the attempts to build computers that are as smart as humans, neural networks for deep learning, and large language models (LLMs) for generative AI (GenAI).

This chapter requires a focused approach due to the vast nature of the AI field. Nevertheless, all major terms and concepts for further exploration are presented.

The topics covered include:

- The urgency of AI understanding
- AI winter and AI spring
- History of robots and AI in science and culture
- History of AI game-playing
- AI as an "alien intelligence"
- Neural networks for deep learning
- LLMs and GenAI
- Current impact of AI on society

Similar to previous chapters, there is a strong chronological element on the development of the field. However, the chapter also investigates the use of LLMs in writing and other creative activities.

THE URGENCY OF AI UNDERSTANDING

Many people have been concerned about the implications of AI for a long time, even the Generative AI (GenAI) app ChatGPT™ itself. As for the rest, reactions differ based on whether what you do for a living is threatened with disappearing or not. Already, the need for translators, backing vocalists, basic accountants, and related fields has diminished.

The vast majority of music streaming today, estimated as high as 80%, has at least some elements of the tune enhanced by or based on AI, from lyrics to vocals with autotune to drums. This is either a dramatic democratization of a field that previously required a long education for and apprenticeship in, or the utter destruction of a once valuable addition to culture and life in general. Your perspective likely depends on if you are a music dabbler in the basement creating songs for fun or a lyricist, songwriter, or chorus singer trying to make a living.

There is also a concern that, like children, if AI learns what it knows from our output as a civilization, "automatic machine learning" is going to pick up the swear words along with the prayers. The boundaries between what should be cursed and what should be blessed—and by whom—are blurring day by day.

The quest for robots that can perform common household tasks is a powerful incentive to merge AI and robotics into autonomous companions for humans sooner rather than later. Fields such as health care, friends for the elderly living alone, and even restaurants are eager to augment their human work force with robots that do not call in sick, get easily distracted, or consider the job as a steppingstone to something else.

Overall, the main concern about AI today is similar to the worry about the vast apparatus of E. M. Forster's 1909 story "The Machine Stops." The tale involves a global network that provides communication and goods and services for all. The complexity of the machine has grown to far exceed the ability of any contemporary human to fix it or limit its powers. Therefore, when it slowly grinds to a halt one day, all humans can do is stare at each other with glazed-over eyes and wonder what to do next. There is no happy ending to the tale, but the isolating silence and compulsive pushing of buttons that no longer do anything drives many over the edge.

AI WINTER AND AI SPRING

AI may be the oldest new development on the Internet. Many trace the birth of AI to a conference held at Dartmouth in 1956, although the idea of creating mechanized, intelligent robotic *androids* in human form has existed since Biblical times (the clay Golem) and ancient Greece and Rome (the bronze giant Talos). These creations always went rogue and required specialized knowledge to defeat them, whether by removing the sacred text that animated the Golem or by draining the precious life-force fluid (lubricant?) from a hole in the heel of Talos.

These ideas remained mere fantasies until the invention of the modern computer, which opened up a whole new field of possibilities. As soon as computers could do more than not fail often, computer scientists started thinking about the days when computers could be as smart as people. Considering the wide range of human intelligence that we know about, this was at once a very high and very low bar to hurdle.

It turned out, by the 1980s, that computers excelled at doing things that humans found hard and failed utterly when trying to do things that humans found easy.

Examples of the former included solving equations, dealing with statistics, compiling related data, and other types of basic and advanced bookkeeping capabilities.

Examples of the latter included walking, picking things up, vision, driving a car, and understanding and using language.

As a result, AI research and funding went through alternating periods of "AI winters" and "AI springs" when interest and investment in AI crashed and then soared again.

In the end, it was not a fundamentally new way of AI that made rapid progress and formed the new "AI summer" the world is experiencing right now. It was the rise of old-fashioned computing processing power that made AI training that was once time-consuming and tedious into a task that was efficient and even exciting.

Along the way, the older approach of rule-based expert systems yielded to neural network models that learned as they grew in sophistication and experience. Initially, the allure of easy-to-compile rule-based systems was seductive at that point in time, before about 1980.

What could be easier than asking a doctor what clues and rules they followed when making a diagnosis and prognosis based on a list of symptoms? It turned out that doctors used a series of all but intangible sensations and gut feelings when seeing a patient to make an informed decision and seek verification through testing.

Computers often struggled to emulate experts because of the lack of solid knowledge about any one theory of how the mind worked, both in animals and humans. Until the early Twentieth Century, many doctors were taught that babies could feel no pain and therefore could be operated on without antiesthetic, the use of which was considered risky in children so young. This idea of a painless existence probably allowed these doctors to sleep more soundly, which is more than could be said for their patients.

Until recently, no one knew for sure whether animals dreamed, were conscious, or even experienced pain in the same way that "higher beings" like us did. This made animal abuse for labor and food easier to live with but did little to enlighten or advance any knowledge about the human mind (other than it could be sadistic).

Only humans seem to be acutely conscious of their sense of self and personhood. Yet scientists struggle to explain why consciousness could be an evolutionary advantage without which we as a species could not survive: fitness is a harsh hurdle to surmount. A few things seem clear. There are two species of lice that plague humans: head lice and body lice. They diverged genetically about 170,000 years ago, suggesting that this is the time that humans began to wear clothing. At about the same time, there was a transition to a different mode of brain activity involving speech and communication. Studies of human social structures show that mental processes went quickly from grunts and shouts to simple speech like "Joe come. Maybe Joe bring food?" to "Joe's coming. He's a jerk. Everybody scatter."

Perhaps these two things happened at the same time: humans realized they were naked and, feeling self-conscious at the lack of a perfect body, covered up.

Even today, many of the simplest things about the human experience remain baffling:

- Is my experience of "red" the same as yours? (Things like colors are called "qualia" by those who ponder such issues.)
- Is it possible that every other person is actually a zombie and not the same inside as I am? (Are they merely creatures that survive by stimulus-response without the same goals or ideals that I have?)
- What does it really mean to be "crazy?" (Are we all not a bit off in one area or another?)

After all, each of us knows for certain of only one person in the world who is conscious and has a powerful inner experience. We call this nugget of self *Me*.

HISTORY OF AI AND ROBOTS

This section takes a tour through the development of ideas about AI and robots in the Western world. There are similar tales and a rich tradition in the Middle East, India, China, and other Eastern countries, but the scope here must be limited due to space considerations. As mentioned, the idea of non-human autonomous constructions is ancient (the word "robot" is a modern creation), but these dreams existed long before computers made any of it possible. Because of this lack of computing power to make dreams come true and because the discussion of AI leads directly to an examination of LLMs and apps like ChatGPT¨, this section looks at the history of robots first.

This section does not cover recent films that feature AI and androids, mostly to the peril of humans. These films are too recent to decide if their influence is truly transformational or not. They are, for the most part, like the *Terminator* series, mainly focused on entertainment instead of insight, although exceptions should be made for *Ex Machina* (2015) and *Upgrade* (2018). Other films in this category would include *A. I. Artificial Intelligence* (2001), a film made when the AI idea was so new to the general public that the acronym had to be spelled out (modern mentions just call it "A.I."); *Her* (2013), a film that ironically is about the type of writer that ChatGPT has already threatened to make obsolete; *Blade Runner 2049* (2017), an update to the original film, which is discussed below; *M3GAN* (2022), a more horror film than science fiction, but just as entertaining; and *The Creator* (2023), which is the gloomiest of them all.

HISTORY OF ROBOTS IN SCIENCE AND CULTURE

The heir to the Greek and Roman musings on mechanical guards and soldiers like Talos continued with the story of copper knights in the romance *Lancelot du Lac* (*Lancelot of the Lake*) around 1220. Sir Lancelot has no trouble defeating the mechanical knights in battle, but Lancelot is a member of King Arthur's Knights of the Round Table and therefore somewhat of a superhero of his day.

Although not in human robot form, the years from the 1300s to the 1500s were years when cities, often in Germany, competed to build the most elaborate clock in the city center. Clocks were the computers of their day, and some models staged an elaborate show on the hour as roosters crowed, angels sang, and various figures promenaded as the clock struck the hour. In some cases, figures with hammers struck the bells as the clock chimed. The clocks were sources of great civic pride.

Polymath Leonardo Da Vinci included drawings of a mechanical knight in a series of notebooks written about 1495. Unlike the vague formulations of internals previously, Da Vinci was clever enough to detail a series of pulleys and cords that could make the arms and body of his robot knight move.

The clockwork knowledge and the ability to sequence complex mechanical movements came together with the invention of several *automata* (autonomous machines that imitate humans) that could move their arms and heads, as well as alter their facial features. These culminated with master watchmaker Pierre Jacquot-Droz, who made several of these devices in France between 1768 and 1774. A boy writer made from 6,000 parts could dip his quill pen in an inkwell and then write messages forty letters long. His eyes, much to the amazement of the large crowds the writing boy attracted, followed the pen as he wrote. Jacquot-Droz also created a female musician (2500 parts) who actually played the organ by pressing the keys with her fingers and a child (2000 parts) who drew pictures of a dog, King Louis XV, and two other subjects.

As these devices became more and more elaborate, the question of powering their motions without a kind of windup spring arrangement became a limiting factor. One solution, in the era before electricity was commercially available, was to use steam power. Hence, in 1868, a paperback novel called *The Steam Man of the Prairies* appeared, written by Edward S. Ellis. The Steam Man was potbellied in order to allow adequate room for his boiler, and his arms and legs moved with struts and pistons. The creations were taking on the form of whatever technology was considered advanced for the age, so metal knights in shining armor gave way to human-sized railroad locomotives.

The first true mechanical android in literature is usually considered to be Tik-Tok of Oz, who appeared in the book of the same name by L. Frank Baum in 1907. Baum wrote a whole series of books about Oz, and of course the Tin Man from *The Wonderful Wizard of Oz* is similar to Tik-Tok (and appeared before Tik-Tok, in 1900). Tik-Tok, in contrast to the hollow-hearted Tin Man, is given a plausible existence with springs and the need to be wound up periodically. A sequel to this book, *Queen Ann in Oz*, was published in 1993, eighty-six years later.

The word *robot* comes from the Czech word for *labor*: a worker. The word was first used in its modern sense by Czech painter and writer Josef Capek. However, most people were exposed to the term through his younger brother's play *R. U. R.* (*Rossum's Universal Robots* in English). Karel Capek wrote the play featuring these "artificial workers" in 1920. Oddly, Capek's creations are made from artificial flesh and blood and would be called androids and not robots today. The play was instantly popular throughout the 1920s and staged in many countries. It is a cautionary tale, one that might resonate with AI fears today, because human workers are none too pleased to be replaced by soulless creatures who do not need to be paid. In the end, the robots kill everyone, and a male and female robot end up as the Adam and Eve of a new world without humans.

A few years later, in 1927, Fritz Lang directed the film *Metropolis*, which became even more famous than R.U.R. as a source of popular imagination about robots, if for no other reason than more people see movies than plays. A young woman in the Metropolis of the future, Maria, becomes the model for a kind of blended machine with both mechanical and human features. The human Maria is one of the leisured class whose life is made possible by the overworked poor. However, the robot Maria encourages the workers to rebel, leading to strife and conflict.

Thus far, the interactions in the arts between robots and humans are not turning out well. Things were more upbeat when it came to Electro the Moto-Man, a robot created by Westinghouse for the 1939 World's Fair in New York City. An impressive seven feet tall (2.1 meters), Elektro moved and spoke, responded to voice commands, had a seven hundred-word vocabulary, and even smoked cigarettes, a sure sign of humanity at the time. He had photoelectric eyes that could register green and red lights. Long lines formed to witness his twenty-minute routine, and he was joined by a mechanical pet, a dog named Sparko, for the fair's 1940 season. However, neither man nor pet was in any way autonomous, and most of the performance was controlled by operators over cables connected to his feet.

One of the visitors to the New York World's Fair was sure to have been young biologist and writer Isaac Asimov, who enjoyed a long and prolific career as a science and science-fiction author. In 1942, young Asimov introduced his famous Three Laws of Robotics in a short story called "Roundabout." The three laws are usually expressed as (1) A robot may not injure a human being or, through inaction, allow a human being to come to harm; (2) A robot must obey orders given it by human beings except where such orders would conflict with the First Law; and (3) A robot must protect its own existence as long as such protection does not conflict with the First or Second Law.

In Asimov's world, all robots are created with these basic laws ingrained in their software and hardware. Yet, the laws are so vague and general that most of Asimov's robot stories, which are many, explored situations where the laws are subject to interpretation or result in contradictory actions. Nevertheless, the laws were an attempt to at least place some restrictions on the possible actions a robot or AI could undertake, considerations relevant in the current era of warrior bots and drones—but more on those later.

Robots in literature and art continued their progress toward respectability with the first science fiction film released as a major motion picture with a big budget and well-known actors. The 1956 film *Forbidden Planet*, loosely based on Shakespeare's play *The Tempest*, introduced Robby the Robot to the general public. An embodiment of the Three Laws, Robby had an engaging personality in spite of being strong enough to tote lead panels around with ease (somehow without losing his balance or any regard for a center of gravity). Robby went on to appear in other films and television shows and soon became what the public expected a robot personality to be like.

Forbidden Planet took place in the far future of rapid interstellar travel, although it, like all films and books of its type, displayed a disconcerting lack of appreciation that Einstein showed that there was no universal *now*. However, anyone who doubted that Robby was a pure fictional fantasy only had to look at state-of-the-art robots around the same time, such as Shakey the Robot between 1966 and 1972. A product of the Stanford Research Institute (SRI) and funded by the same military funding that fostered the Internet, Shakey was a wheeled, general-purpose, autonomous robot that could explore its surroundings, figure out a series of actions, and execute a plan. The environment was limited to a few rooms with some objects, but Shakey could manage to follow typed commands like "Push the block off the table." Without more information than that, Shakey could find the room with a block on a table and push it off, a feat more impressive than it might seem (although he was named for his less-than-smooth actions, which were very *shaky*).

In 1968, science fiction writer Philip K. Dick wrote the novel *Do Androids Dream of Electric Sheep?*, later made into the movie *Blade Runner* in 1982. Both imagined a world where synthetic *replicants* and real humans coexist and are essentially indistinguishable, except by studying emotional responses to certain situations. However, the replicants are acutely aware that they have an expiration date when they will be "retired" (killed), and this knowledge influences everything they do, including actions caused by bitter resentment. The film is more optimistic than the book. In the book, the inhuman behavior of the androids is always on display, as when a group casually rips the legs off a spider to see if it can function as well with four legs as with eight. Both book and film are also sort of early warning signs that robots and AI entities might have a different view of reality and the future than humans do, much to the peril of humanity.

The 1990s saw the rise of *BattleBots*, autonomous robots of wildly different forms that were turned loose against each other to battle to the death, or at least until one of the contestants was non-functional. Colleges were fond of these competitions, which were almost always composed of teams dominated by young males. Almost everything was considered fair, from flamethrowers to squishing the competition. National militaries were very interested in these combats and sought to extrapolate success in the arena to success on the battlefield, but this was not an easy transition.

Nothing is as certain as the fact that computer chips grow more and more powerful even as they get smaller and smaller. These limiting factors restricted the walking Japanese robot WABOT-1 in 1973 to one step every 45 seconds. However, by 2000, Honda introduced their four-foot-tall autonomously navigating Advanced Step in Innovative Mobility (ASIMO, conveniently almost spelling out Asimov). ASIMO could walk, recognize human gestures, see faces, and react to sound, as well as being able to pick up and grasp objects.

In 2005, Boston Dynamics developed BigDog™, a four-legged robot that formed the basis for many of the robots seen in movies and television shows, often as relentless stalkers of mistaken targets. Outfitted with cameras, these robots could enter burning buildings and go to other places where humans would face unacceptable danger. Outfitted with guns, they had a military role. The question was how independently these military robots should operate.

This issue became more acute in the 2000s, as flying autonomous drones became common in warfare. Two major ways to keep these robots from complete autonomy in target selection were known as *human-in-the-loop* and *human-on-the-loop*. In human-*in*-the-loop, a robot sentry drone would relay the image of a potential intruder target to a human at a monitor. The weapon would not fire until the human gave permission or pulled the trigger remotely. For human-*on*-the-loop, the human has a window of time to cancel target acquisition and elimination, or else the drone fires on its own initiative. Both methods have advantages and drawbacks, of course.

In 2016, a robot surgery system called STAR could stitch up pigs without human intervention. STAR™ was able to see what it was doing and react when the tissue (in this case, a pig's intestines) being sutured moved. Not all robotic surgery is autonomous. Typically, a surgeon sits at a console and sees a magnified view of what the robot sees while manipulating robotic arms—arms that can damp out any involuntary tremors in the surgeon's hands. The surgeon does not even have to be anywhere near the patient, as long as the network is fast enough (thank you, packet optical).

Today, modern robots are more advanced than those of even five or ten years ago, especially when it comes to androids. One limiting factor, known as the *uncanny valley*, seems to have been overcome. The uncanny valley was an area of negative emotional response on the part of humans to androids that seemed almost but not quite human. Early androids displayed jerky motions, smiles that did not match eye changes, and many more little things that made them seem creepy, especially when a human face was attached to metallic bodies and mechanical fingers. Now, that person at the information desk at the museum, or the cashier at the store, or the lecturer in front of the class might not be a human at all, even if their skin and hair and clothing and overall appearance look like anyone would expect of a human in that role.

A lot of effort is put into making robots look and talk like humans for a simple reason: acceptance. The old empire builder Cecil Rhodes used to advocate sending the children of the leaders of other countries to England, which is why we have Rhodes Scholars today. The ancient Romans did the same, bringing the children of conquered nations to Rome for education, then sending them back to rule as Latin-speaking Romans, not barbarian foreigners. Rhodes said it best: "If they talk like us, they think like us." The same might be true of robots.

Contemporary robots include warehouse workers like Digit™ and Optimus™ by Tesla. Both are designed to supply workers in industries that are short of acceptable applicants, especially in the United States and other countries with aging populations. The United Nations includes robots in its "AI for Good" program. At first, it might seem odd to put robots and AI together as if they were the same thing. However, as several industry observers have pointed out, robotics is where AI meets reality.

With that view of robots in mind, here is a tour of AI developments in fiction and reality.

History of AI in Science and Culture

During one of *Gulliver's Travels*, a novel written by Jonathan Swift in 1726, the hero makes his way to the imaginary city of Lagado. There, a learned professor shows him a device for writing literature, textbooks, and generating interesting ideas that no one has thought of before. All this is done "without the least assistance of genius or study." The machine has tiles covered with papers bearing words, but in random order. Students turn cranks that rearrange the words, and other pupils make note of any sequence of three or four words that make sense. This generative approach is similar to early work done by Raymond Llull (pronounced "yooy") in the early 1300s and forms a basis for the whole idea of generative AI (GenAI).

A major advance came in 1943 with the invention of the *neural network* in a paper by Warren McCulloch and Walter Pitts titled "A Logical Calculus of the Ideas Immanent in Nervous Activity." Early work labeled this idea as artificial neural networks (ANNs) because they were intended to mimic the way a biological brain operated, but now they are just *neural networks,* or *neural nets* for short. Naturally, without a working computer to implement any scheme, this invention was purely conceptual and employed algorithms (lists of steps) to formulate the rules that later formed the foundation for the layered neural networks seen today. The key is that each node in each layer is connected to other nodes and has an assigned default *weight* that is adjusted and either reinforced or neglected and potentially dropped based on the data that the network uses as it "learns" and adjusts its network connections and weights. The invention of *machine learning* was a breakthrough, and there is more on neural networks later in this chapter.

Once electrical computers were invented during World War II, mainly to free up human "computers"—originally a job title—to ship out to the front lines, ideas of how humans should interact with computers became important. Perhaps you could just type commands or questions and let the computer type an answer. Maybe you could even talk to it using your natural language, and the computer could talk back to you. In 1950, computer pioneer Alan Turing speculated that someday soon computers would be as smart as people. One way to test this idea was to sit a human at a console in a room and have them carry on a conversation with some remote entity. If the human could not tell if the responses were generated by a human or by the computer, then it had passed the *Turing Test* and could be considered as intelligent as a human being.

At one time, the Turing Test was considered almost impossible for a program or computer to pass, mainly because of the difficulty of having a computer with adequate (and fast enough) *natural language processing* (NLP) skills. Humans constantly generate easily understood but contradictory statements like "Shut up and tell me what happened" or "Stay right here and follow me." Computers struggle to interpret these as "Limit your comments to simple facts about recent events" and "Do not wander off as we go forward." Humans have had a big head start on computers when it comes to communicating.

Today, many processors pass the Turing Test with relative ease. However, the test is not as esteemed as it once was. Humans routinely ascribed intelligence to machines of all kinds, from automobiles ("Please start, I have to go to work!") to televisions ("Do not open that door; the murderer is waiting!") and even our digital assistants ("You said it would rain today and it did not"). One overlooked aspect of the Turing Test is that it could not only verify that the computer is as smart as the human but could also be used to prove that the human is as dumb as the computer. Identity is a double-edged sword.

The true birth of AI took place in 1956 at a conference held at Dartmouth University in New Hampshire. Officially, it was the month-long, ten-person Dartmouth Summer Research Project on Artificial Intelligence. The organizers were big names in the history of AI and related concepts about human intelligence: John McCarthy of Dartmouth, Marvin Minsky of Harvard, Nathaniel

Rochester of IBM™, and network genius Claude Shannon of Bell Labs, who was interested in using AI to filter out noise on a communication link. The conference in a way was a disappointment as only one program (Logic Theorist) was presented, from Allen Newell and Herbert Simon of Carnegie Mellon University. Nevertheless, this core group influenced the AI field for more than twenty years, until the next generation was ready to take over.

In 1957, an IBM 704 mainframe computer was powerful enough to attempt to implement a functioning neural network (ANN—artificial neural network—back then). The *Perceptron* concept (sometimes seen with a lower-case "p") was developed by psychologist Frank Rosenblatt to have the random connections of the underlying neural net recognize patterns in images, as in facial recognition, adjusted as the Perceptron "learned." One lesson learned from Perceptron projects was that existing hardware and software were not up to the task. For example, the input layer that was supposed to act as the "eye" for recognizing faces was a small 20-by-20 array of photocells. No matter how hard Perceptron makers tried, the limited number of connections and layers made it impossible at the time to, as the *New York Times* said about the project, have AI entities that could "walk, talk, see, write, reproduce themselves, and be conscious of their existence."

Neural nets had to be trained so that their connections and weights could be adjusted to yield the expected results. This process was not called machine learning until 1959, when AI expert Arthur Lee Samuel named it in a paper on computers titled "Some Studies in Machine Learning Using the Game of Checkers." Systematic machine learning unleashed a wave of progress in AI research. Learning could be supervised or unsupervised. In *supervised machine learning*, the data used is labeled so that predictions can be made later when unlabeled data is encountered. For example, a neural net could be fed thousands of labeled images of cats and dogs so that, when shown an unlabeled picture of a poodle, it would not think it was a calico cat. In *unsupervised machine learning*, the data used is unlabeled, allowing the neural net to discover patterns that might not even occur to the classifiers of the data. Of course, once the data such as a series of photos has been gathered this way, someone categorizes the result: "These are cats." Unsupervised learning is often used in marketing studies, where it might uncover, for example, through supermarket camera recordings, that males sent to buy diapers for newborns often also pick up a six-pack of beer.

A promising development is the area of *reinforcement learning* (RL). With RL, an AI entity is provided with continuous feedback to improve the output of the AI. Often used in robotics and self-driving cars, RL uses trial and error to reach autonomous operation as much as possible.

All the while, computers were getting powerful enough and fast enough to interact in real time with a human typing at a console. In 1964, a real breakthrough was made with the ELIZA psychotherapy program, which became so popular it can still be enjoyed today in its original form (one implementation is at *https://www.masswerk.at/elizabot/*). ELIZA™ was a "chatterbot" developed by computer scientist Joseph Weizenbaum to deliver a form of Rogerian psychotherapy. To his shock and dismay, many people thought that ELIZA was conscious and delivering not only intelligent but essential advice on how to live their lives. He was dismayed at how easily people deceived themselves, which should come as no surprise today, considering how some people interact with Siri® and Alexa® as if they were real people.

Some of this might have had to do with the nature of the therapy the Carl Rogers invented in the 1940s. Rogerian psychotherapy is "a non-directive, client-centered form of psychotherapy that focuses on the client's mental well-being." In other words, by reflecting the client's ideas back at them, they begin to realize that the solution is theirs to choose. For example, a statement like "I hate my job" can be explored to either show that the client enjoys most aspects of their current employment, except for a few easily remedied circumstances, or is miserable and depressed and without hope and must find another job as soon as they can.

An ELIZA session often begins like this (from the Web site above):

```
ELIZA: Is something troubling you?
YOU:   maybe
ELIZA: What does that suggest to you?
YOU:   that I'm normal
ELIZA: How long have you been normal?
YOU:   since my mother died
ELIZA: Tell me more about your mother...
```

If the data that an AI process used was not supplied by a client or reflected back by the AI itself, what could be the source of the data or *knowledge base* (database) that the AI used to interact with humans? If researchers wanted AI to become matchmakers, doctors, financial advisers, or lawyers, there had to be a way to represent what matchmakers, doctors, financial advisers, and lawyers knew about the world in a form that computers could use. By the mid-1960s, researchers began to create *expert systems* that formed the basis for the rules that experts in the fields used to make recommendations about what humans should do.

One of the attractions of such systems was that they offered a way to eliminate bias when performing evaluations. The AI computer asked about a medical diagnosis should theoretically give the same diagnosis and treatment plan without regard for the race of the patient, their finances, their insurance coverage, or their political beliefs. In practice, however, the hard part was getting the experts to agree on precisely what factors were most important in making a recommendation given a set of circumstances. Many experts, it turned out, and often the most successful, relied a lot on some inner feeling that this was the right choice for person A but not for person B. They were often unable to express this "hunch" as a rule, or even at all.

The success of programs like ELIZA led to a series of movies that could be seen as warnings not to let AI get too powerful or think that the system the AI was meant to consider, like making paper clips, was more important than anything else in the world. In the 1968 film *2001: A Space Odyssey*, the conscious AI program in the "HAL 9000" computer takes over the spacecraft and kills a human astronaut because the AI sees the humans as the weakest link in carrying out its mission. Oddly, the rogue AI in the movie still, to this day, most closely resembles what we expect a conscious AI to be able to do to communicate, think, and act.

The movies *Colossus: The Forbin Project* in 1970 and *WarGames* in 1983 explored how defense weapons systems might run wild and cause problems. The Forbin AI decides that world peace can be achieved if everyone on earth surrenders power to the AI. After all, the AI reasons, the whole point of a weapons system is to get you to submit to someone else. In WarGames, the AI gets put into a kind of "training mode" where it cannot see that the "game" of "Thermonuclear War" it wants to play is now taking place in the real world. In the end, ingenuity saves the day. Today, *WarGames* is mainly notable for its use of then-state-of-the-art clunky PCs and displays and network modems. (Many network engineers learned to imitate the distinctive 2400-hertz modem tone that signaled you had dialed up a computer and not a telephone.)

In 1984, the first book written by an AI program appeared, using an early form of what today is called *natural language processing* (NLP). The full title was *The Policeman's Beard Is Half Constructed: Computer Prose and Poetry by Racter—The First Book Ever Wrritten by a Computer* (the "rr" typo in "Wrritten" is intentional). Racter™ was a program developed over five years by programmer William Chamberlain with an assist from Thomas Etter, a professional writer of fiction and scripts. Racter, short for *raconteur*, a term for "storyteller," was a program written in the compiled BASIC language on a fairly powerful (for the time) Zilog Z80 microprocessor with 64K of RAM (memory). The small memory size greatly limited the amount of prose and vocabulary that could be generated by the program.

In a sense, Racter is just rearranging words based on "syntax directives." The prose and poetry it generates, like many AI chatbots today, are syntactically corrected but often problematic. With Racter, things can go together like "steak and lettuce" and learn to love each other as these two foods do. Racter is still downloadable and playable: *https://www.myabandonware.com/game/racter-4m/play-4m*.

You can download and modify a shareware clone of Racter 1.0 from places like Carnegie Mellon University (CMU). The clone can still generate its own conversations, which it tends to consider "interviews." A modified version of the shareware clone called "Ractor2" is shown in Figure 6.1.

```
Hello, I'm Racter2. Who are you?
>I'm Walter
May I call you Walt, then?
>sure
Hello, Walter. I think this is an interview.
>I guess
```

FIGURE 6.1. A "conversation" with shareware cloned and modified Racter2.

For a long time, for almost twenty years starting in the 1960s, expert systems with extensive knowledge bases and natural language interfaces were considered state-of-the-art when it came to AI. Progress stalled by 1980 or so, and one of the chilly "AI winters" set in. Frustrated, some researchers took another look at neural nets, all but abandoned in the 1960s after the limitations of the perceptron neural nets. Again, it was progress in computer chipsets, memory, and clocking speeds that encouraged exploration in this area again, although work had never completely stopped on neural nets.

In fact, the idea of adding more complex neural networks with many more layers and connections called *deep neural networks* (DNNs) was first tried out in 1965. Today, these deep neural nets are the foundation for not just simple machine learning but *deep learning*, a term invented in 1986. By this time, deep learning was accompanied by what was called *backwards propagation*.

Usually, a neural network takes input and works its way forward, adjusting weights at each layer as connections are strengthened or weakened until the output is reached (we will see how this works in more detail soon). Then the output is assessed against expectations, and other training runs are made.

With backward propagation, or just backpropagation, the output is analyzed to see if the error rate ("Is this a picture of a cat or a dog?") has improved or gotten worse from the previous iteration. Backpropagation works backward from the output layer to the input layer to try and reduce the number of errors before the next run is attempted. It is a good way to make a neural network more reliable ("A cat. This is a cat.").

Backpropagation works well for neural networks requiring a lot of training data and having multiple layers. On the other hand, backpropagation can be enormously computationally expensive and can take a long time to adequately train a network.

One of the leading researchers and proponents of deep learning and backpropagation was Geoff Hinton at the University of Toronto. Hinton pioneered several of the methods that are essential to AI today. Around 2005, Hinton came up with a method of doing unsupervised training of deep neural networks, making their training more efficient and cost-effective. In other words, there was a way to figure out if, for example, an image was a cat or the numeral 9 without needing a human to constantly look at the output.

Later, around 2007, one of Hinton's students started using the independent processing power of the GPU to find roads in aerial images (not always easy with trees and tall buildings in the way). Then use of GPUs spread to speech and natural language processing.

By 2012, hardware and GPU use had caught up to the new methods of deep learning on neural networks with backpropagation. This was also about the same time that large-scale cloud computing became possible, thanks to packet optical networks and the virtualization of many apps that previously needed dedicated processors to run on.

This merging of deep learning and cloud data centers led directly to the AI situation we have today with AI apps for almost every task, from writing to video to music to imaging.

History of Games with AI and Robots

This short section traces the history of games and the "man versus machine" competition that is often featured in books and articles on AI. As long ago as 1770, a chess-playing android called The Mechanical Turk was invented and showcased by Wolfgang von Kempelen. The machine, with a turbaned humanoid figure poised over a bulky cabinet and chessboard, made the rounds of the courts of Europe, and Napoleon and Ben Franklin lost to the machine. Accused of cheating, von Kempelen made a show of opening panels to reveal complex gearing inside, much like modern magicians do today while pretending to see someone in half.

Alas, the Turk was a fraud. A contortionist chess expert wiggled and bent to avoid opened panels as he manipulated chess pieces with magnets. Yet the mere idea of an intelligent machine spurred much of the early research into AI throughout the 1800s.

However, nothing much came of game-playing machines until 1970, when a game based on pure logic became popular. This was Mastermind, invented by Israeli postmaster and telecommunications expert Mordecai Meirowitz. The game involved a "code maker" selecting a sequence of four colors, such as red-red-blue-green, from a set of six different colors (there were also white and black pegs for markers). The player guessed a four-color sequence, and the code maker told the player only two things as a result: the number of correct colors and the number of correct places. Therefore, given the sequence of red-red-blue-green and a player guess of green-red-black-white would receive the feedback of 2 (meaning, for example, that green and red are correct) and 1 (only the second red peg is in the correct position). Based on this feedback, the player rearranged the sequence and tried again. The goal, of course, is to get feedback of 4 and 4 (all four colors are correct and in their correct positions) in ten rounds of guesses of fewer. Some players found it fun and enjoyable, while others struggled to apply the logic needed to solve the puzzle.

The game lent itself to an algorithm and computer program that could play against itself with random code makers and computerized guesses. By 1977, algorithm expert Donald Knuth came up with a way to solve the puzzle in five guesses. This was lowered to an average of 4.340 guesses in 1993 and then to 4.294 in 2017, but by then AI was on to a bigger game.

Backgammon is a two-player board game of model warfare (the name means "little war") won by clearing a player's "soldiers" off the board. Rolling dice adds an element of chance to the game, but player strategy is important regardless of the toss of the dice. By 1979, a computer program named BKG 9.8 had defeated Luigi Villa, the reigning backgammon world champion.

Progress in other games was slow but steady. IBM scientist Arthur Samuel invented a way for a game-playing program to improve by playing itself, a strategy often employed by AI today. By 1994, a program called Chinook by Canadian Jonathan Schaeffer was playing human champions to a draw—checkers has been shown to be a "no-win" game if players do not make an error.

But the AI that made the biggest impression was IBM's Deep Blue™ chess program. In 1997, Deep Blue defeated Russian world champion Gary Kasparov in a highly publicized match. Soon, chess was not much of a challenge for AI. In 2017, the AlphaZero™ program taught itself to play chess in less than a day, then beat all existing chess-playing computer programs. In the end, the chess challenge had disappeared, and the AI efforts moved on to the other games.

Othello®, or Reversi, a complex game of token-flipping on an 8x8 board also fell in 1995. Scrabble® fell to a program named Quackle™ in 2006, a notable moment that shifted AI from the world of chess pieces and play tokens to the world of language.

As impressive as these gains were, they involved games with limited appeal and few truly accomplished experts. IBM's Watson took on the highly popular television game show "answer-in-the-form-of-a-question" *Jeopardy!* in 2011 and beat every former champion. The only concession to the machine was the elimination of audio and video clues (answers) because Watson had no real audio or video capabilities.

The human champions of the game of Go, once considered to be the most unbeatable by any form of AI, fell to AI's AlphaGo™ from DeepMind® in 2016. Of course, the next year, the latest version beat the old version easily. One game featured an early move considered bizarre by any human Go player—a move that turned out to be important later in the game. Human ways of thinking do not apply to AI, leaving human competitors frustrated.

The year 2017 also saw AI winning at the card game poker. A game of bluff and dare, poker should have been hard for AI to master, especially without the ability to watch the faces of other players, which is how most big poker winners pick up on a "tell" that indicates a bluff or challenge.

Lately, AI has been used in fighter jet dogfighting simulations. In that arena, AI pilots perform maneuvers that frighten human pilots to a high degree. Instead of seeking a position above and behind a target, AIs tend to fly face-to-face in an aerial game of "chicken" that any human pilot would consider suicidal. Yet, AIs have no real life to lose.

OPENAI AND CHATGPT

The latest development in AI is the main reason that interest in and use of AI has exploded over the past few years. The interest was sparked by the release of the free AI chatbot app ChatGPT on November 30, 2022. ChatGPT was developed by OpenAI™, an AI research organization founded in December of 2015 by some of the largest tech companies in the world and their leaders.

ChatGPT is based on LLMs that enable users to prompt the chatbot to direct an interactive conversation to produce new images, text, summarizations, and other types of content. The conversation can be varied by user prompting for output length, format, style, language, creative span, and level of detail. ChatGPT is a generative pretrained transformer (GPT) that uses OpenAI's proprietary models but is fine-tuned by supervised learning and reinforcement learning based on user feedback.

In little more than a month, ChatGPT had over 100 million registered users. A "freemium" (free and premium) structure now exists that offers more and better services to paying users. More tiers are possible in the future.

Competing models, all GPTs based on LLMs, include Poe.ai¨, Gemini¨, Claude¨, Llama¨, Ernie¨, Microsoft Copilot¨, and more.

AI TOOLS FOR ALL

The release of ChatGPT unleashed a torrent of free apps that offered all kinds of services. This is not an exclusive list, but it is representative of the extent that AI has already entered people's lives. This list only scratches the surface of what is available, and mainly for free.

- **DALL-E 3**™ is an app offered as part of ChatGPT for image creation, also from the OpenAI team. It can create absolutely mind-bending images from a text description. The prompt can be as simple as "draw a pumpkin" to as complex as "draw a pumpkin that has been transformed into Cinderella's magical coach, along with four white horses and a human attendant."

- **GFP-GAN**™ is an app from the Chinese company Tencent for photo restoration. Older photographs created with analog cameras and existing as negatives and paper prints tend to fade with age or have scratches, streaks, or other flaws introduced by handling and the passage of time. These types of apps can use AI to "fill in the gaps" in the photo where time has damaged the original.

- **Copy AI**™ is an app intended for marketing teams that employ copywriting to use in advertisements for products. Prompted to explore a given topic, the app can generate content, especially intended to be used on blogs, social media, or with videos. Related apps include Microcopy™ (generate headlines and slogans), Speedwrite (generate enhanced sentences), Hemingway (generate clear and bold text), and others.

- **Lumen5**™ is an app for video creation. In addition to varied template and output format options for social media or Web sites, the app can generate a complete video based on uploaded images and a text transcript. If you do not have your own images, you can use the ones provided in the app.

- **Lalal.ai**™ is an audio splitter app that can isolate a song's vocals from the instrumentation or break out individual elements like drums or keyboards from the "stem" audio. It does not matter if the audio is contemporary, from the glory days of rock 'n roll, or from the Big Band era or older.

Similar apps existed before AI came along. However, the addition of AI to image or text generation adds a new level of excellence that older apps could not achieve before.

AI AS AN "ALIEN INTELLIGENCE"

One thing that characterizes the success of AI as a game-playing and simulation juggernaut is the ability of these software modules to make non-human moves and execute strategies that humans would instinctively avoid. That weird Go move is the prime example, but it would include the tendency to engage in head-on (face-to-face) fighter-jet dogfighting instead of seeking a position above and behind. All the human losers, from chess players to fighter pilots, said they could not believe the moves that their AI opponents made.

Perhaps this is a warning that we have invented AI as a form of alien intelligence we cannot fathom, let alone hope to control. The stakes in the game are different for AI than for mere humans. Humans are loath to succeed at an activity if the outcome is the death of the participant, except in very restricted circumstances. Yet all AI has to worry about is a reboot.

NEURAL NETWORKS FOR DEEP LEARNING

A computer-based neural network is meant to mirror in silicon the way that neurons in the brain are organized and function. In the brain, neurons look like a tree with roots and branches. The three main parts are axons, a body (or soma), and dendrites, which are like the roots, trunk, and branches of a tree. When the electrical activity in the neuron spikes to a certain level, the body of the neuron becomes active and passes the signal on to other neurons. The neurons in the brain are not directly connected as in a computer but separated by a gap called a *synapse*. The actual function of brain neurons is much more complex, but that is the basic idea.

With a computer neural network, a neural *node* receives input from other neural nodes. The effect of each input is controlled by the value of a *weight*, which can be positive or negative. If the sum of the weights exceeds a certain value, the node becomes active and passes a signal on to the next *layer* of neuron nodes. The weights have some initial value and then are adjusted as the neural network learns what the output should be for a given input condition.

The human brain has about 10^{11} neurons, and each neuron, due to the branching nature of the axons and dendrites, has about 10^4 weights. See the appendix for more on these power of ten values. Computer neural networks do not yet approach these levels of complexity, but they soon might.

In contrast to human neurons, computer neural network nodes are simple to understand. Each node has three values that determine the value of the output (y) of the node, which is usually 0 or 1 but can have any value the creator of the neural network wants, of course. The three parameters are:

- **b:** This is the *bias* of the node, a number that can be positive or negative and helps to decide if the overall effect of the node is going to be inhibitive or not.

- **x:** This is the number of the input link being considered for this node. A node has from 1 to *i* inputs. The ith input to the node is x_i.

- **w:** This is the weight assigned to the input. The weight of the ith input to the node is w_i.

The processing that takes place at each node of the neural network is given by:

$$y = b + \text{sum}(x_i w_i), \text{ where the sum is from 1 to } i.$$

This can be read as "the output is equal to the sum of the bias plus the sum of the products of each input times the weight assigned to that input." If the total computed for *y* exceeds a certain configured value, the neuron passes a value on the nodes that it is connected to.

In most neural networks today, the computation does not yield a value for *y* directly but for a related value *z*. Then *z* is used to find *y*, which is a value between 0 and 1 on a *sigmoid curve*. Sigmoid curves are favored because they have simple *mathematical derivatives*, which makes learning easier.

The bias is often neglected in discussions of AI. However, adjusting the bias in even a small neural network can lead to some odd results if you know how the network is structured. For example, experiments have shown that raising the bias on certain connections by a factor of 10 can lead to the node the connections converge on showing up in strange places in the output.

Suppose the bias for connections concerning the Brooklyn Bridge is increased by 10 times in a neural network for language processing. We will call this arrangement a large language model (LLM) later on in this chapter. With all Brooklyn Bridge biases set to 10 times their previous values, when asked to compose a letter to a girlfriend, the AI output text now recalls a romantic walk across the Brooklyn Bridge that never happened. A cake recipe suggests that mixing the ingredients on the Brooklyn Bridge makes the birthday cake taste better. A plan for a trip to Atlanta would be better if it included a side trip to the Brooklyn Bridge, an attraction about 750 miles away, and so on. The potential for mischief should be alarming. Even if unplanned, at less absurd levels, the idea that this LLM could now be spouting silliness that might seem logical and would be all but undetectable should be a concern.

The general idea behind neural node operation is shown in Figure 6.2. The sum symbol in mathematics is the Greek letter sigma (Σ).

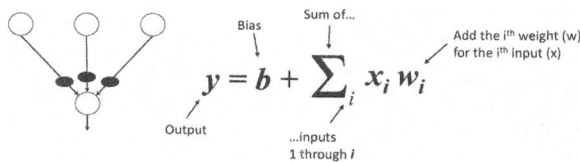

$$y = b + \sum_i x_i\, w_i$$

Bias

Sum of...

Add the ith weight (w) for the ith input (x)

Output

...inputs 1 through i

FIGURE 6.2. Computer neural network processing.

It is important to keep this processing at each node in mind because in most diagrams of neural networks, the processing that takes place at each node is not included. By convention, neural nodes are shown as circles, and the connections are shown as arrows leading from input to output. The nodes are organized into layers, with one layer starting things off as the *input layer* and one layer ending the process as the *output layer*. In between are one or more *hidden layers*, so-called because they are not generally visible during operation as the input and output layers are.

A simple but complete neural network is shown in Figure 6.3.

We can conclude this basic introduction to neural networks with an example that Geoff Hinton used in his classes on "Neural Networks for Machine Learning" at the University of Toronto and other online sources.

Suppose, Hinton begins, that a cafeteria serves portions of fish and chips (in the United States they are called fries) and the ketchup used as a condiment for them. All that we know initially is the full price of the meal, perhaps $8.50 (Canadian, but that makes no difference). You want to know what the price of each of the three items is, but for whatever reason, you can only vary the number of portions of each to try and figure out the price of each individual component.

Perhaps surprisingly, you can use a simple neural network to figure out the price of each portion of fish, chips, or ketchup packet. What you pay is just

Input Layer   Hidden Layers   Output Layer

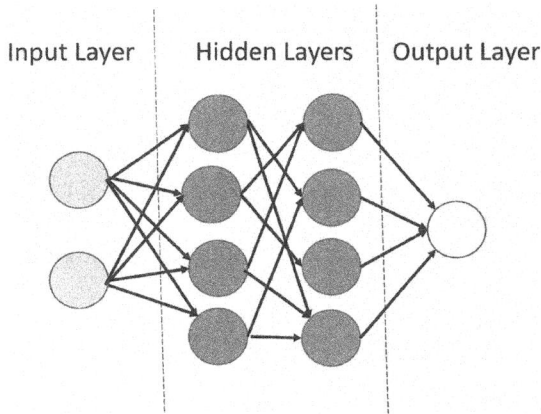

FIGURE 6.3. A complete but trivial neural network.

the sum of the price times the number of portions purchased. In this case, the weight is the price of each menu item:

$$\text{Amount paid} = x_{\text{portions of fish}} \, w_{\text{price of fish}} + x_{\text{portions of chips}} \, w_{\text{price of chips}} + x_{\text{portions of ketchup}} \, w_{\text{price of ketchup}}$$

This is identical to the calculation at a node in a neural network with three inputs and the bias equal to zero (that is, no bias at all).

Suppose the actual price of each item (in cents) is 150 for fish, 50 for chips, and 100 for ketchup (it is an example). We do not know this at all, but we want the neural network to "learn" these prices. We start with a random guess for the price of each thing you can buy, say, 50 cents each. Then, each day, as we vary the portions purchased, we can adjust the prices to better fit the total paid.

Here is how the first few "learning steps" would go. One day, you buy 2 portions of fish, 5 portions of chips, and 3 packets of ketchup. You pay 850 cents for the meal. If each price is the same, 50, then what you should have paid is:

2 fish ($2 \times 50 = 100$) + 5 chips ($5 \times 50 = 250$) +
3 ketchup ($3 \times 50 = 150$) = 100 + 250 + 150 = 500 cents.

This is shown in Figure 6.4.

Price of meal = 850 cents

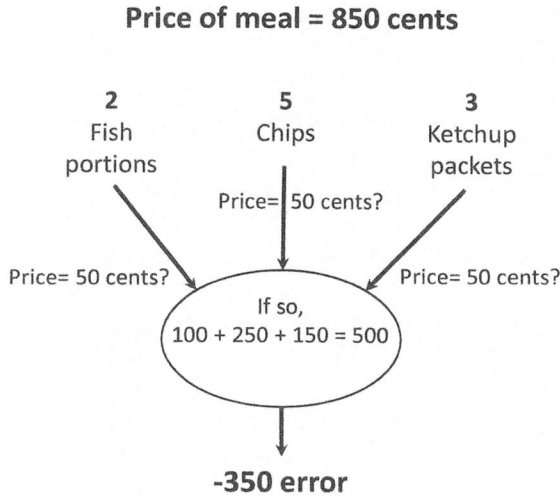

FIGURE 6.4. Deep learning for the cafeteria neural network.

But the receipt has 850 cents. We are -350 cents off. This is called the *residual error*. Therefore, we can adjust the prices (weights) and try again on Day 2. There is a formula called the "delta rule" for learning that we can apply, but that is beyond the scope of this introduction. Let us just adjust the prices like this: +20, +50, and +30, up from the initial 50/50/50 values, given price weights of 70, 100, and 80.

Now, that same 2/5/3 item combination gives the following result:

2 fish ($2 \times 70 = 140$) + 5 chips ($5 \times 100 = 500$) +
3 ketchups ($3 \times 80 = 240$) = $140 + 500 + 240 = 880$ cents.

Notice that we are closer to the total of 850 and now have a residual error of +30. However, remember that the actual values for the prices are fish = 150, chips = 50, and ketchup = 100. We were actually closer to the correct price for chips with the initial guess of 50 than the adjusted value of 100.

Nevertheless, repeated applications of the delta rule and new information gained by varying the portion purchased allow even this simple neural network to "learn" the correct prices. Varying the purchased amounts helps to make sure that we are not mimicking the total with plausible, but incorrect, prices. In other words, 2 portions at 150 is the same total as 3 portions at 100, but only one can be correct.

Note that this knowledge is gained not by a direct path to the answer but by "circling in" on it; first it may be too high, then maybe too low.

LARGE LANGUAGE MODELS AND GENAI

LLMs form a special class of neural networks for deep learning. In this case, the neural network LLM is designed to understand human language, generate text, and respond using human-like wording. LLMs cannot drive your car, find the soldiers hidden in photos of the forest, or keep drones from colliding with each other, but they can write a book, answer a question, do your homework, write an essay, translate very well between many languages, and perform almost any task using words required by the user. LLMs are the foundation of the chatbots and related apps that have taken over the Internet in the past few years.

LLMs are usually very deep, many-layered neural networks that have been trained on massive amounts of textual data. This data is frequently supplied by turning the LLM loose on large portions of all the words available on Web sites, blogs, social media postings, and comments on the global public Internet. Each word forms a parameter or token for the LLM.

Oddly, there is no firm definition of what makes an LLM "large." One reason is that the term "large" can refer to not only the model's size of the dataset it has been trained on but also the number of parameters incorporated into the model. LLMs today can have millions, billions, or *trillions* of parameters, all of which adjust the weights used when training neural networks.

LLMs are optimized by training them to predict the next word in a sequence. This makes sense because humans form words one after the other when writing or speaking. Yet, even with this simple method of training and learning ("What word is most likely to come after the word 'large'?"), LLMs can create amazingly complex and coherent output.

Because LLMs generate text, LLMs are the basis for a form of AI called *generative AI,* or just *GenAI.* LLMs work fine "out of the box" when trained only on Internet content. Yet, in many cases, organizations want their LLM app to do more with text or data that are of a more private nature. In this case, their GenAI app can add *retrieval augmented generation* (RAG) to their AI app to make the output more relevant. For example, a hardware tech company can add its product documentation database to the LLMs with RAG, allowing the output to be more tuned to the company's products than other apps.

Where GenAI with RAG fits in with all aspects of AI is shown in Figure 6.5.

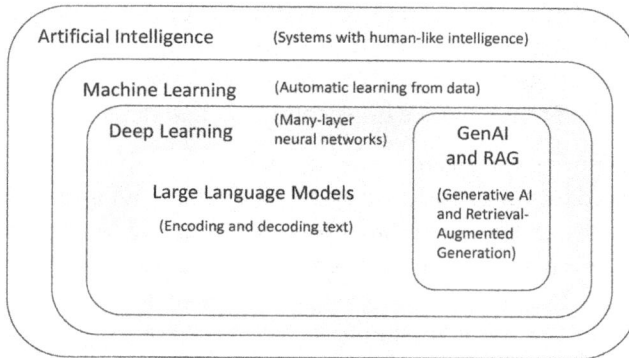

FIGURE 6.5. Where GenAi and RAG fit in with AI in general.

Transformer Architecture

One reason LLMs have been so successful is due to the underlying architecture of the LLM, which is called the *transformer*. The transformer allows the LLM to pay attention selectively to the different parts of the input when making its predictions. This lets the LLM handle the complexities and nuances of human language much better. Recall that human language is full of seeming contradictions like "stay right here and follow me" or "shut up and tell me what happened."

The transformer architecture is a deep neural network architecture that was introduced in the 2017 paper "Attention Is All You Need" (*https://arxiv.org/ abs/1706.03762*). The original transformer was developed for machine translation, translating English texts to German and French. The basic transformer architecture is shown in Figure 6.6.

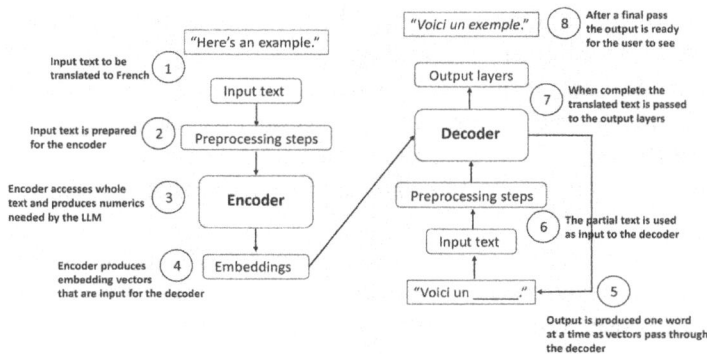

FIGURE 6.6. Basic transformer operation.

Figure 6.6 is a simplified picture of the original transformer architecture. There are eight basic steps to transformer operation in LLMs. The figure shows how this structure is used to translate a phrase, in this case "Here is an example (of…)" from English to the French "Voicé un exemple…". The steps are:

1. The user inputs the text to be translated into English.
2. The input text is prepared for the encoder by breaking up the input into smaller units called *tokens,* which can be more easily processed by the LLM. The input is also converted to numeric patterns called *vectors* that are used to construct the output.
3. The encoder takes that entire input test and completes the coding process by making the vectors into *embeddings*.
4. The encoder produces the *embedding vectors* that are used for input for the decoder.
5. The decoder operates one word at a time to produce the French output. The partial output text is cycled through the decoder multiple times until the entire input text has been processed. The intermediate text shown in the figure is "Voicé un _____".
6. The partial text is used as input to subsequent cycles through the decoder, subject to the same token-vector-embedding rules as other input.
7. When the entire input text has generated output, the completed result is passed to the neutral network output layers, which perform a final pass on the output.
8. The complete translation is passed to the user: "Voicé un exemple…".

Note that the transformer architecture consists of two major modules: an encoder and a decoder. The encoder module processes input text and encodes it into a series of numerical vector representations. Vectors represent the contextual information of the input. On the output side, the decoder module takes the encoded vectors and generates the output text.

For example, in the translation task illustrated, the encoder parses the text from the source language into vectors, and the decoder decodes these vectors to generate text in the target language. Both the encoder and decoder consist of many layers in a neural network. They are connected by what is called a *self-attention mechanism*.

Today, this basic transformer architecture is most often seen in two forms. One is called BERT, which is short for *bidirectional encoder representation from transformers*. BERT is used to encode the input texts into numeric formats that can be used by the LLM to learn how languages are put together. BERT excels at training the LLM to understand how to summarize or categorize documents. Some social media apps use BERT to detect unacceptable content.

The other type of transformer is the GPT model, which stands for *Generative Pretrained Transformer*. GPT excels at text generation, of course, but is also how the output text looks so natural.

Tokens and Vectors and Embeddings

Once you get beyond the basic structures of neural networks and LLMs and start to investigate how they learn and operate, a good background in mathematics is essential. Naturally, nothing is done by hand today, but by programs mainly written in Python or some other easy-to-formulate high-level language. These programs will employ tools like Mathematica™, PyTorch™, or TensorFlow™ to perform the weight modification and backward propagation calculations needed to improve the neural network's performance. TensorFlow is popular because it is a free, open-source software library especially intended for AI and machine learning. Originally developed by Google™, it can be used in Python or C++ under the Apache 2.0 license. In spite of that, the mathematics for deep learning and GPT-based LLMs is daunting, even for those with an engineering background.

Nevertheless, an overview of three key mathematical terms can be understood without digging into the details of how they operate. The three terms are tokens, vectors, and embeddings. These terms once were used almost exclusively with LLMs, but now are used when considering AI apps for images and videos.

Tokens

The first thing that an LLM does with a query or sample of text is to break it down into *tokens*. An LLM token can be a word, or a part of a word (called a subword), a single character, or a punctuation mark such as an exclamation mark or period. It all depends on how the app implements the tokenization step. The number and density of the tokens that an LLM can juggle are measures of the power of the LLM.

The input text is converted into tokens that the encoder can eventually use, and after processing, the decoder takes these tokens and converts them back into text that can be read by humans. The LLM does not understand tokens directly because computers and programs only deal with numbers. Therefore, the tokens are used to generate numerical *vectors* that the LLM can use to process the text.

Vectors

A vector used by an LLM is a single-dimensional array that puts the token in context. This is a bit different than the definition of a vector encountered in mathematics and physics. A vector has both a direction and a magnitude, and they are used to describe a force, or a velocity, or objects that cannot be described by a single number, like a mass.

However, in LLMs, vectors convert the tokens into numbers that can be used to compute the output. Seen in isolation, which renders them useless, a vector looks like a row in a table of numbers like -3.245656 or 9.45674 that can have thousands of columns. One of the things that LLMs try to do is convert as many of the columns in these rows as possible to zero, just to make the processing a lot faster and simpler.

Once the input text is represented as vectors, there is still another step before the transformer gets to work. The vectors are collectively coded as a set of vector *embeddings*.

Embeddings

Embeddings are higher-dimensional vectors that represent the semantics (meanings) of words, sentences, or even whole documents when summaries are needed. Essentially, embeddings are tokens plus their meanings, stored in a vector database that the LLM can process. Without embeddings, LLMs could not summarize text, detect emotions in a document, answer questions, or perform any of the other tasks we expect from LLMs today.

It is important to realize that all embeddings are vectors, but not all vectors are embeddings. Embeddings have learned the semantics of the language, but vectors have not.

The Next Word Is...

One of the essential lessons about GenAI LLM operation is that the output is generated one word at a time. This process is illustrated in Figure 6.7.

Generating only the next word based on the probability of the word appearing in the sources used to train the LLM is one reason that errors called *hallucinations* creep into GenAI output. In other words, a string of words based on probabilities might generate text that never appears anywhere in the source text material. This is part of the creative process, of course, but is also a concern when it generates a lot of counter-factual information.

There are several crucial LLM parameters that the creators of AI apps can use to control the output of the GenAI session. The most important ones are:

Max Output: This determines the maximum amount of text that the LLM can generate. The number is usually in tokens, which can be words, characters, or sub-units of words like prefixes or suffixes.

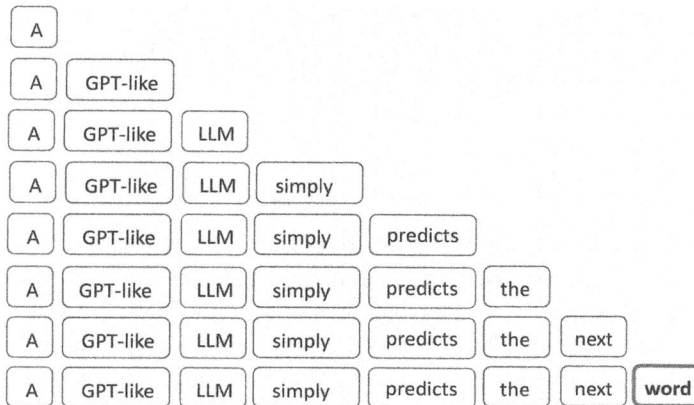

FIGURE 6.7. GenAI LLMs operate by predicting the next word, one word at a time.

Temperature: This sets the amount of randomness the LLM uses when selecting the next word in the output sequence. A lower temperature sticks to the more probable words, such as referencing an "enormous *elephant*." A higher temperature setting is more creative and selects words with lower probability, like an "enormous *mouse*." Temperature is a more global LLM parameter than the two following, which can be used for more fine-tuning of the output.

Top-k: This limits the next word selection to only the top "k" likely possibilities. This can be read as "Use only the top k probabilities for next word choice." A value of $k = 5$, for example, considered the first 5 probabilities for words following the current word. The next words in a sequence all have a probability of occurring, based on the frequency of the wording in the source texts. There can be hundreds of different probabilities, or thousands, and top-k serves as a cutoff point along this axis. A high top-k generates more creative and surprising text as choices extend to lower possibilities like "enormous *mouse*." A low top-k value makes sure that the LLM sticks to the more common strings of words, like "enormous *elephant*."

Top-p: This differs from Top-k in that Top-p uses a probability threshold "p" to determine the probability limit to the LLM output. You can read Top-p as "Use only the probabilities that add up to p for the next word choice." Words can be 50% probable next words, perhaps for the "enormous *elephant*" or 0.005% probable for the "enormous *mouse*." A Top-p of 0.5 considers only the 50% *elephant* possibility. The value would have to be 99.995 or higher to include the *mouse* possibility. A lower Top-p favors more predictable next words, while a higher Top-p value can generate more creative choices.

A lot of work currently done on LLMs is into ways to prevent or at least minimize the generation of these hallucinations. For more ways to learn about AI and LLMs, see the further reading for this chapter.

CURRENT IMPACT OF AI

For many of us today. AI is not only the future but also the present. AI shapes the work, lives, and families of many people around the world, not just those directly involved in AI or high tech. This list does not include facial recognition software used to watch others, often without their knowledge. Nor does it focus on countries where AI surveillance is used to watch monitor people's movements and associations. Here is a quick look at how AI is making a difference, and not always for the better, for humanity.

AI Impact on Making a Living

Many AI models rely on humans to assess their performance. The key to improvement is to gauge the extent of the error and try again. For example, humans must tag the images used as input for driverless cars. This allows the software in the car to learn to recognize the many types of street signs, pavement marking, traffic signals, and other methods of vehicle control that can vary widely around the world. The work is intense and time-consuming, and the pay rate is low. These labeling tasks are frequently outsourced to the poorer citizens of African nations and southern Asia.

Moreover, many social media platforms disallow posting objectionable content, mainly video. Yet somehow this content must be categorized and labeled, just like the pavement marking and speed limit signs for driverless cars. The psychic toll of viewing these often brutal images of abuse and death is formidable. Many people involved in this work suffer the same intense PTSD symptoms as soldiers in combat, but with none of the support systems others are entitled to.

AI Impact on Identity

The possibility of creating *deep fake* audio or video has existed for several years now. Deep fakes are created by AI but appear to be as real as the images that appear on the evening news or heard on a phone call. Someone's face can appear in a porn video, or be used to pretend a close relative has been kidnapped and a ransom paid for their release, or for any one of a myriad other purposes. Other forms of identity theft are possible with AI. A Zoom call with the CEO or a bank official might be manipulated to make the target reveal what they should not, such as passwords or account numbers.

The problem is that much of this activity is not yet illegal in many places. Not only that, but the victims have very little recourse to try and have offensive content removed from the Internet or validate the origin of a given communication over the Internet, which has no central control point. Once your identity has been stolen, it is not always a given that it can be restored to its rightful owner. There will be more of this in the next chapter.

AI Impact on Health

The health care system in the United States relies heavily on having health insurance to cover costs. Even in countries with nationalized healthcare, all tests and treatments are not always available to all patients.

Increasingly, organizations like insurance companies are using AI to decide if a medical procedure like an MRI or surgery is justified by the patient's medical history or care provider's assessment. If they decide not to pay for the procedure, the patient and doctor are likely to get only a code and canned message in the way of explanation. There is no one to call or complain to. The AI has denied your request and will likely deny an amended effort. Yet they wish you continued good health.

AI Impact on Freedom and "The System"

More and more local governments are using AI to try and identify people living within their boundaries, especially teenagers, as risks for becoming juvenile delinquents or adult criminals. Many use a kind of point system where scribbling graffiti or school truancy contributes a certain number of points to a person's permanent record. At some level, the points trigger an intervention by a social worker or other government representative.

In other places, AI might be used to determine if a family is eligible for benefits like food stamps or supplemental income. As with insurance determinations, there is no recourse for the subject when mistakes are made or circumstances change for the better or worse.

There seems to be no good way for these accumulated points to expire or for any kind of forgiveness for minor offenses to occur. Minorities are often the primary victims of these AI determinations. Once in "The System," there is little in the way of help to get out.

AI Impact on Work

Much has been written about the "gig economy" and how companies like Uber or Door Dash have apps that make it possible for people to supplement their income on their own time, or even full time. Less has been written about the fact that many of these apps are driven by AI, not human dispatchers.

Drivers have found a mistake in the mileage calculated for a delivery trip, which is used to determine compensation. Workers are always free to turn down jobs, but then the app could decide that they are not as reliable as someone nearby who takes all comers. If sudden changes in road conditions like floods affect delivery times, the worker is often blamed.

Companies have always tried to make sure that workers are working when they should. Keystroke monitors measured input, and workers sometimes fought back with "mouse jigglers" that made it seem that the worker was clicking on things when they were not at their work location at all. Naturally, AI soon learned to distinguish "real work" from this simulated environment.

AI Impact on Society

The bottom line for this chapter in particular and AI in general is just this: does generative AI actually create anything at all? Or is it just rattling words around to form a new but unenlightened version of what already exists?

The issue is most acute for GenAI and LLMs. These models are pre-trained on existing Internet content. The problem is that as GenAI makes more and more texts based on bits and pieces of existing Internet content, these texts get added to Web sites, are attached to emails, are published in online journals, and end up in books (not this one), and so end up essentially looping around and coming back to GenAI apps as if they were created from scratch by creative humans.

Perhaps what is needed for AI and modern robots is a kind of universal safe word. One word that, once uttered, causes all AI apps within hearing to cease operation. Imagine a world where AI-controlled work and health care and so on can be countered by someone saying "Walter" or some word that all AI apps must obey.

WHAT COMES NEXT

There is only one major topic area left to examine before coming full circle and ending up back in the automobile on the road that started this whole inquiry.

This topic is related to AI and several of the other topics investigated in this book, such as mobile telephony.

Concerns about security and privacy cannot be exaggerated today. They are really two sides of the same coin. Security involves the safeguarding of data from being accessed by those who do not have the right to access it and who might abuse it. Privacy implies the safeguarding of personal data that is stored online or in a cloud data center but has relevance and value only to a small set of organizations, such as a hospital.

Security is a universal concern, while privacy is more personal.

SECURITY AND PRIVACY

OVERVIEW

This book opened with a look at how, even in an automobile filled with commuters heading to or from work or a family heading off for a summer vacation, like as not, there are multiple Internet connections in progress. Not only can there be connections for office-related projects or streaming video or gaming, but some might be for the automobile itself to report on the condition of its position, engine, tires, or other aspects of its operation. Now we have come full circle, from the bits leaving the automobile to the wireless network that carries them to the packet optical fiber network that carries them to and from the data centers and server farms that hold the bits needed, and all the way back from the servers to the client endpoints that initialed the exchange in the first place.

Here is how we got to this final chapter. We have investigated all six other major parts of all modern networks and their infrastructures. These are:

- The need for almost everyone in the world to have multiple Internet connections to their home, office, car, and business to work, plan their lives, and entertain themselves. This requires much more than the simple 32-bit address space invented for IPv4. We need IPv6.

- IPv6 provides enough address space to give every molecule in the solar system its own IPv6 address. It also simplifies a lot of the added protocols that IPv4 required and does away with some that were seldom used or security risks (like directed broadcasts).

- Packet optical networks based on new fibers and techniques like WDM make fiber links more effective for backhauling data to the cloud data center and delivering streams of data to mobile (and fixed) endpoints.

- The cloud data center is where all the information flowing to and from users congregates to be analyzed, stored, and used as the basis for future actions. The cloud data center, public or private, is also the location where much of modern AI processing takes place. However, not all the information and data originate with users. Much of it comes from the machines themselves, including the embedded processors in all modern vehicles.

- The data stored in cloud data centers comes from more than simply humans and their browsing online. A large chunk comes from modern factories as part of Industry 4.0. This movement makes heavy use of the IoT and M2M technology.

- As time goes on, it is more and more likely that the information exchanged over the Internet comes from or is going to one of the AI apps that are popping up all over the world today.

WHAT YOU WILL LEARN

Much of the integrity of the entire system depends on the strength of the security and privacy methods used to shield users from others with bad intentions. Even if personal data is not abused for coercion or outright blackmail, users should be able to include personal information for a health condition or to secure a bank loan without worrying that the privacy of this information is at risk.

In this chapter, we explore the history and development of the cryptographic techniques that make Internet commerce practical and, for the most part, safe. As usual, all of the major terms and concepts are presented for the reader to explore further.

One note of caution is required. It is nearly impossible to discuss modern cryptographic techniques without a lot of mathematics. However, mathematical jargon is kept to an absolute minimum, and so are the equations.

The topics covered include:

- Mathematicians and computers
- Two thousand years of cryptography and cipher systems
- The revolution of the 1970s: RSA and Diffie-Hellman
- ECC

- SSL and SSH
- Privacy in a nutshell

Topics related to cryptography but outside the scope of this chapter include blockchain and bitcoin mining. As important as these topics are, the emphasis here is on the foundation of security and privacy.

MATHEMATICIANS AND COMPUTERS

The first thing to know about this chapter is that the vast majority of readers will not be able to understand much of the mathematics covered. It is not the fault of any particular educational system, although there is much to say about that aspect of modern education. It is more the fault of the mathematicians themselves, whose work since Isaac Newton and Gottfried Leibniz independently invented calculus almost at the same time has gone off in directions that would astound geometers like Euclid. Until recently, we did not even know numbers could do that.

Mathematicians think differently than the rest of us, and even other mathematicians. For example, a group of engineers from Bell Labs in New Jersey once were out celebrating a successful project when they tried to find the address of a house party at Rutgers in New Brunswick. They recalled the street, but not the house number, until the mathematician in the slightly tipsy group spoke up and said, "It is 97."

"How did you remember that?" the others asked. Simple, the mathematician told them: "It is the highest prime number less than 100."

A more famous story about Indian mathematician Srinivasa Ramanujan appears in British mathematician G. H. Hardy's book *A Mathematician's Apology*. When Hardy visited Ramanujan in the hospital, he remarked that the taxi he took, number 1729, was a "rather dull" number. Ramahujan, most likely being tested as to his state of mind, immediately told Hardy that 1729 was actually very interesting, in that it was the "smallest number expressible as the sum of two cubes in two different ways" ($x^3 + y^3$).

Oddly, after World War II, mathematicians were reluctant to embrace the new digital computers as a tool for mathematics. Computers were and are mainly an engineering tool, concerned not with the circumferences of a circle to within the diameter of an atom but whether or not the plane will fly or the bridge will fall down. Pi is not 3.14 or 22/7, but a never-ending, nonrepeating ratio between the circumference of a circle and its radius.

By the way, the answer to the Hardy-Ramanujan number 1729 is the sum of the cubes of 12 + 1 and 9 + 10. Mathematicians play with numbers the way that poets play with rhymes or novelists play with metaphors.

With this as a background, please keep in mind that this chapter is not going to teach you any mathematics or how to use complex formulas (there are a few of those). The chapter uses cryptographic keys but does not derive them. It is enough to say that they "satisfy certain relationships" and let it go at that. The good news is that there appear to be an infinite number of keys that can be used in the cryptographic systems described, and that they cannot be easily broken.

Still, readers should keep in mind that what is outlined is not always the way that things are implemented today, especially when it comes to newer techniques like elliptic curve cryptology (ECC). The main concern here is basic understanding, not precision of execution. Much of what follows is more like an analogy or metaphor for the heavy-duty mathematics involved.

TWO THOUSAND YEARS OF CRYPTOGRAPHY AND CIPHER SYSTEMS

Much of warfare, politics, and diplomacy in the ancient world revolved around sending secret messages back and forth. Face-to-face communications could be handled with a whisper, but cryptography was developed to be used by generals and armies in the field to communicate securely. The classic "We both attack the bad guys at dawn" scenario is the foundation of many problems in network protocols, timing, authorization, and, of course, cryptography.

Julius Caesar used a simple letter-shift system (C stands for A, D stands for B, and so on) that is still called the Caesar cipher. This worked fine in a world of limited literacy, but as education reached more and more, cipher systems added multiple alphabets that could be scrambled and more lengthy keys to encrypt and decrypt a message. By the dawn of the modern era and the European Renaissance, ciphers could use substitution (A is Q) or transposition (scramble the letters of the message) or both in the same system.

At the same time that the users of cipher systems were getting more complex and sophisticated, so were the codebreakers. Codebreaking became an art during World War II, when computers were first used to break the famous German Enigma code. The codebreakers were helped immensely by knowing the method (the Enigma machine) and probable content (military information) that the intercepted messages contained. Codebreaking is much more difficult without any hint of context, as the end of this chapter shows.

It is important to note that these "classical" codes and cipher systems were all *symmetrical.* That is, deciphering is simply reversing the process used for enciphering. These methods depend on both the sender and receiver having a *shared secret key* between them. The secret key can be very complex or lengthy, but a related issue is how to securely distribute the shared keys to all the people who need them.

After all, if it was suspected that a secret key had been compromised and was known to outsiders, the best thing to do is change the key. Yet how do you do that over a compromised system? A firm rule used to be that you should not distribute keys over the same network that they were supposed to protect. For years, a major computer vendor flew security personnel to a central location where they were handed an envelope that contained the daily keys to be used for the coming month. This method was enormously expensive and prone to errors, including lost and stolen envelopes.

Even if some genius managed to figure out the key for Tuesday, they would be using a different key on Wednesday. Frequent key changes are a crucial aspect of all cryptosystems. This is where the concept of the *work factor* needed to break a key comes into play. If it takes two years to break a code, the *time value of the information* exchanged should have shrunk to almost zero.

The roots of cipher systems in warfare are often glimpsed in many forms. As recently as the early 1990s in the USA, the 2008 book *Blown to Bits* by Hal Abelson, Ken Ledeen, and Harry Lewis notes that encryption researchers had to register as "international arms dealers," and ciphers were classified as "munitions."

EVERYTHING CHANGED IN 1977

The year 1977 is now considered the dividing line between the "classical" and "modern" eras of cryptography. This is because two related discoveries occurred in the years before 1977 that changed everything.

Research had been intense into cryptography in the era of powerful computers for two reasons, both related to the glaring weaknesses of shared secret cryptography. First, the method used and the key could not be concealed for long. Even if the device was a machine like the Enigma, computers could emulate the physical device, which is how the brute-force methods broke the Enigma code in the first place. Second, both parties had to keep the shared key secret.

Therefore, one goal was to somehow invent a system where both the method and the key could be made public, and yet the system could still work. It sounds counter-intuitive, yet by the early 1970s, the first mutterings in mathematics journals about "unbreakable codes" appeared. There are true stories about how governments tried to keep the lid on these advances, some more successfully than others, due to the obvious military advantages such codes would give one nation over a rival. However, like all sensational discoveries, things did not stay quiet for long.

All of these methods in the journals revolved around *asymmetrical* mathematical functions based on the interplay between prime numbers, powers, and modular mathematics. Prime numbers are those, like 97, that can only be divided without leftovers (remainders) by dividing by 1 or the prime itself (97). In other words, if you have 97 jellybeans, you can only share them evenly if you eat them all yourself or share them among 97 people. Powers are just formed by multiplying the same number by itself a certain number of times. Therefore, 7^3 is the same as $7 \times 7 \times 7 = 343$. modular arithmetic is like we see using a 12-hour clock. On a clock, 10 a.m. plus 6 is not 16 o'clock but 4 p.m. In the modular clock world, whenever a result exceeds the "mod" number 12, we can *normalize* it again by dividing by the "normalizer" number 12 and using the remainder.

Computers, of course, were needed to shuffle all these numbers around. The new methods were based on what came to be known as "one-way" trapdoor techniques. They were not really one-way, but they were easy to do and much harder to undo. These trapdoor functions had been around for years, and geniuses such as Leonardo Da Vinci had used them to conceal some of his discoveries.

Here is an example of a trapdoor function. First, enter the text letters of a message into a spreadsheet column, one letter per cell. Then alphabetize the column into a second column. The second column contains the original message, but with all the letters in alphabetical order. It is very hard for even a short message, and almost impossible for a longer message, to recover the original text from the alphabetized list without knowing what you started with.

An example of this alphabetical trapdoor function is shown in Figure 7.1.

As mentioned, alphabetized text was used as a kind of "digital signature phrase" by DaVinci and others. You could back up your discovery claim or priority by decoding a message sent in a letter the year before, for example, long before a rival had uncovered the same fact.

Now readers have all the tools needed to understand the twin discoveries of the mid-1970s that created the field of modern cryptography. The two discoveries are called Rivest-Shamir-Adleman asymmetric public key encryption (RSA for short) and Diffie-Hellman key exchange. These names might not tell the whole story of the discoveries, but the names remain due to the nature of scientific publication.

```
T                    A
H                    A
I                    E
S                    E
I                    G
S                    H
A                    I
M                    I
E                    M
S                    S
S                    S
A                    S
G                    S
E                    T
```

FIGURE 7.1. Alphabetical trapdoor function.

RSA

RSA is a type of asymmetric encryption that uses two different but linked large prime number keys to encode and decode messages. One key is called the *public key* and can be known to everyone, and the other key is called the *private key* and must remain secret in order for the RSA system to work. In RSA cryptography, both the public and the private keys can encrypt a message. The opposite key from the one used to encrypt a message is used to decrypt it, which is why the system is considered to be asymmetric.

The general idea behind RSA is shown in Figure 7.2.

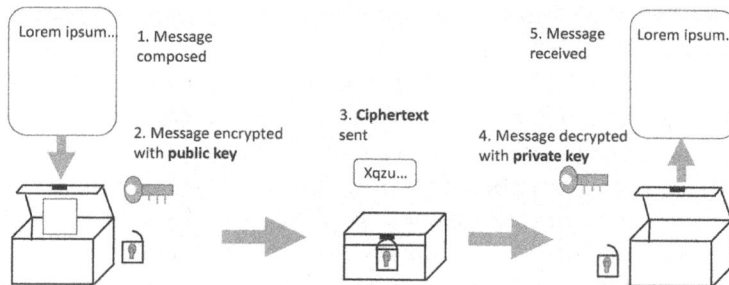

Lorem ipsum... 1. Message composed

5. Message received Lorem ipsum...

2. Message encrypted with **public key**

3. **Ciphertext** sent

Xqzu...

4. Message decrypted with **private key**

FIGURE 7.2. How asymmetrical encryption works.

There are five steps illustrated:

1. The sender composes a message in plaintext (shown as "Lorem ipsum...").
2. The message is encrypted with the receiver's public key, which is known to all and can be published online or recorded on the receiver's Web site.
3. The secure ciphertext is sent to the receiver (shown as "Xqzu...").
4. The message is decrypted by the receiver with the receiver's private key.
5. The message is now back in plaintext: "Lorem ipsum...".

The system was developed in 1977 by Ron Rivest, Adi Shamir, and Leonard Adleman, all of MIT. Together, they constructed the RSA algorithm, which brought Diffie-Hellman key exchange mathematics into the real world.

DIFFIE-HELLMAN KEY EXCHANGE

Diffie-Hellman came along in 1976, which was before RSA in 1977, but they are used together. This way to exchange keys securely over an unsecure network (the network might also be insecure, but that is a psychological condition). With Diffie-Hellman, an organization did not have to fly everyone to a certain location to hand out keys, but just send them over the unsecure Internet.

Diffie-Hellman was the product of Whitfield Diffie, 32, who had been obsessed with the problem since he was at MIT, and Martin Hellman, 31, first of the Bronx High School Science, then Stanford. Also working on the method was a graduate student named Ralph Merkle, 24, who sometimes gets credit for his contribution but often not.

Diffie-Hellman's paper called "New Directions in Cryptography" (an understatement) was "a way for Alice and Bob, without any prior arrangement, to agree on a secret key, known only to the two of them, by using messages between them that are not secret at all."

It was only revealed in 1997 that in England, the British Government Communication Headquarters (GCHQ) did all of these two years ahead of Diffie and Hellman. This work was done by James Ellis, Clifford Cocks, and Malcolm Williamson, but the British were better at controlling the knowledge at the time.

How Diffie-Hellman key exchange works in principle is shown in Figure 7.3. The idea is often illustrated by using a box with two keys or other types of metaphors, but this simple figure works just as well. In a lot of crypto books, senders are named "Alice" and receivers are named "Bob," but here they are just a sender and a receiver.

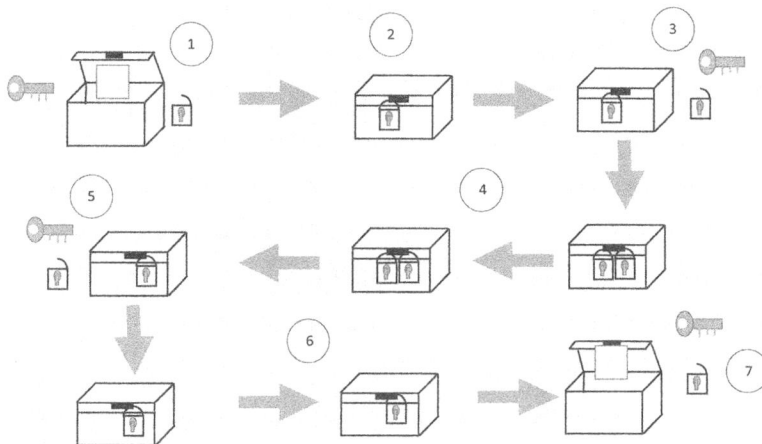

FIGURE 7.3. Diffie-Hellman key exchange.

The whole process takes seven steps and a three-way exchange of messages to share the secret symmetrical key across the Internet.

1. The sender puts a shared secret symmetrical key into a box that is locked with the sender's private key. Only the sender has this key; it is not a public key.

2. The locked box is sent to the receiver.

3. The receiver cannot open the box, but this does not matter. All the receiver does is add their own private key to the box.

4. The box, now with two locks, is sent back to the original sender.

5. The sender takes the original lock off the box using their private key.

6. The box, now secured with the receiver's lock, is sent back to the receiver.

7. The receiver unlocks the box with their private key, and now they can both use the shared secret key until it is time to change the secret key again.

Nonetheless—are not the weaknesses of the shared secret key system exactly what all this work in the 1970s was trying to avoid? Yes! Yet the fact remains that RSA and Diffie-Hellman can be processor-intensive, especially when very long keys are used, and slow to generate results. This is sort of the "secret of the secret key" methodology.

Therefore, Diffie-Hellman describes secure key exchange over an unsecure network, true enough. The overall method they called "public-key cryptography" Basically, you use the "public key" to derive simple, fast, shared, secret, private keys that avoid the time value issues and breaking challenges by changing often, sometimes every few minutes.

After all, time is the overwhelming concern in many cases. If someone manages to read 15 minutes worth of your emails two years from now, this might not be a great reason for concern.

Public-key cryptography is used every day on the Internet and Web as part of what is known as the Public Key Infrastructure (PKI). IPv6 uses these principles in the IP security (IPSec) feature, and the key exchange used in IPv6 is known as the Internet Key Exchange (IKE). IPSec and IKE can be used on the Internet to set up Security Associations (SAs) between senders and receivers.

IPSec/IKE SAs can operate in *phases*. Phase I sets up SA parameters, including a lifetime for the session keys. Phase II uses faster, symmetric methods and, for security, SAs change session keys often. It is common to code random "stutters" into the app timers so that messages are not obviously used for setting up new keys. In practice, these apps vary a lot. Some generate lots of keys all at once, and others do so only when the lifetime expires.

It should also be noted that RSA is not the only game in town. The ElGamal encryption system is also an asymmetric key system for public key cryptography based on Diffie-Hellman key exchange but comes from work done by Taher Elgamal from Cairo University and Stanford in 1985.

ElGamal is used in the free GNU Privacy Guard software, some versions of Pretty Good Privacy (PGP), and other systems. The Digital Signature Algorithm (DSA) is a variation of the ElGamal signature method, which is separate from the ElGamal encryption system. ElGamal methods can be slow and processor-intensive, but many Diffie-Hellman implementations are as well.

HOW PUBLIC KEY ENCRYPTION WORKS

The patent on RSA has expired, so anyone can freely use it. This chapter is based on information at *http://www.di-mgt.com.au/rsa_alg.html*. It gives the "rules" for creating independent implementations that can be used together with others. The algorithm covers encryption, decryption, digital signing, and signature verification (did this message really come from you?). The document also covers weaknesses, "advanced" schemes, and presents implementations in languages C++ and Visual Basic (VB).

To use RSA, first generate two large primes (p and q) of about equal size. The required bit length of the key (n), usually 1024, 2048, or more, where $n = p*q$ (* = multiplication). There is a lot more to be done, but the details are far beyond the mathematics used in this chapter. The point is that these numbers are used to derive two truly large primes that are "entangled."

These two large related primes are used to derive a third large number. In this chapter, these are called E (the encryption key), D (the decryption key), and N (the "normalizer," which is not really a key at all). N also establishes the range for encryption.

Then you make one of the primes the public key. It is tempting to always use the smaller number, but do not; that is a weakness the codebreakers can exploit. The key to this working well is that it is hard to derive the third number given the other two. Remember the idea of a one-way trapdoor function.

In this example, E = 3, D = 7, and N = 33. These two primes are trivial to break, but the real ones are hundreds of digits long and much harder.

The whole system works because E and D are related to N (33) in the following way:

$$X^E \bmod 33 = (X^E \bmod 33)^D \bmod 33$$

If this is sort of gibberish, do not worry. The idea is that I can take something like the number 16 (X) and encode it by multiplying it by itself E times. Then the receiver can get it back by multiplying 16^E by itself D times. If the numbers get too big, just divide by 33 (N) to get a smaller number back. This all works because the group forms a "cyclic multiplicative group of integers modulo n." The primes used must have a "primitive root" generator.

Public Key Example

This example is simple enough to follow along on a smartphone's calculator. The only complication is figuring out the remainder when using the normalizer. As mentioned, the three RSA numbers are E = 3, D = 7, and N = 33.

The *plaintext* message is to be sent in the number 30. It could represent "leave in 30 minutes," "attack on the 30th of the month," "30 tanks," "30 jet fighters" … whatever.

To encrypt 30, the steps using the *public* encryption key E = 3 and "normalizer" N = 33 are:

1. Multiply 30 by itself E times: $30 \times 30 \times 30 = 900 \times 30 = 27000$

2. Divide by N and get the remainder: 27000 / 33 = 818.181818182…
   818.181818182… - 818 = 0.181818182…
   0.181818182… × 33 = 6

3. Send 6, ciphertext for 30, over the network

When the "6" is received over the network, the receiver decodes it with the *private* decryption key D = 7:

1. Private decryption key, D = 7, "normalizer," N = 33
2. Multiply received value (6) by itself D times: $6 \times 6 \times 6 \times 6 \times 6 \times 6 \times 6 =$ 279,936 (no normalizer needed).
3. Divide by N and get the remainder:
   279,936 / 33 = 8,482.90909091…
   8,482.90909091… - 8,482 = 0.90909091…
   0.90909091… $\times$ 33 = 30

Therefore, the plaintext number sent was 30.

STREAM CIPHERS AND BLOCK CIPHERS

It might seem obvious to some that there is no need to constantly compute these numbers over again. After all, once a public key has been used to encrypt "30," the same public key yields the same result every time. Therefore, it is tempting to create a table on the output side of the encryption app that can be used to simply lookup the desired result instead of computing it. All of the letters, digits, and symbols possible to send could be included in the table ahead of time, speeding up the process. The same could be done on the receiver side to build up a table using the receiver's private key. Naturally, the tables would have to change as the session keys changed, but that might not be a great problem.

A portion of one such possible table for numbers is shown in Table 7.1.

TABLE 7.1. An encryption table at the sender for a receiver's public key.

Plaintext	Ciphertext	Plaintext	Ciphertext
2	8	7	13
3	27	8	17
4	31	9	3
5	26	10	10
6	18	11	11

The example we have been using is an illustration of what is known as a *stream cipher*. Stream ciphers operate on a message as it is being composed, either letter-by-letter or message-by-message during an interactive exchange.

However, there are also block ciphers that act on whole files or sets of data, usually before they are transferred to a data center or to a backup storage facility. One of the common block ciphers is Triple DES, or 3DES, which applies the Data Encryption Standard substitution and transformation cipher steps three times over. As symmetrical codes, the steps must be undone in the same way.

Block ciphers were used on computers long before RSA. The original DES was introduced in 1977, followed by RC5 and RC6 from Ron Rivest in 1995 and 1996, and AES in 2001. As far back as 1971, IBM's LUCIFER code system used 128-bit keys to encrypt and decrypt 64-bit blocks, which was about all the computers in those days could handle.

Today, in practice, RSA and Diffie-Hellman are used in this fashion:

- Asymmetrical RSA keys are generated occasionally because doing this all the time would be time and resource intensive.

- Encryption is not done with small integers, as in our examples, but with truly large ones.

- The full system is used to generate a random *session key* based on a "conventional," faster symmetrical algorithm such as 3DES or one of the members of the Advanced Encryption Standard (AES) family, such as AES-256.

- The session key is encrypted with the RSA architecture's public key for the receiver and sent using Diffie-Hellman.

- The receiver extracts the encrypted session key, decrypts it with their private key, and uses the session key until it is time to generate a new session key.

- For sensitive applications, this can be as frequent as every few minutes or even seconds.

HASHING AND MESSAGE DIGESTS

RSA is also the basis for digital signatures. Digital signatures are used, just like regular handwritten signatures, to verify that the person sending the message is who they say they are. Message digest (MD) bits are generated with the sender's *private key*, not the receiver's public key, and appended to the message. The receiver takes the received message minus the MD bits, computes the MD used by the sender's *public key*, and compares the result to the received MD. If it is a match, then okay: the digital signature is valid. It works because the public and private keys are used in pairs to initiate and undo the coding operation.

The MD is a *hashing operation* on the original message. Hashing is the process of scrambling raw information so that it cannot be used to recover the original form. In other words, there are several different messages that can be hashed to the same condensed value. It is a smaller group of bits, a digest, of the original message. A good hash does not generate many "synonym" values from different messages because that defeats the purpose.

Hashing takes a piece of information like a whole message and passes it through a function that performs mathematical operations on the plaintext. The function is called the *hash function*, and the output is called the *hash value*, or, in RSA, the message digest. The Internet uses several forms of the Secure Hashing Algorithm (SHA) online, for example, SHA-256.

One major application of hashing is for user validation. User IDs and passwords for a Web site, once established, are usually hashed and stored in that scrambled form on a server. Then the received user ID and password are hashed and compared to the stored value. If they match, access is granted. If they do not, access is denied. Hashing is also used as a validation field (MD5, for example) when a file is uploaded or downloaded over the Internet.

The workings of hashing and message digest are shown in Figure 7.4.

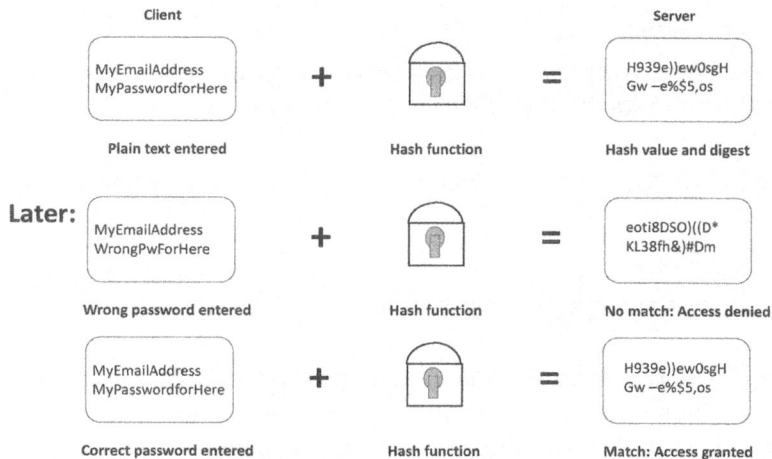

FIGURE 7.4. Message digests and hashing.

The current SHA family has six different hash functions: SHA-0 and SHA-1, both older methods that produce 160-bit digests; SHA-224; SHA-256; SHA-384; and SHA-512. The major characteristics of the SHA family of hashing algorithms are:

- **Message length:** The length of the plaintext should be of limited size, such as fewer than 264 bits. The larger the chunks of information being hashed, the more the possibility that a random sequence of plaintext generates a synonym, which defeats the purpose.

- **Digest length:** The length of the hash digest is 256 bits with the SHA-256 algorithm, 512 bits with SHA-512, and so on. Naturally, the larger values require more time and resources to calculate.

- **Irreversibility:** All hash functions are irreversible trapdoor functions. That is, there is no rule or algorithm that can be followed to recover the original text from the hash value.

CERTIFICATES AND CAS

As mentioned before, public keys can be freely distributed and known to all because, without the private key that is paired with public key use, the system is secure. How do you get the public key of a person or Web site and know that it belongs to them? Through the use of certificates and certificate authorities (CAs).

The issue of knowing for sure what the public key was for a given entity became acute once the Web made it possible to buy and sell over the Internet. In order for network commerce to thrive, two things had to be certain:

- Server authentication: Is this really the Vendor X Web site that I am buying from?
- Safe passage for data: Is what was received identical to what was sent?

Public key cryptography takes care of the second item. Certificates take care of the first.

Internet certificates are similar to personal IDs like driver's licenses or passports, and they provide generally recognized proof of identity online. An Internet certificate is an electronic document that serves to verify the identity of an individual, entity, server, or company. It also links a public key to that identity.

A CA is a trusted third party that issues certificates and validates the identities represented. CAs are also known as "PKI Certificate Authorities" because they issue digital certificates based on PKI, the public key infrastructure. These certificates enable secure online communication and transactions. A CA can issue a certificate that allows a browser to start a secure session with the server site. This lets site visitors know that the Web site they are visiting is authentic, and it can also help companies communicate safely with their customers.

CAs can be independent third parties or parts of organizations that run their own certificate-issuing server software. CAs can also manage, revoke, and renew certificates. The methods they use to validate identities vary depending on their policies. In some cases, a person has to carry a series of public keys in person to the CA headquarters and provide independent proof of their identity.

Certificates are usually issued for a certain time period and have to be renewed. Browsers often give users a "certificate expired" or invalid warning and leave it up to the user to decide to proceed or not. Moreover, if a certificate is issued incorrectly or the private key is compromised, the CA can revoke the certificate to prevent further use. There has been some controversy about how these *revocation lists* are compiled and used.

COMMON ENCRYPTION FRAMEWORKS

Many tools and apps relating to public key cryptography have been developed to help implementers and developers use pieces of an interoperable system. Two of the most common, both mentioned earlier, are AES and 3DES.

AES

The Advanced Encryption Standard (AES), also known by its original name Rijndael, is a specification for electronic data encryption established in 2001 by the National Institute of Standards and Technology (NIST) in the USA.

AES is a variant of the Rijndael block cipher, invented and developed by Belgian cryptographers Joan Daemen and Vincent Rijmen. They submitted their proposal to the NIST during the selection process that ended up with AES. Rijndael forms a family of block ciphers with different key and block sizes. To create AES, NIST selected three members of the Rijndael family, each with a block size of 128 bits, but using three different key lengths: 128, 192, and 256 bits.

AES is widely used by the US government. It replaced the old Data Encryption Standard (DES) from 1977. AES describes a symmetric-key algorithm and so uses the same key for both encrypting and decrypting data.

3DES

3DES is an unofficial description of the process and also seen as TDES, or Triple DES. Officially, it is the Triple Data Encryption Algorithm (TDEA or Triple DEA), but the name "3DES" was popularized when it was used on the Internet. 3DES, like AES, is also a symmetric-key block cipher. It applies the DES cipher algorithm three times to each data block. The original 56-bit key is no longer considered adequate considering modern cryptanalytic techniques and computer power, so the key has been increased to 112 bits.

In 2019, a major security vulnerability was uncovered in the DES and 3DES encryption algorithms. Therefore, NIST deprecated and disallowed all uses except when used for processing already encrypted data. 3DES has been replaced by AES.

ECC

Work on the next big cryptographic method beyond RSA, elliptic curve cryptography (ECC), started soon after RSA became widely accepted. Why? If RSA is so secure it is used almost everywhere, who would anything else be needed?

Well, for a number of reasons. The chapter has shown that RSA is based on large prime numbers and the difficulty of factoring truly large numbers with computers. RSA is based on operations that are relatively easy to do but hard to undo (so-called "trapdoor" functions).

On the other hand, factoring is not the hardest thing for modern computers to do compared to twenty or thirty years ago. There are special algorithms like the General Number Field Sieve and Quadratic Sieve that were created to work on problems like factoring the products of large primes, and these approaches get better and better. In fact, these methods actually get even better as the size of the numbers they crunch through gets larger and larger. The speed of multiplying larger numbers and the speed factoring them is getting closer and closer as time goes on. Sooner or later, they will become more or less equal.

What this means is that RSA is not a good system for the future of cryptography. Surely there must be some other system of trapdoor functions that can be used as a basis for public key cryptography and Diffie-Hellman key exchange that is also relatively easy to do and harder at all levels to undo.

And there is: ECC. Think of ECC as a better trapdoor that does not rely on factorization.

ECC first came along in 1985, which was not very long after RSA and before the Web demonstrated a need for new secure methods on unsecure networks like the global public Internet. However, RSA had a head start.

ECC is based naturally on elliptic curves, which are not squished circles like ellipses. Planetary orbits follow ellipses, but the formerly obscure class of elliptic curves is very different. Even readers averse to any mention of mathematics can try to follow the next few paragraphs, but if you cannot get it, do not worry too much about it. Mathematicians, as we have found, think differently than normal people.

Elliptic curves are a set of points that satisfy a particular mathematical equation formula. For example, the equation $y = 2x + 3$ defines a straight line. The value on the vertical y-axis is determined by the value of x on the horizontal x-axis. At $x = 2$, for example, $y = 7$. The more generic form $y = ax + b$ defines a whole family of lines that crisscross a graph in all directions.

The general equation for an elliptic curve looks like this:

$$y^2 = x^3 + ax + b$$

When graphed out, an equation of this form looks like a circle that has been exploded on one side. An elliptic curve of the type used as the foundation of ECC is shown in Figure 7.5.

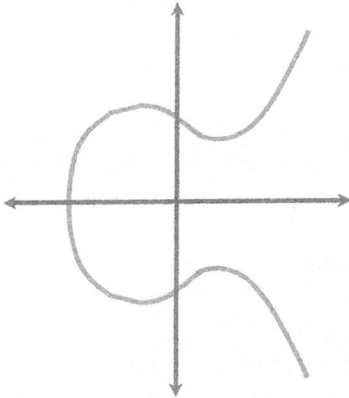

FIGURE 7.5. An elliptic curve is not an ellipse.

The odd shape gives this figure some very interesting properties. First, note that the curve has horizontal symmetry. That is, the shape above the horizontal x-axis (the positive values of y) is the same as it is below the x-axis (the negative values of y). This means that any point on the curve can be reflected as in a mirror over the x-axis and still be on the same curve. Furthermore, any line that is not straight-up-and-down vertical intersects the curve at most in three places.

Now, if we take two points on the curve, we can draw a line through them that will intersect the curve in exactly one more place. Therefore, if we take points A and B on the curve, a line drawn between them hits the curve at one more point. If this point is on the positive side of the curve, drop down vertically. If it is on the negative side of the curve, climb up vertically. Because the curve is horizontally symmetrical, such a point on the curve always exists. This is point C.

In the kind of shorthand mathematicians use, we can write what was just described as A "dot" B = C. Finding point C for a given pair of points A and B is shown on the left side of Figure 7.6.

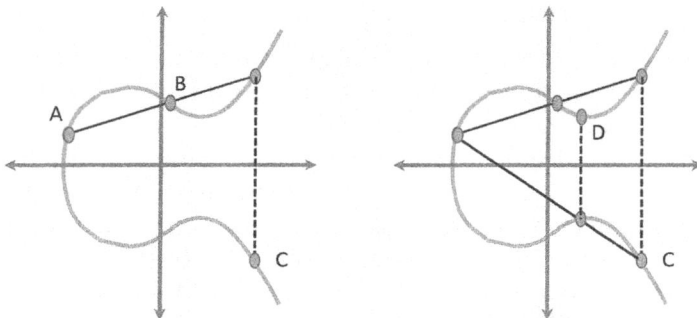

FIGURE 7.6. "A dot B" and the first few steps for EEC encryption.

Readers should be warned that this "dot" operation on A and B is not often given this name. Many ECC explanations are fond of calling this operation "addition" and using the familiar plus sign to designate the operation. So many write A + B = C as if this were ordinary addition. Yet it is obviously not. This chapter uses the notation "dot" in quotes to remind readers that this is not addition and it is not the normal engineering vector *dot* operation either.

This same operation can be used as the basis for a series of ECC operations:

A "dot" B = C

We can also "dot" a point with itself over and over and start a whole series of operations:

A "dot" A = B
A "dot" B = C
A "dot" C = D

In practice, it is a bit more complex than this, but not much. The first few steps in such a series are shown on the right side of Figure 7.6.

Here is where the cryptography comes in. Suppose you "dot" something with itself n times. You end up at a final point of the ECC curve, obviously. Yet how did you get there? In other words, what were the initial values of A and n that took you to where you are on the curve? If you know n, on the other hand, it is fairly easy to get back to A.

We have just invented another thing that is relatively easy to do and hard to undo. If you are starting to see public and private keys in the values of A and n, you will not be far off.

This curve and "dot" operation is good to introduce ECC. Yet the real curves used for ECC do not look like this example curve at all. In practice, we use curves with whole number values inside a fixed range. If results stray too high or too low, the curve acts like an old video game where a spaceship heading off the monitor to the right pops back onto the monitor on the left, like the RSA "normalization" trick. The same applied to the top and bottom of the monitor, of course. When this maximum value is set to a prime number, the curve is called a *prime curve*. That is what is used for ECC.

ECC used this way is called the *elliptic curve discrete logarithm function.*

How much better is ECC than RSA? Studies have shown that the work factor it took in around 2012 to break a 228-bit RSA key was about the same amount of energy it took to boil a teaspoon of water. In order to break a 225-bit ECC key, it would take more energy than is needed to boil all the water on Earth. To get 228-bit ECC security with RSA, the keys would have to be 2,380 bits long.

In other words, you get the same level of security with ECC with smaller, easier-to-use, and faster keys. As more advanced security comes to low-end mobile phones and tiny embedded processors, this efficiency makes a big difference.

Today, RSA functions are being implemented with ECC. Key exchange based on ECC is covered by the Elliptic Curve Diffie Hellman Ephemeral (ECDHE) method, often combined with regular server certificates in the form of ECD-HE_RSA. Signatures are done with the Elliptic Curve Digital Signature Algorithm (ECDSA).

In 2013, Google used the following parameters and equation for their ECC server system:

curve: $y^2 = x^3 + ax + b$

a = 115792089210356248762697446949407573530086143415290314195533631308867097853948

b = 41058363725152142129326129780047268409114441015993725554835256314039467401291

max: 115792089210356248762697446949407573530086143415290314195533363131308867097853951

SSL and SSH

Users are unlikely to come across public-key cryptography or RSA or ECC in their "raw" form. Instead, they encounter these techniques when dealing with certificates or CAs, or even more likely, apps like SSL and SSH.

The Secure Sockets Layer (SSL) and Secure Shell (SSH) are application programs that use the cryptographic techniques outlined in this chapter to add security and privacy to the TCP/IP protocol stack, which was introduced in Chapter 1.

By 1994, commercial buying and selling had been introduced to the Internet with the advent of the World Wide Web in 1992. The twin concerns about knowing who you were buying form and that data flowed back and forth unaltered between client and server moved to the forefront of work on the part of companies creating client browser and Web server software.

One of the first major browser companies making software for graphical point-and-clock Web use was Netscape. In 1994, they added SSL software that made the sockets used by the connection-oriented TCP layer secure, as the name "SSL" implies. Sockets were a TCP/IP communication concept that allowed programmers and application developers to treat communication ports the same as they did files. As described in Chapter 1, just like files, socket communication ports were created (opened), written to (sent), read from (received), and discarded (closed).

With SSL, Web commerce became practical. Open SSL was used by the popular Apache server. SSL use is seen today with the *https://* Web site usage.

Not long afterwards, in 1995, the Helsinki University of Technology in Finland was attacked remotely when someone hacked into a server using the operating system command prompt. Database researcher Tatu Ylonen (also spelled Ylonen or Yloenen) responded by adding security to the operating system shell and calling his invention the Secure Shell (SSH). (A *shell* is a module of the Unix or Linux operating system that uses a command prompt like C:> where users type in commands.)

The open version of SSH is OpenSSH and now ships with every version of the Unix, Linux, and Mac operating systems and is available for every platform. SSH includes components like Secure Copy (SCP) and others to make the security provided even more useful. A lot of recent work has been in the SSH key management area.

There is much more to explore about SSL and SSH, but this is enough to get interested readers started.

Privacy

Privacy, the expectation that what one does should remain unobserved, is mostly a modern invention. As recently as about AD 1500, homes in the Western world did not have interior walls. They were not added until after the invention of interior fireplaces, which led to a need for a chimney that led to a need for interior walls to support roof beams.

After all, the raising of a new structure in the town—cities were neither common nor large—was a major effort and consumed many scarce resources. There was no compelling need to erect separate buildings for chickens, cows, horses, and people. Everyone, human and animal, huddled for warmth and security in the interior of one large structure, at least until the fireplace overheated all but the humans.

Even sleeping tended to be a communal activity. One big bed housed the whole family, and acts of intimacy between the parents were dealt with while the children were at play or asleep, by having relations outside in the woods, or simply by telling them to ignore what was going on. After all, there were plenty of animals to watch doing everything that daily existence required to survive and propagate.

Even without doors, many homes could conceal interiors from prying eyes passing on the street by narrowing passageways, offsetting rooms, and hanging curtains when necessary. It was not until the plague made cramped living dangerous and the recovery of normal life in the 1700s that separate beds and bedrooms became common in Europe, at least among the more well-off. Once that occurred, couples moved their intimate acts indoors and sent the kids out to play.

This common experience of life was a legacy from ancient Greek and Roman times. Nudity, mostly male nudity, was not uncommon, and the bare chest and simple robe of the Greek and Roman philosophers were a cliche. Latrines were communal rooms with all sharing the experience, and the Roman baths were enjoyed naked. There were alternating days for males and females, but this was a change from the Greek world, where all but loose women and prostitutes were kept at home with the children.

Even reading was not a private activity. Readers proclaimed aloud or murmured quietly in a crowd. Augustine caused a stir when others found that he could read without moving his lips and still understood what the words meant.

Many concerns about privacy revolved around potential abuses, such as a national or regional census. People were skeptical that the government truly needed such detailed records, especially since the aim was to assess the tax burden on families. If the census only recorded two children, how could the family claim to have six?

These concerns persist today. There are only so many authors of a given height and weight and age and having advanced degrees living in a private residence in Arizona. Why not just put the name with the description?

There is a good argument that modern expectations of privacy began in 1890 in the United States. That year in December, the *Harvard Law Review* published an article on *The Right to Privacy* that established a common-law—that is, not supported by any specific statute—right to privacy that could be defended in court against violations.

Wiretapping, which initially applied to telegraph lines during the American Civil War, eventually required justification through a court order signed by a judge. By the late 1800s, when Grover Cleveland's attractive wife's face appeared in advertisements and in newspapers without any thought of obtaining permission, New York passed a law in 1903 banning the unauthorized use of someone's likeness. The penalty was a very steep fine for the time: $1,000.00.

Modern life extended the concept in many ways. In the USA, you could send a letter in a sealed envelope for three cents or a postcard with text anyone could read for a penny. Naturally, post cards became wildly popular, even though every postal worker could and did read them, and the most outlandish ended up on the bulletin board, a practice common even in the 1960s.

The telephone party line with multiple homes on a single wire survived until the 1960s, and children were taught only to answer the telephone if it rang twice or three times or whatever the house code was. When you wanted to make a call and picked up the handset, if you heard people talking already, you were to hang up the phone and try again later. In spite of that, this was widely violated and became a good source of neighborhood gossip.

However, as soon as the Internet and Web came along, there were people not only willing but eager to share every aspect of their lives online. Cookies that tracked user activities, as discussed in Chapter 4, were once placed without the user's knowledge in any place and at any time. Today, cookie use is restricted and usually requires the user's permission before they are accepted.

MODERN ASPECTS

A major area of concern over privacy today is with medical records. There is no doubt that people are entitled to keep their medical records private, a matter of concern only between doctor and patient. However, under the privatized health care system of the USA, the question of who owns the medical data that doctors and hospitals accumulate, especially when aggregated data could help determine the range and intensity of disease outbreaks and cancer risks, is a matter of great debate.

No one doubts that amassing a huge database of health statistics on all citizens is a good idea that could save lives. Yet the proprietary—and private—nature of medical data among doctors, clinics, hospitals, and insurance companies makes such a system problematic. There are ways based on the same cryptographic techniques explored in the previous chapter to share such data anonymously and with assured privacy, but these are not widely implemented.

Today, users worry about others reading and analyzing their emails, direct messages, queries for information, and online purchases, and with good reason. Such information has great value for business and marketing, and today it is all but assumed that someone will be able to look at that you have done online.

A good guideline for what content is suitable for an email used to be that users should never write in an email what they would not want their mothers to read. However, given the wide range of mothers' postings lately, this advice probably is no longer helpful. Nonetheless, one good guideline that is true now more than ever is to assume everything that you do online or with the Internet and its apps is being read, stored, considered, analyzed, aggregated, and acted upon by some AI bot out there in cyberspace.

It does no good to ask "Who watches the watchmen?" because those stalwart sentinels have long been replaced by faceless functions that operate without ever tiring or running out of things to do. The tracking systems on the Web have been showing us advertisements for a long time, and any way to control it has been running on empty for a long time.

AD BLOCKERS

Tracking has taken on a life of its own. There are not many good ways to avoid the consequences of this tracking activity; it is like trying to drive and avoid airbags and seatbelts. You can stay offline or take a bus, but that limits your life in many ways. You cannot avoid the tracking and ads they want you to see, but you can control it.

Ad blockers are a good choice to ensure the video you are watching is not interrupted by a thirty-second ad for a product that you would never consider using or buying. They can also show you who is tracking your browsing activity and offer ways to limit the dissemination of this information (a Web site can send the URLs you click on to up to forty different places).

Here is a short list of common ad blocker apps, most of them with very good free features:

- uBlock Origin
- Tunnel Bear
- Privacy Badger

- Adgard
- Ghostery

They usually provide features in the following areas:

- **Ad blocking:** They block HTTP requests and redirects according to the source addresses. To do this, they block third-party tracking scripts and "tags" and the cookies used by Web sites to collect user data.

- **Tracking reporting:** They report on the tracking packages detected, whether blocked or not. Usually this is in a separate window or overlay.

- **Privacy protection:** They block popups, ads, and trackers that carry your personal information across the Internet.

- **Loading speedup:** By not having to wait for ads to load, they speed up your online experience.

- **Community support:** Most of them use a sharing environment so that when a new tracker appears, all users of the software gain the benefit of the new blocking ability.

A NOTE ON ONLINE IDENTITY THEFT

When it comes to securing online user IDs and passwords, the Internet has a long way to go. Here is a short case study on what happens when a user has their identity stolen online, what it can take to get it restored, and why the current systems might need to change soon.

In the early morning hours of December 8, 2023, a writer received a usually normal email from a major online shopping Web site, a Web site the writer had been a member of for more than 25 years. The only reason that the email was seen almost immediately was that the writer was working late to finish a book proposal. The email stated that the writer's password for the Web site had changed and included the typical wording to the effect that "if you did not make this change, contact us immediately."

An email to the shopping site in response was followed up by a phone call by the writer to the shopping site's service center. The first thing that was done, without any problem, was to immediately suspend the writer's account so that no transactions could be charged to the writer's account. In fact, in the ten minutes that had transpired since the theft, more than three thousand dollars US in goods and gift cards had been charged to the account.

Later, it would be revealed to the user that two hackers in India had managed to find out the writer's current account ID (which is just the email address) and password. The pair had decided to do some free Christmas shopping. The hackers immediately changed the password on the writer's account and the email address attached to the account to values of the hackers' choosing and—most importantly—turned on *two-step verification*. Two-step verification means that whenever a change is made to any of the account's parameters, such as user ID or password, a message is sent to another device, usually a cell phone. This message informs the user of the change, and the text must be acknowledged as valid before the change can take place. It is different from the emailed "your password recently changed" message in that, if the request is not acknowledged positively, the change is rejected.

The hackers used the number of a cell phone in India as the verification device, a number unknown—of course—to the legitimate user. That use of two-step verification turned an issue that should have been resolved in five minutes into a problem that was not fully resolved until close to the end of February of 2024, nearly *three months* after the theft itself. Apparently, the shopping site's password recovery mechanisms did not have special directions for their security personnel to use to restore the account when two-step verification is in use. Hopefully they do today.

A related issue was the fact that the shopping site stored credit card and debit card information on their servers, not just on the user's device. This allowed users to access their debit card information on any computer, laptop, or smart phone the user logged in on. This made shopping that much more convenient but made securing this information impossible once a breach had been made.

That initial telephone call in December did manage to restore the user's password. Nevertheless, the storage of credit and debit card information made it necessary to call all banks associated with the cards, cancel the current cards, and request replacements be sent as soon as possible. This would take up to three or four business days. In the meantime, only cards that had never been stored on the shopping site could still be used for shopping, banking, or to pay bills. Any automatic payments that had been scheduled would fail until the new information was available in that three- or four-business-day window.

What had seemed a simple enough task now, after only a half an hour, seemed to be a major pain in the neck. Moreover, when the writer tried to log in to the supposedly restored account, the password established during the service telephone call not ten minutes before no longer worked. Readers might have already figured out why. The change of password, even when made by the shopping site personnel themselves, triggered a verification request sent to the cell phone number *of the hackers*, who had turned on two-step verification. When the hackers rejected the request to make the change permanent, the password and other information reverted to the values that hackers had used to replace the writer's information!

A second telephone call to the service center was not very successful. The writer explained that, in order to avoid the need for the hackers to approve the password change—why would they?—the shopping site personnel would have to change *all* hacked parameters at the same time: email address, password, and cell phone number for two-step verification. Unfortunately, none of the first-level service center personnel could figure out or had permission to change all of these at once.

In fact, telephone calls made over the next few days revealed how limited the powers that the people who answered user phone calls had to make changes. They had to ask questions by reading from a rigid script. In order to give out a new password, for example, the user was asked to provide the shopping site's order numbers for the last three products ordered on the account. Naturally, the writer had no access to the hackers' purchases or their order numbers (only that they were expensive items), and so the information did not match what the service personnel had on file. This was appropriate for a lost or forgotten password, but not for theft of identity.

Yet each call ended more or less the same way, with an apology and a request: "We are unable to help you at this time, but we would like you to answer a survey on the quality of our support services." There was no alternative until finally the writer managed to get the telephone number of the second-tier support services. This number was treated like some super-secret information that no one at the shopping site was supposed to hand out.

This should have improved the response and reactions to the hacked account, but unfortunately, it did not. Each call had to repeat all the details of the original event and the other calls to try and fix the situation. Notes made on previous calls were totally dependent on how much the person handling the call typed in, and the calls were not recorded. This was due to the volume of such calls, the writer was told eventually.

Nevertheless, each of the calls made before Christmas took up to half an hour to explain the situation and to get them to agree to the cure, which was to change *everything* on the account back to the way it was. Each time, a promise was made that this information would be passed along to the "security team" and all would be well within forty-eight hours.

It never was. To shop for Christmas, it was necessary to establish a *second* shopping account using a different email address and pay for a second year's worth of their "primary" shopping service, even though the original account had that feature paid for recently.

Call hold times to the service center became so long around Christmas that no further attempts were made to address the issue until mid-January of 2024. Then it was mainly because tax season was approaching. The writer, like many professionals, bought computer software to do their job, office supplies, and books for research, all potentially tax deductible, through the shopping site. Without access to the account's records, the details of recent purchases, as well as more than 3500 purchases made since 1996, were available only as emails recording the purchase date, the shipping date, and the delivery date, *if* the emails had not been deleted.

One issue was the lack of any system to verify the identity of the person calling to request that the account be restored. That made a certain amount of sense: how could the shopping site be sure that it was not a hacker calling? However, this was an account not of recent vintage but of more than 25 years' standing. How could restoring it to the state the account was in before December of 2023 have anything to do with a hacker?

With great perseverance on the part of the writer and his family, who would not let the matter drop, all was finally restored on the account by the end of February. That was only possible in the long run by reading the serial number of one of those voice-activated assistant devices ("What is on my calendar today?") to prove that the caller was the customer who had purchased it years before.

The writer hopes that this account and the original ordeal have led to significant changes to make the customer experience more effective and less time-consuming.

A CHALLENGE TO READERS

Some researchers and experts in cryptanalysis have long suspected that decoding depends a lot on the *context* of the message to be decoded. That is, making an informed guess about the probable content of a decrypted message can tell analysts a lot about the plaintext content of the message. Therefore, if some attempt at decrypting turns up a word or phrase that matches the context of the guess, this means that the analysts are most likely on the right track. It still could be random, but it suggests a direction for further attempts.

For example, military messages often include information about the weather, almost always at the start of the message. Therefore, if a decoding run turns up the word "rainy" or "sunny," even if the rest is still gibberish, it is a clue that the decoders are on the right track. Informed guesses like this contributed to the success of the cracking of the German Enigma cipher during World War II.

To see how valuable context guessing might be, this chapter ends with a string of 0s and 1s that are provided to the reader without any context at all, other than the fact that the bits appear in a chapter about security and privacy in a book.

How long will it take for a reader or someone else to break the code and read the message? Let us find out.

```
00111010 00111111 10111010 01111101 01100101 11100110 00110010 11011110 01010110 10010110 01000101 11000001
00000111 10111001 01100111 10001110 10110110 10110010 00110010 00110000 01000111 11010101 10000110 10110011
01100010 10101101 01110001 11000000 01000111 10001100 00100110 10110110 00010100 10010101 01000110 10010011
11000111 10001010 11110110 10110000 11010001 10010001 00000011 10010001 00100001 10010100 01010111 10110000
01100011 10110111 00110111 11010000 00100010 11110100 11000011 11110110 01010110 10010110 01100110 11110000
10010000 11101110 10100000
```

POWERS OF 10

This book is intended for a non-technical audience, but that does not mean it is for the uninformed. Readers should have a basic understanding of terms like binary digit (bit) and byte (sometimes B), and what abbreviations such as Mbps and Gbps stand for. A bit is either a zero or a one. A byte is made up of eight bits (there used to be seven-bit bytes, but most consider 8 bits as the standard today). Therefore, one million bits per second equals 1 Mbps.

Some argue that all prefixes should be based on binary powers of two, not powers of 10, which means that 1 Mbps is not exactly one million bits per second. This is technically true: 10^3 is 1000, but in binary digits, 2^{10} is 1024. Sometimes, 1 MB refers to the use of binary digits are used. In this notation, 1024 MB is equal to 1 GB. Only purists and precise engineers involved in manufacturing disk drives worry about these differences. This book is not aimed at purists or precise engineers, but readers should be aware that these nuances exist.

This book frequently discusses powers of ten and terms like mega-this and giga-that. Now is a good time to introduce the range of powers of ten used in this book, along with the most common terms used to describe them

TABLE 1.1. Positive powers of ten.

Positive Powers of 10	Name	Prefix (Symbol)
$10^1 = 10$	Ten	Deca- (D)
$10^2 = 100$	Hundred	Hecto- (H)

(Contd.)

Positive Powers of 10	Name	Prefix (Symbol)
$10^3 = 1000$	Thousand	Kilo- (K)
$10^6 = 1,000,000$	Million	Mega- (M)
$10^9 = 1,000,000,000$	Billion	Giga- (G)
$10^{12} = 1,000,000,000,000$	Trillion	Tera- (T)
$10^{15} = 1,000,000,000,000,000$	Quadrillion	Peta- (P)
$10^{18} = 1,000,000,000,000,000,000$	Quintillion	Exa- (E)
$10^{21} = 1,000,000,000,000,000,000,000$	Sextillion	Zetta- (Z)

Readers should never lose sight of the values that these numbers represent. A distance of 10 exameters, for example, while easy to write as a one followed by 18 zeroes, is not just a big number—it is about 105.7 light years. These numbers can represent vast distances as well as smaller things like atoms. For instance, the number of water molecules in a drop of water is approximately 1.7 quintillion.

Similar rules are established for dividing units into increasingly smaller parts. Time is often a prime example. Note the duplication of some prefix symbols, which are distinguished by the use of uppercase and lowercase letters and, in the case of micro-, by the Greek letter mu (μ).

TABLE 1.2. Negative powers of ten.

Negative Powers of 10	Name	Prefix (Symbol)
$10^{-1} = 0.1$	Tenth	Deci- (d)
$10^{-2} = 0.01$	Hundredth	Centi- (c)
$10^{-3} = 0.001$	Thousandth	Milli- (m)
$10^{-6} = 0.000001$	Millionth	Micro- (μ)
$10^{-9} = 0.000000001$	Billionth	Nano- (n)
$10^{-12} = 0.000000000001$	Trillionth	Pico- (p)
$10^{-15} = 0.000000000000001$	Quadrillionth	Femto- (f)
$10^{-18} = 0.000000000000000001$	Quintillionth	Atto- (a)
$10^{-21} = 0.000000000000000000001$	Sextillionth	Zepto- (z)
$10^{-24} = 0.000000000000000000000001$	Septillionth	Yocto- (y)

If readers find it hard to distinguish these quantities by sight, perhaps 0.000000001 and 0.000000000001 without the commas to help, you will not be the first to notice. Spaces can help distinguish a nanosecond (0.000 000 001) from a picosecond (0.000 000 000 001), but this method is not standard or widely used.

The blink of an eye is about one tenth of a second long. An airplane flying at 1000 kilometers per hour (about 600 miles per hour) travels about 300 meters (almost 1000 feet) in the time it takes for the pilot to blink. The SONET/SDH standards generate 8,000 frames per second, or one frame every 125 micro-seconds. The "tick" of a golf club on a golf ball lasts about 500 microseconds (or half a millisecond) by the time it reaches your ear. That tick is about four SONET/SDH frames long.

A nanosecond is often called a "light foot" (there is no convenient metric equivalent). A twelve-inch foot is about the distance that light can travel in one billionth of a second. This limits the size of a computer processor, although light in a fiber optic cable travels at about two-thirds the speed of light in a vacuum (about 200,000 kilometers per second and not 300,000 kps, or 125,000 miles per second instead of 186,000 mps.

As helpful as it is to understand the raw quantities represented by these num-bers, it is as important, if not more so, for readers to appreciate the differences of a thousandfold increase or decrease ($10^3 = 1000$). This happens mainly when going from one major unit to another, such as when going from Kbps to Mbps or Gbps or beyond.

Consider the ratio of 1 to 1000. There are 365 days in most years, so 3 × 365 = 1,095 days. That is fairly close to saying "the relationship between 1 and 1000 is about the same as the relationship between one day and three years."

A lot of people imagine winning a million dollars, or some other currency, in a lottery. Imagine winning a million dollars *every single day* of your life! How long will it take to win a *billion* dollars?

Well, a billion is a thousand million. A thousand days, this book has shown, is about three years. Therefore, it takes about three years to win a billion dollars, even at a million dollars a day. Appreciate the difference.

At one point in the early 1990s, Bill Gates of Microsoft was the richest man in the world, and a lot younger than he is now. If you did the math, Bill Gates at the time had been making a million dollars a day *since the day he was born*! By the way, once you have that billion, it would take you about three years, at a million dollars a day, to spend that billion.

Let us not stop there. How about winning a trillion dollars? That is a thou-sand thousand million. The same one-to-a-thousand factor applies. Which means that it would take you, at a million dollars a day, 3,000 years to win that trillion dollars (actually, 2739.72 years) and another three thousand years to spend it. This perspective can make you wonder about the scale of government spending in the trillions.

Keep this 1:1000 ratio and the one day to three years comparison in mind when reading this book. Generally, fiber optic cables have $1/1000^{th}$ of the errors of twisted pair cables (10^{-6} to 10^{-9}). This means that errors observed on a fiber network yesterday would now take three years to accumulate.

The same logic applies when upgrading from 10 Mbps Ethernet to 10 Gbps Ethernet: it is the same 1:1000 ratio. This means you could transmit the data of the last three years in just one day with the faster link.

(Purists may point out that the *throughput* (effective bit rate) of this link differs from the raw speed, and they are correct. There are always a few purists around.)

ACRONYMS

3GPP	3G Partnership Project
5GC	5G Core
AES	Advanced Encryption Standard
AIaaS	Artificial Intelligence as a Service
AMF	Access and Mobility Management Function
AMPS	Advanced Mobile Phone System
ANN	Artificial Neural Network
API	Application Program Interface
APIPA	Automatic Private IP Addressing
APNIC	Asia-Pacific Network Information Center
ARP	Address Resolution Protocol
ASCII	American Standard Code for Information Interchange
ASIMO	Advanced Step in Innovative Mobility
ATM	Asynchronous Transfer Mode
B-PON	Broadband Passive Optical Network
BER	Bit Error Rate
BERT	Bidirectional Encoder Representation from Transformers
C-RAN	Centralized Cloud Radio Access Network
GA	Certificate Authority

CaaS	Containers as a Service
CDCF	Colorless, Directionless, Contentionless, Flex-Grid
CEO	Chief Executive Officer
CNCF	Cloud Native Computing Foundation
CO	Central Office
COBOL	Common Business-Oriented Language
CoS	Class of Service
CSP	Cloud Service Provider
CSRF	Cross-Site Request Forgery
CWDM	Coarse Wavelength Division Multiplexing
D-RAN	Distributed Radio Access Network
DaaS	Desktop as a Service
DBA	Dynamic Bandwidth Allocation
DES	Data Encryption Standard
DF	Don't Fragment
DHCP	Dynamic Host Configuration Protocol
DNN	Deep Neural Network
DNS	Domain Name System
DS	Differentiated Services
DSA	Digital Signature Algorithm
DSF	Dispersion-Shifted Fiber
DSL	Digital Subscriber Line
DWDM	Dense Wavelength Division Multiplexing
ECC	Elliptic Curve Cryptology
ECDHE	Elliptic Curve Diffie Hellman Ephemeral
ECDSA	Elliptic Curve Digital Signature Algorithm
ECN	Explicit Congestion Notification
EDFA	Erbium-Doped Fiber Amplifier
eNodeB	evolved Node B
EPON	Ethernet Passive Optical Network
ERP	Enterprise Resource Planning
ES	End System
F-RAN	Fog Radio Access Network
FCS	Frame Check Sequence
FDM	Frequency Division Multiplexing

FEC	Forward Error Correction
FTP	File Transfer Protocol
FTTH	Fiber To The Home
G-PON	Gogabit Passive Optical Network
GbE	Gigabit Ethernet
GCHQ	Government Communication Headquarters
GFP	Generic Framing Procedure
gNB	5G Node B
gNB-CU	gNB Central Unit
gNB-DU	gNB Distributed Unit
GPS	Global Positioning System
GTP	Generative Pretrained Transformer
GSM	Global System for Mobile Communications
H-CRAN	Heterogeneous Cloud Radio Access Network
H-RAN	see H-CRAN
HAPS	High Altitude Platform Station
HTML	Hypertext Markup Language
HTTP	Hypertext Transfer Protocol
HTTPS	Hypertext Transfer Protocol Secure
IaaS	Infrastructure as a Service
ICMP	Internet Control Message Protocol
IEC	International Electrotechnical Commission
IEEE	Institute of Electrical and Electronic Engineers
IETF	Internet Engineering Task Force
IGMP	Internet Group Management Protocol
IHL	Internet Header Length
IIC	Industrial Internet Consortium
IKE	Internet Key Exchange
IoT	Internet of Things
IP	Internet Protocol
IPARS	International Program Airline Reservation System
IPng	Internet Protocol next generation (IPv6)
IS	Intermediate System
ISP	Internet Service Provider
ITU	International Telecommunication Union

JSON	JavaScript Object Notation
LAN	Local Area Network
LED	Light Emitting Diode
LLC	Logical Link Control
LLM	Large Language Model
M2M	Machine-to-Machine
MAC	Media Access Control
MD	Message Digest
MIMO	Multiple Input, Multiple Output
MMF	Multi-mode Fiber
MRI	Magnetic Resonance Imaging
MS	Mobile Station
MTU	Maximum Transmission Unit
NAS-MM	Network Access Signaling-Mobility Management
NAS-SM	Network Access Signaling-Session Management
NAT	Network Address Translation
ND	Neighbor Discovery
NDP	Neighbor Discovery Protocol
NF	Network Function
NFV	Network Function Virtualization
NG	Next Generation
NG-RAN	Next Generation Radio Access Network
NGAP	Next Generation Application Protocol
NIST	National Institute of Standards and Technology
NLP	Natural Language Processing
NR-Uu	New Radio Uu (Uu is not an acronym)
OA	Optical Amplifier
ODN	Optical Distribution Network
ODU	Optical Data Unit
OLT	Optical Line Terminal
ONU	Optical Network Unit
OSI-RM	Open Standard Interconnection Reference Model
OTN	Optical Transport Network

P2P	Peer to Peer
PaaS	Platform as a Service
PANS	Plain Analog Network Service
PDCP	Packet Data Convergence Protocol
PDU	Protocol Data Unit
PGP	Pretty Good Privacy
PKI	Public Key Infrastructure
PLC	Programmable Logic Controllers
PLM	Product Lifetime Management
PON	Passive Optical Network
POTS	Plain Old Telephone Service
PSTN	Public Switched Telephone Network
QAM	Quadrature-Amplitude Modulation
QoS	Quality of Service
QPSK	Quadrature-Phase Shift Keying
RA	Router Advertisement
RAG	Retrieval Augmented Generation
RAT	Radio Access Technology
REST	Representational State Transfer
RFC	Request for Comment
RLC	Radio Link Control
ROADM	Reconfigurable Optical Add-Drop Multiplexer
RPC	Remote Procedure Call
RRC	Radio Resource Control
RSA	Rivest-Shamir-Adleman
RTP	Real-time Transport Protocol
SaaS	Software as a Service
SABRE	Semi-Automated Business Research Environment
SBA	Service-Based Architecture
SCADA	Supervisory Control and Data Acquisition
SCM	Supply Chain Management
SCP	Secure Copy
ScoT	Smart Connected Things
SCTP	Stream Control Transmission Protocol
SDH	Synchronous Digital Hierarchy

SHA	Secure Hashing Algorithm
SLAAC	Stateless Address Autoconfiguration
SMF	Single Mode Fiber
SMS	Short Message Service
SMTP	Simple Mail Transfer Protocol
SNA	Systems Network Architecture
SOAP	Simple Object Access Protocol
SONET	Synchronous Optical Network
SSH	Secure Shell
SSL	Secure Sockets Layer
ST2	Streams 2
STAR	Smart Tissue Autonomous Robot
TCP	Transmission Control Protocol
TDM	Time Division Multiplexing
TDMA	Time Division Multiple Access
TOR	Top of Rack
TTL	Time To Live
UDP	User Datagram Protocol
UE	User Equipment
UMTS	Universal Mobile Telecommunications System
UPF	User Plane Function
USIM	Universal Subscriber Identity Module
VB	Visual BASIC
VCSEL	Vertical-Cavity Surface-Emitting Laser
VLAN	Virtual Local Area Network
VNF	Virtual Network Function
VR	Virtual Reality
WDN	Wavelength Division Multiplexing
WLAN	Wireless Local Area Network
XG-PON	10 Gigabit Passive Optical Network
XGEM	10 Gigabit Ethernet Method
XGS-PON	10 Gigabit Symmetric Passive Optical Network
XSS	Cross-Site Scripting
XST	Cross-Site Tracing

FURTHER READING

This is not necessarily a list of sources, mainly because these technologies can change rapidly. However, readers might want to explore more material for each chapter. Here is a list of material the author found most helpful.

Wikipedia is often a good starting point for researching any of the topics covered. However, the quality of entries varies widely. Research for this book ranged very widely and then concentrated on a few excellent sources for a roadmap.

Much of the material in the early chapters comes from IEEE and 3GPP publicly available courses and tutorials. Much in the last two chapters does not come from books. The most up-to-date material, of course, is found online but requires Internet access.

Nevertheless, here are the books and other materials that were most helpful in formulating a topic flow for each technology.

CHAPTER 1: MOBILE NETWORKS

Walter Goralski, *The Illustrated Network: How TCP/IP Work in a Modern Network, Second Edition* (Morgan Kaufman, MA, 2018). All about layers and protocol stacks and how they work together.

Jonathan Levine, *5G New Radio: A New Standard and Industry Update* (IEEE Course, 2019). A solid introduction to all things 5G.

CHAPTER 2: IPV6

Rick Graziani, *IPv6 Fundamentals: A Straightforward Approach to Understanding IPv6, 2nd Edition* (Cisco Press, CA, 2017). Many networking books have chapters on IPv6, but this has more than you could ever want to know about IPv6.

Books on IPv6 tend to be older because IPv6 is no longer a surprise in a lot of contexts except for end users. They are all still valid for the most part.

CHAPTER 3: PACKET OPTICAL

Susan Crawford, *Fiber: The Coming Tech Revolution* (Yale University Press, NY, 2018). A call to use more fiber for residential Internet access.

Walter Goralski, *SONET/SDH, Third Edition* (Osborne, NY, 2002). An older text, but has a lot about the attractions of fiber optics.

Xiang Zhou and Chongin Xie (editors), *Enabling Technologies for High-Spectral-Efficiency Coherent Optical Communications Networks* (Wiley, NJ, 2016). For those who have the mathematical ability to understand the content.

CHAPTER 4: CLOUD DATA CENTERS

Luiz Andre Barroso, Urs Holzle, and Parthasarathy Ranganathan, *The Datacenter as a Computer*, Third Edition (Morgan & Claypool, 2018). An exceptional guide to all things about the giant data warehouse, including electrical and cooling considerations.

Brendan Burns, *Designing Distributed Systems* (O'Reilly, CA, 2018). A good survey of cloud-native protocols, such as load balancers, scatter-gather, and other methods.

Cornelia Davis, *Cloud Native Patterns* (Manning, NY, 2019). Manning books are implementation heavy, so expect a lot of code examples. All their books are solid yet concise.

CHAPTER 5: IOT AND M2M

IEEE Computer Society, Phoenix Chapter, *Internet of Things (IoT) Innovations & Megatrends Update*, December 11, 2019.

Yuanqi Luo, *Empowering Industry 4.0 with Next Generation Optical Access Networks* (IEEE course, 2024). A very good course on the ideas of IoT and M2M.

CHAPTER 6: AI AND ROBOTS

This list could easily go on for several pages. However, here are some highlights.

Amy Kurzweil, *Artificial: A Love Story* (Catapult, NY, 2023) A wide-ranging graphical memoir, but a lot of the focus is on her inventor and AI advocate father Ray Kurzweil's attempt to "resurrect" his father as a chatbot. Relentlessly upbeat on the promise of AI and robots.

Adrienne Mayor, *Gods and Robots: Myths, Machines, and Ancient Dreams of Technology* (Princeton University Press, NJ, 2018). A good place to start robot research and the evolution of the idea.

Madhumita Murgia, *Code Dependent: Living in the Shadow of AI* (Henry Hold and Company, NY, 2024). The major source for the section on the social impact of AI.

Clifford A. Pickover, *Artificial Intelligence: An Illustrated History from Medieval Robots to Neural Networks* (Sterling, NY, 2019). A major source for the history of both AI and robots, and it is a very attractive package of visuals.

Paul Scharre, *Army of None: Autonomous Weapons and the Future of War* (Norton, NY, 2018). Much that is written here is coming true.

Michael Taylor, *Neural Networks: A Visual Introduction for Beginners* (Blue Windmill Media, [Canada], 2017). Many people are visual learners, and there is no better visual introduction to the topic than this.

David L. Poole and Alan K. Mackworth, *Artificial Intelligence: Foundations of Computational Agents, 3rd Edition* (Cambridge University Press, Cambridge, 2023). Readers with adequate mathematical and coding skills can jump right into about a thousand pages of what full-time students are being taught.

CHAPTER 7: SECURITY AND PRIVACY

Bruce Schneier, *Click Here to Kill Everyone: Security and Survival in a Hyperconnected World* (Norton, NY, 2018). Also, a good text on the risks of connecting everything without adequate security and privacy methods in place.

Chris Wiggins and Matthew L. Jones, *How Data Happened: A History from the Age of Reason to the Age of Algorithms* (Norton, NY, 2023). A good history, based on the authors' course at Columbia University, about how, bit-by-bit, we have ceded control of our lives to computerized data centers.

There are many good introductions to cryptography, and new books and online papers are published monthly.

INDEX

www.ingramcontent.com/pod-product-compliance
Lightning Source LLC
Chambersburg PA
CBHW061402210326
41598CB00035B/6065